"RISE UP AND STEP INTO YOUR DESTINY!"

An Inspirational Guide to Become the Awesome Supernatural Person God Created You to Be.

Christipher Joy

Rise Up And Step Into Your Destiny!
An Inspirational Guide to Become the Awesome Supernatural
Person God Created You to Be.
by Christipher Joy

Printed in the United States of America

ISBN 9781615795284

www.xulonpress.com

6/27/10

Awesome Minister Jane & Awesome Bianca

May Awesome God richly bless you with
His love, joy, health, peace and prosperity!

Awesome Christopher

DEDICATION

This book is dedicated to the memory of my late father Maurice Joyner, Sr, and my Big Mama Mattie E. Smith.

Thanks, love and much appreciation to my wife KJoy and son Michael Joseph for your support and caring. Along with the Lord Jesus, you two comprise the three heart beats of my life.

Thanks and love to my grown sons Terry, Sean, all the grandchildren along with Mom Pearl, Alicia and all of our family for being a constant source of love and inspiration.

Thanks so much to Pastor Jimmie Flakes, Minister L.M. Rivers and Attorney Ashton Cumberbatch, Jr. for being the foundational blocks of Love Crusades Evangelistic Ministries.

Thanks to Rhonda Walker and Susan Lewis for your insightful information on healthy foods and physical fitness. Thanks to Yvonne Williams and Marlow Hooper for your caring expertise on real estate purchasing and mortgage financing.

Thanks also to Ogden Bass, Troy Moss, John Finney, Gordon Hannon, Bobby Bryant, Tracee Johnson, Harry Carter, Theresa Jackson, Rickey Hughes and James Walker for donating your valuable time, supplies, finances and sharing your expertise, helping me to navigate LCEM through the electronic world.

A special thanks to the multitude of pastors, church congregations and individuals for your faithful commitment in supporting me over the past twenty-seven years in ministry. Your support and encouragement has been the strong foundation that enabled me to maintain a godly perspective and build a strong spiritual house.

I thank you all from the debts of my heart.

ACKNOWLEDGMENTS

"Outstanding presentation of the gospel message in print! Christipher Joy has captured the timeless message of Jesus as our Destiny and outlined it in a simple pattern for everyone to see themselves as the Spiritual, Physical and Business person they were created to be. Evangelist Joy juxtapositions his own personal testimony to help the reader see how they too can be used in the supernatural way the LORD has destined for each of us."

— Dr. Robert E. Wilson, Executive Pastor of Christian Education, Decision Point Ministries, Atlanta, GA

"Rise Up and Step into Your Destiny gives us practical ways of growing and becoming mature as believers. The life stories show the realness of this growth, change and transformation. The Apostle Paul said: "Follow me as I follow Christ." If we follow the principles in this book, we too will grow, change and be transformed."

— Dr. Decker H. Tapscott, Sr., Senior Pastor, Faith Christian Church and International Outreach Center, Warrenton, VA

"No matter where you are on life's journey or your Christian walk, when you read this book you will be inspired and encouraged to develop and enhance your godly perspective to Rise Up And Step Into Your Destiny to become the Awesome Supernatural person that God created you to be."

— Pastor Charles E. Singleton, Senior Pastor, Loveland Church, Ontario, CA

Table of Contents

PART 4: ABUNDANT LIFE

Foreword

Though I was raised in a Christian home, surrounded by generations of pastors, preachers, and missionaries, I was a young adult before I came into an authentic saving relationship with Christ. Sure, I attended church faithfully; I could recite scriptures with confidence and had a fairly solid grasp of all "thou shalts" and "thou shalt nots". But I did not have anything approaching an intimate, vibrant relationship with Jesus as the very center of my being-nor did I sense the need for such.

All that changed when, in my early 20's, I had an overwhelming encounter with the person of Christ (not just the pronouncements of Christ). Immediately my focus shifted. More than anything I wanted to learn the details about this new love of my life and what He wanted me to be and do as the result of it. Mere church-going, scripture-quoting and living by a clean-cut moral code were no longer enough.

I sensed the need for a spiritual mentor, a well-seasoned guide who had traveled the road I was now traveling, someone able to "shepherd me after God's own heart."

Enter Christipher Joy.

Now, he is a renowned evangelist who powerfully shares the word of God around the world. Back then he was just Chris, my patient, spiritual big brother who spoon-fed me foundational biblical truths-and the best of his native Texas cuisine.

Christipher was, and still is, consumed with passion for God. Through his generous watchful friendship I began a discipleship process that completely transformed my life and shaped my calling.

How was he used to such monumental effect? Christipher taught me, not just what I could and should do for God, but the rich resources God has provided for me, His child. He taught me the truth about my identity in Christ. He pointed out the reality of the vast privileges that are ours on account of Him "who has chosen us in Him, predestined us, accepted us, and what is the hope of His calling, and the exceeding greatness of His inheritance..." **(Ephesians 1:4, 5)**

Bottom line, Christipher Joy taught me that if I understood and appropriated the facts of my identity in Christ, then a life of super-abounding joy, and kingdom-effectiveness was not only possible, but inevitable.

A couple of exciting decades have passed since God profoundly used Christipher to jumpstart me into my destiny. Since then he has gone on to share those same transforming truths with countless others across the country and around the world.

They, like I, have been challenged to live abundantly as true heirs of promise.

Now it is your turn. You hold in your hands my early mentor's highly compelling message of truth. Believe me, it is as biblical and practical as it is personal and relevant to your situation.

Want to know-without a doubt-who you are and what you possess in Christ? Are you yearning to live a soaring life of faith and triumph rather than merely existing until Jesus comes back? If so, you've come to the right place.

Take a deep breath and turn the next page with unbridled expectancy. You're not too early and you're not too late. Now is the perfect time for you to rise up and step into your destiny!

Ronn Elmore, Psy.d

INTRODUCTION

Having spent many years in the entertainment industry as an actor, writer, producer, before at age thirty-six, truly accepting Jesus Christ as my Savior and Lord, I sometimes tend to look at life through the lens of my past experiences. Spiritual insight from God has led me to understand that my journey on earth, along with all mankind, is God's great human drama. God's human drama allows you and me to experience all the nuances of life, including love, joy, passion, pain, peace, failure, discouragement and success as we fulfill our purpose on earth.

Many years ago I remember sitting in a movie theater mesmerized by the great epic "The Ten Commandments". The film was directed by Mr. Cecil B. DeMille, who was a master at chronicling biblical dramas on film. His movie made an indelible impression on my brother, Maurice, Jr. and I. We did not stop talking about the movie for weeks, and I have never totally dismissed it from my consciousness.

I had heard about God as a small child but never realized that He played such a significant role in my human destiny. I later wondered if God played such a major part in every life as He had in the life of Moses. Did God orchestrate the events in my life as He had in Moses life? This was of particular interest to me because, like Moses, I was separated from my mother at a very early age. Unlike Moses though, God had not ingeniously reconnected me with my mother — as He had Moses with his mother. My mother passed away three months before the fourth year of my journey on earth.

One truth that rose above all others in the movie was that God had a plan for Moses' life. And God was with Moses throughout the duration of his life, directing, orchestrating and motivating him to fulfill his purpose. Could God have a plan for my life, for your life? Perhaps not like the magnitude of His plan for Moses life; but, nevertheless a plan. Is God a part of my life and your life? Is He directing our steps and orchestrating the events of our lives without our knowing it, just as He did in Moses' life?

Yes! Yes! Yes! In my growing relationship with the Father, through my Lord Jesus Christ, the help of the Holy Spirit and God's word, I have come to know that God has always been a part of my life. He has been directing, orchestrating and motivating me to fulfill the glorious plan He has for my life. God created me for purpose and God is my destiny! He conceived you and I for a purpose that is dear to Him. Sometimes I am overwhelmed at the thoughts of how much God loves me, how He gave himself for me on the cross of Calvary, then patiently waited for me to surrender to Him after He was introduced to me so early in my life. **Truly God is Awesome, Amazing and He is long suffering!**

Early in my walk with Christ I had to fight off and dismiss guilt about wasted time and opportunities. There were many times when I did not "respond to" or pursue my destiny, when God had orchestrated events and people, giving me an opportunity to know Him. Perhaps you find yourself overwhelmed in like circumstances. I reflected on the life of Moses and found comfort in the fact that he did not walk into God's plan to fulfill his purpose until he met God, his destiny, in a burning bush at approximately eighty years of age.

I was further encouraged by the Lord to know that He had been orchestrating the experiences of my life to prepare me to fulfill my purpose as His messenger. Like Moses, He had allowed me to be trained in an environment that prepared me for His call on my life. As a full time evangelist, my background of writing, producing, directing and acting in stage, television, and film projects was great preparation for ministry. God gifted and enabled me, through my experiences, to write messages with good word pictures, organize crusades, church meetings, write, produce, direct drama ministries and speak to hundreds and thousands of people as His anointed messenger. My challenge now was to rise up and step into my destiny. **GOD IS MY DESTINY! HE IS MY GREAT FORTUNE! IN HIM I LIVE! IN HIM I MOVE! IN HIM I HAVE MY BEING!**

The more I thought about the movie, the revelation of three primary things became clear to me. And these three things were necessary to step into destiny. First, Moses had a relationship with God and God had a call on his life. The Spirit of God was upon him, and God directed Moses' path. He had been taught about the God of Israel and about the role of the true and living God in the lives of His people. Second, Moses grew up to be a physically fit young man. He developed and disciplined his body. He was later given the strenuous task of destroying a city by Sethi, the Pharaoh. And Moses had to be physically fit when God called him to lead the children of Israel for forty years in the wilderness. In the movie "The Ten Commandments," Charlton Heston, who played the role of Moses, and Yul Brynner, who played the role of Rameses, had to be physically fit to be believable in the performance of their roles in the movie. There were lots of action scenes in the movie, including fighting in hand to hand combat. Third, God had strategically placed Moses in the house of the Pharaoh, to learn the ways of Egyptian hierarchy. He learned how to organize people and resources in order to build cities. In dealing with the vast wealth and resources of Egypt he also learned how to negotiate and handled their business contracts. Moses was in their world and for awhile he was a part of it; thus he knew how to conduct business and successfully occupy the land where he dwelled.

I can't help but remember my first year in acting classes at Los Angeles City College. My instructor stressed three primary things to all of us young, aspiring thespians. First, if we were going to succeed, we had to have a passion, a calling to be an actor. Without the passion we would never make it, because acting takes so much from you for such a long time before it gives anything back. We had to have a passion and a calling for the craft in order to endure the demands that it would place on us. Second, in addition to our passion we would need healthy fit bodies that were trained and disciplined to handle the various strenuous activities of performing in movies and television. Before we embarked on scene development, acting in small vignettes and plays, we all had to take specialized classes in body movement, dance, stretching, voice and diction. We also did tongue, facial and breathing exercises to learn how to enunciate and use our diaphragms. The classes were primarily designed to familiarize us with our bodies, to strengthen our bodies and to learn how to control our bodies through daily exercises and simple dance movements. We learned that our bodies were our instruments. And our instruments had to be trained and kept in excellent condition to be available to respond to our every command. Third, he would state loud and emphatically: "This is show business, ladies and gentlemen! Show—-Business! Don't just study and learn the 'show' part, learn something about the business!" I was inspired to take business courses, including contract law and accounting to prepare me for the business of entertainment. These courses along with the business acumen that my father had instilled in me, growing up in Texas, well prepared me for handling the business affairs of life.

Amazingly, these three principles carried over into my life and in my walk with God. I have a passion for God, and a call on my life from God. I am constantly in my holy script learning my part. To this day I am watchful and careful of my diet and I exercise regularly, keeping my body fit and healthy. I have been blessed to be exposed to and learn the ways of business in the world where I live. This has greatly enhanced my dominion over my personal and ministry business affairs. Now that I have a leading role in the greatest human drama of my life, I definitely want to be ready for any action that my role calls for. I want to please my Writer, Producer and Director, by knowing my script, having a healthy well trained instrument so that I can do all that my leading role demands of me, and be able to negotiate and conduct His business for my family and ministry. My lead role in God's epic drama demands that I rise and step up. **Me!**

THE SPIRITUAL YOU

You! God has a plan for your life. You, like me, were born for purpose, and you are here on earth as part of God's story. Our lives are really extensions of the God who created us. His great desire is to reveal your true identity; which apart from Him, you will never fully know. Children of God, unlike creatures of God, come to a true revelation of who they are, whose they are and why they are here on earth. To simply be born, live and die on this earth only equates to creature status and often aborted purpose. To be a child of God requires that you believe and confess the Lord Jesus Christ as the Son of God, and accept His death and sacrifice on the cross as payment for your sins. He then opens the door of true identity and reveals His great potential and purpose that is imbedded in you screaming to be released. God has patiently waited for you to surrender to Him. He has been directing and orchestrating the events of your life to bring you to the place where you are at the reading of this book. All the experiences of your life were either designed or orchestrated by God to prepare you for His call on your life. His call and your affirmative response to Him is the beginning of you stepping into your destiny. The moment you said yes to Jesus, your life shifted into a higher gear. You were chosen by God to play a vital role in His kingdom story. God, the greatest writer, producer, and director of human life cast you in a leading role. **YOU ARE THE STAR OF THIS DRAMA.** God desires to tell His love story through you. It's His life lived and told through you. God the Father is the Executive Producer. He is the Limited Partner in your Limited Partnership for Unlimited Success. As the Limited Partner, He supplies all the resources needed for your part in His story. Jesus created the story, wrote the script and He's the agent who cast you in a leading role. The Holy Bible is your script. The Holy Spirit is your director - your guide.

You are the General Partner in this partnership. You have to do all the work. And you do the work by allowing Jesus Christ who lives in you to direct your steps to reach a most successful conclusion. The Apostle Paul understood this phenomenon once he had surrendered to Christ. Being inspired by the Holy Spirit, he wrote: **"I have been crucified with Christ; it is no longer I who live, but Christ lives in me: and the life which I now live in the flesh I live by faith in the Son of God, who loved me, and gave Himself for me."** (Galatians 2:20 NKJ) **LIGHTS!**

Have you ever heard of someone having been stamped as great and successful by the world, and in frustration, change their lifestyle in the evening of life, with a full cup, because they felt so empty? Not knowing who you are is one of the great tragedies in life. Fulfilling your purpose and stepping into your destiny is inextricably tied to knowing who created you and why you exist. One can never truly know who they are without knowing who created them and why. The creator is always a part of his creation. The manufacturer is always a part of his product. Who you are is so much more than your title or possessions. After a lifetime of worldly achievements, many people still feel completely empty.

THE PHYSICAL YOU

The second component to having dominion is the physical you. Do you compromise your availability to God because you do not give proper attention to maintaining the physical you? No way am I suggesting that you have to be a body builder or the next poster person for a physical fitness advertisement. However, you do have a responsibility to develop your body and practice discipline in the care of it. Most parents spend quality time during childhood years encouraging their children to eat nutritional foods with a healthy, proper balance of vegetables, fruits and carbohydrates. Years ago, before the advent of television, technical toys and games, physical exercise was a prominent part of a child's daily routine. Even today in schools, physical education (exercising body extremities) is still a part of the curriculum. However, much less emphasis is put on developing the body and maintaining discipline in the care of the body. I do remind you that your body is the temple of the Holy Spirit. To give the Spirit of God full access and availability, you need to be careful and protective of what you put in your temple and how you maintain it. We are commanded to glorify God in our temple. **"Or do you not know that your body is the temple of the Holy Spirit who is in you, whom you have from God, and you are not your own? For you were bought at a price: therefore glorify God in your body, and in your spirit, which are God's."** (1Corinthians 6:19, 20 NKJ)

To glorify God in your body you have to refrain from immorality, unrighteousness and also be careful of the intake of improper foods. That, along with sin, gives the devil place and access to attack your body and inflict great harm to you. Be on guard and avoid anything that gives the devil access to you. **"And that you put on the new man which was created according to God, in true righteousness and holiness. Nor give place to the devil."** (Ephesians 4:24; 27 NKJ)

Obesity and poor health has deterred and denied many well meaning individuals from fulfilling their purpose and meeting the daily challenges of life. For a born again saint of God it is imperative that you feed your spirit with the proper diet from God's holy word and exercise your spirit by walking in faith. You are a new creation in Christ; therefore, it is also imperative that you feed your natural body with the proper diet and keep your body physically fit through consistent physical exercise.

You now have a new way of living. You may have lied, stole or maimed people before salvation; but now you are a new creation in Christ Jesus. Jesus has made us to be kings, queens and priests unto God the Father. You are blessed because your sins were forgiven and washed away by the blood of Jesus. God has called you to a new way of life. If you smoked or drank before you got saved, you need to stop now. The Holy Spirit does not want to live in a contaminated infested body any more than you would want to live in a rat and roach infested house. Nicotine in cigarettes is the same poison in insecticides that are used to kill insects. Alcohol is known to tear down and destroy human cells and body tissues. Mind altering drugs, especially non-prescribed street drugs, can impair your reasoning abilities and hinders the work of the Holy Spirit to lead and guide you to victory. Refusing to exercise the body and eating a constant diet of fatty, non nutritional foods breaks down and destroys built in body protections from God. Without the proper portions of fruits, grains, nuts and vegetables, your body's capacity to defend itself against life threatening diseases is diminished and the door is opened for the devil to attack you with strokes, heart attacks, cancer, high blood pressure, high cholesterol, diabetes, kidney disease and liver diseases. Proper preparation of food is also essential to maintaining good health. Avoid excessive amounts of fried food and high saturated fat in food. The lack of a healthy fit body also effects personal self esteem. To be available to God and fulfill His purpose for your life, you have to maintain a healthy fit body. You are fearfully and wonderfully made. God has done His part by designing and making your body in a miraculous way with many built in protections. Are you doing your part by taking care of it?

Many churches across our nation have started programs emphasizing the need to change our eating habits and start a physical exercise regimen. Two or three people, who are seriously committed to living a better quality of life, can come together and start programs in the church or at a community facility. Those who are already engaged in a healthier lifestyle can share with others. You can walk together in the mornings before work or school. You can also have a group that walks in the evenings after work. Exercise can be a great way to promote family activities. Husband and wives, parents and children, can walk or run together. Families can ride bicycles together in the park or other places in their neighborhoods.

We also spend a lot of time preparing food and eating together at church functions. Why not take the lead as an organizer or food preparer to prepare healthier meals? Also, encourage others to prepare healthier meals and cut back on all the fried greasy foods. I love fried chicken but I have drastically cut back on my personal consumption of it. And I definitely try to avoid eating fatty foods late at night shortly before my bedtime. Making wise choices, in what I eat and when I eat, is doing my part to take care of my body.

THE BUSINESS YOU

Too often a devout Christian struggles to maintain and have dominion in daily business activities that are required to successfully occupy the land. You can be filled with and led by the Holy Spirit, but if you are ignorant of the world's system and refuse to seek knowledge on how to navigate through it's treacherous activities using godly principles, you will constantly be deceived and victimized by the system. Take note of Jesus parable of ten pounds. **"So he called ten of his servants, delivered to them ten minas, and said to them, 'Do business till I come.'"** (Luke 19:13 NKJ). In the King James translation of the Scriptures he said occupy till I come. Occupy means to engage in business, to trade, to busy oneself with business matters. We are in this world but we are not of it: meaning that we are to live in it, engage and do business in it, but we are not to be devious, dishonest or use unjust weights as many in the world do.

Jesus Christ saved you, that you might be a witness for Him. He has commanded you to propagate the gospel of His kingdom until He comes and receives you unto Himself. **"And he said unto them, 'Go into all the world and preach the gospel to every creature."** (Mark 16:15 NKJ) Knowing how to transact business, engaging in trade and acquiring prosperity enables you and me to successfully carry out the great commission of going into the world to win souls for Christ. Do you minimize your ability to go into the world as Christ's ambassador because you have not been able to receive all that God has for you, due to a lack of business knowledge? Do you forfeit God's blessings and minimize your dominion on the earth due to your business ignorance? Are you forfeiting His additions in your life due to your lack of knowledge of finances, how to handle a bank account, maintain a good credit rating, obtain reasonable interest rates on loans, purchase a home, cars, life, auto and health insurance policies, and have solid investments and retirement funds? Put God first in all you do, including your business practices, and God will richly bless you with His add on's. Jesus said: **"But seek Ye first the kingdom of God, and his righteousness, and all these things shall be added unto you."** (Matthew 6:33 KJ)

God will not bless you with abundance if you lack the business capacity to handle it properly. His desire is to add His blessed additions to your life when your priorities are in order and you are occupying the land. Being ignorant of business and lacking the knowledge to successfully navigate the channels of commerce will cause you to forfeit Destiny's additions to your life. Perhaps the first and foremost business principle rooted in the word of God is to know that God gives you seed to sow into other lives. He also gives you bread for your food; but seed for you to sow into others is always first. And God only multiplies the seed you sow. Therefore, put God first, give generously to others and God will increase your harvest. He will cause your seed to be multiplied through divinely inspired and favorable business transactions. Have a kingdom mentality and take the time to learn about business. **A kingdom mentality is a mindset focused on the things of God and how you can occupy**

this earth to propagate His gospel. Please do not think that God is going to handle everything for you. The Holy Spirit is your helper and He will divinely lead and bless you to engage in business and commerce until the Lord Jesus returns. **To be available to God and fulfill His purpose, you have to live a new Spirit filled life, maintain a good portion of health, and know how to transact business.** You are fearfully and wonderfully made as a triune being. God has done his part by filling your spirit with His Holy Spirit, designing, crafting your body in a miraculous way, and giving you a mind and a will to learn and engage successfully in world commerce. God has designed and equipped you to be awesome. Are you doing your part by walking in the Spirit and taking care of your body? Are you stepping up to the plate and allowing God to spread the gospel and occupy the land through you and your business acumen? **AWESOME YOU!**

GOD IS YOUR DESTINY! As a born again child of God, rejoice to know that God is your destiny. Heaven is not your destiny. Destiny is not a place for you, Destiny is a spirit being. God created you in His image and after His likeness. Heaven is your ultimate destination where you will enjoy eternal life with your Destiny. **"And this is eternal life, that they may know You, the only true God, and Jesus Christ, whom You have sent."** (John 17:3 NKJ)

Destiny has birthed purpose in you. The Holy Spirit indwells you to release your potential and fulfill your purpose. It is your responsibility to surrender to the Spirit, allowing Destiny, the Father of purpose, to cultivate and maturate your purpose. Throughout your new walk you will have to choose between purpose and popularity. A close study of the life of Moses, and other biblical characters that God used, reveals they had to choose between popularity and purpose. **"By faith Moses, when he became of age, refused to be called the son of Pharaoh's daughter, choosing rather to suffer affliction with the people of God than to enjoy the passing pleasures of sin, esteeming the reproach of Christ greater riches than the treasures in Egypt: for he looked to the reward."** (Hebrews 11:24-27 NKJ)

Moses made a willful choice to serve God and suffer with the people of God rather than enjoy the popularity and opulence of being a member of Pharaoh's royal family. You can choose to abort your purpose but you can never deny it was birthed in you. Worldly accomplishments, stuff, and activities, can never fill the painful gap of a life lost and lived without it's creator. Worldly position cannot eradicate the scars of aborted purpose. Separated from your Destiny, life is void of spiritual fruit and scarred by aborted purpose. Jesus said: **"I am the vine, you are the branches. He who abides in Me and I in him bears much fruit; for without Me you can do nothing. If anyone does not abide in Me, he is cast out as a branch and is withered; and they gather them, and throw them into the fire, and they are burned. If you abide in Me, and My words abide in you, you will ask what you desire, and it shall be done for you. By this My Father is glorified, that you bear much fruit: so you will be My disciples."** (John 15:5-8 NKJ)

Christ lives in you and I to fulfill His purpose for our lives. He wrote the script for your life. He knows your story better than you. He knows what lies ahead. He knows how present day situations impact tomorrow's events and challenges. The writer knows the entire script before one frame of film is shot; therefore, He alone should be trusted with the direction of your life. **"Trust in the Lord with all thine heart; and lean not unto thine own understanding. In all thy ways acknowledge him, and he shall direct thy paths."** (Proverbs 3:5, 6)

In the human drama, self direction is often an exercise in futility. It is not always prudent to make decisions based on past experiences or present day situations. A director who knows the entire script can best direct each chapter of your life, and even more so when the director is also the writer. Jesus knows you and He will lead you. **"My sheep <u>hear my voice</u>, and <u>I know them</u>, and <u>they follow me</u>."** (John 10:27) Listen and learn the voice of the great shepherd. **Rise up in Jesus!** You can rise above the debris of past mistakes, decadent living, and step out of the muck and mire of those sins that so easily beset you. **STEP INTO GOD YOUR TRUE DESTINY!**

ABUNDANT LIFE

CAMERA! God chose you! The writer, producer and director all agree that **Awesome You** should be cast in the leading role of this great human drama. And in your starring role you must develop a kingdom mentality to walk in the authority (exousia), and the power (dunamis-dynamite), that God has equipped you with. He has given you His word and equipped you with the empowerment of His indwelt Holy Spirit. In the minefields of human drama, His inspired word, the Bible, is the true anointed evidence for your divine teaching, holy correction, righteous instruction, and a light for living in a world of darkness. **"All scripture is given by inspiration of God, and is profitable for doctrine, for reproof, for correction, for instruction in righteousness."** (2 Timothy 3:16 KJ) **"Thy word is a lamp unto my feet, and a light unto my path."** (Psalms 119:105 KJ)

Together with God you have all the ingredients to become an epic hit drama. The writer, producer and director have many epic hits to his credit. **Awesome You** can become His next epic. He knows how to keep harmony on the set as He brings all the significant parts together. He is well prepared and a Master at producing human epics. All he asks of His leading player is to learn the script and follow His directions.

Because I recognize that we often have similar experiences in life, frequently I will share personal thoughts and events to illustrate and emphasize a point. However, throughout this manuscript, it is my desire to allow God to speak directly to you in the first person. Although I recognize that there are supporting characters, featured and bit players in the drama with you, I remind you that you have the distinct honor of having been twice chosen by God for a significant part of His story told through you. Your mother nor your father chose the sperm that would impregnate the egg that produce your biological life. God did. And no one can come to God unless he or she is drawn by God's Spirit. **God twice chose Awesome you to be His leading character in His epic drama of your life. It is God's story told through you.** You, no matter what took place in your past, are uniquely gifted by God for purpose and great accomplishment. There is a triune you that I strongly desire to address in this book: the SPIRITUAL YOU, the PHYSICAL YOU and the BUSINESS YOU. **This book is written to you! It is designed to stimulate, inspire and motivate you** to reach beyond any guilt of wasted time, reach beyond the failures of yesterday, reach beyond the comforts of today and **RISE UP AND STEP INTO YOUR DESTINY! ACTION!!!**

CHAPTER ONE

THE SPIRITUAL YOU: IDENTITY UNVEILED, EMOTIONS HEALED AND PURPOSE REVEALED!

WE ARE A GREAT PEOPLE!

Throughout the pages of this book it is my intent to inform us and reinforce the fact that you and I were created in the image of and after the likeness of Awesome God! And thus, in our created blueprint we are designed to be awesome human species with dominion and power over all God's creation. God told us to subdue and rule over every living thing upon the earth. Ruling over God's creation begins with knowing who you are and how you are suppose to operate. For just a moment, let go of your past and see this moment as a dynamic new beginning for **Awesome You!** It is time for **Awesome You** and **Awesome Me** to rise up and step into our destiny!

> **"And <u>God said</u>, Let <u>us</u> make man in <u>our</u> image, after <u>our</u> likeness; and let them have dominion over the fish of the sea, and over the fowl of the air, and over the cattle, and over all the earth, and over every creeping thing that creepeth upon the earth. So God created man in his own image, in the image of God created he him; male and female created he them."** (Genesis 1:26, 27)

This text in Genesis tells us that we are a great people! Who's great? What people are great? I'm talking about those of us who are born again in Christ. And to those who have not received Jesus Christ as your savior, I'm talking about who you can become. **GREAT!** The word great is tossed around so loosely in our world today. In fact, a step above mediocrity is often great in the eyes of some. What is greatness? How does one come to be great? What possession makes the difference between ordinary and great? Let's walk together and discover who you are or who you can become. Let's discover how you can have dominion on and over this earth.

Me. My first vivid memory is of growing up in Teals Prairie, Texas, on a big farm. My mother Daisy died before I was four years old, and my daddy, Maurice, Sr. took my older brother and I to the country to live with my deceased mother's mother, Mattie E. Smith, who we affectionately called Big Mama. I remember trying to keep up with Big Mama as she walked, back-bent, dragging a big sack behind her, down what appeared to be endless rows of stick-flowers with white fluff balls protruding from thorny pockets. I could never keep up with Big Mama, and too often my brother and I would cut our fingers trying to snatch those white cotton fluff balls from their thorny pockets. Big Mama definitely knew how to pick cotton.

My Big Mama was a great woman. In her day she had to be great to own two hundred eighteen acres of land, raise children, grandchildren and pick as much cotton as she did. She also taught us how to shuck corn, milk cows and churn buttermilk. My first awareness of the name of Jesus, was listening to Big Mama in her rocking chair on the garry (porch) singing, "What a Friend We Have in Jesus", "Blessed Assurance", "Near the Cross", while I chased lightning bugs in the front yard. Sometimes, Big Mama would get happy and shout out "Thank you, Jesus! Thank You!" "Hallelujah!" "The Lord am good! Mighty, Mighty Jesus!" She was definitely on a first name basis with her Jesus. For the life of me I cannot ever recall Big Mama calling me by my first name. I vividly remember her calling me "Lil' Bit" or "Honey Chile". She taught my brother Maurice, Jr. "Junebug," and I about Jesus. She also insisted that we had to do chores and play outside. We learned to milk cows, feed the horses and clean the barn and the yard.

Big Mama was a tower of strength. She was never afraid like us children were when riding in the wagon at night coming home from church. Big Mama held up her trusty lantern in one hand to give light to our path and held the reins of the horse in the other. She would get out of the wagon at the old rickety bridge, grab the horse's bridle and lead him down into a gully that ran alongside the bridge and up to the other side of the road. Even the horse was skittish about crossing that old bridge at night. And we kids were scared of all the sounds of pitch black country nights and the thought of stepping on a rattlesnake or some other critter. None of the things that frightened us kids ever fazed Big Mama. She was so secure in her Jesus. She always said: "Just trust in the Lord and He will keep you and guide you through." **My spiritual introduction.**

A few years passed before my daddy, Maurice Sr., remarried. He came to get Jr. and I, and we moved back to Austin with him and my new mama, Lillian, "Honey J". Daddy affectionately called me "Midget" because I was smaller than the other children; but, he often made me feel like a giant when he would take me to business meetings with him. After a polite greeting I was never allowed to say anything. I was told to sit and listen so I could learn how to do business. Three principles that my father drummed into me were: "Your word is your bond, Midget. So always keep it, even if you have to suffer loss. Keep your word, son!" "Always respect time. Be on time! Do not be late! Time is money." "Be kind and help folks. You never know when you may need a hand." Throughout my life these principles have proven to be very valuable. As a child in Austin I always worked, caddying, shining shoes, working in a fast food place. Just before I was in my teen years my father put my brothers and I in business. We opened up "Four Brothers Taste 'N Tell." A burger and malt place where our school friends and others could meet, eat, dance and have a safe time. I learned how to handle a checkbook, do banking, and business negotiations. **My business introduction.**

While growing up in Austin it became obvious that I had been bitten by a dancing bug. I loved to entertain people. During the time I was getting a formal education I was dancing and singing at schools that I was not allowed to attend as a student. I performed in local talent shows, special events and appeared on local television. In my mind I was pursuing greatness. I was seeking to be the next Sammy Davis, Jr, Fred Astaire, or Bill "Bojangles" Robinson. Mr. Cactus Pryor, a local radio and television personality, along with Mr. Lavada Durst and Mrs. Catherine Lampkin were great sources of encouragement and help in my early career. Later, I went off to college in Los Angeles in pursuit of a career in show business. In Hollywood, I changed my name legally. I achieved some fame, had my name up in lights on theater marquees, starred in television, movies and on stage. At Desilu Studios I was chosen along with four other acting students to spend two weeks with a great lady and master comedienne- Ms. Lucille Ball. She allowed us to participate and learn every aspect of doing the "I Love Lucy" Show. I shall never forget her advice to me after asking what I really wanted to do. I said I wanted to act, write and produce. Enthusiastically she said: "Great! Work hard at it; because the more control you have behind the camera, the more control you will have in front of it." I later received Emmy consideration as a co-writer of an episode of "Starksy & Hutch", directed by Mr. Paul Michael Glaser. I also met and worked with Mr. Bing Crosby, Mr. Redd Foxx, Mr. Billy Dee Williams, Mr. Demond Wilson, Mr. William "Smokey" Robinson, Mr. Burgess Meredith, Ms. Pam Grier, Ms. Nichelle Nichols, Ms. Jayne Kennedy, Ms. Patty Duke, Mr. Gene Corman, Mr. Judd Hirsch, Mr. Jeff Bridges, Mr. Ed Asner, Mr. Hal Williams, Mr. Max Julian, Mr. Leon Isaac Kennedy, Mr. Robert Blake, Mr. Georg Stanford Brown, Mr. Bernie Casey, Mr. Ron Glass and my all time idol, Mr. Sammy Davis, Jr. But I never felt complete, never felt whole, never great. I never really knew who I was.

You. Knowing who you are is much more than an awareness of name, address, physical characteristics, personal acquaintances and life's achievements. The Bible tells you that you are made in the image of and after the likeness of God. To know who you are you have to know something about Awesome God, your creator. God is great; therefore, since you are made in His image, you have the potential for greatness. Humanity lost greatness in Adam's sin, but the potential is still there. "After God's likeness" means that you are to think and operate like God. God has an identity and He established order- cosmos out of chaos. He is in charge of His worlds, heaven and earth, and He tells you to take dominion over the earth-your dwelling place. God is love. His thoughts and actions toward humanity are seasoned by His love and desire for us to be great. And yet many believers and all non believers live life under a veiled identity clouded with distortion and missed purpose. There is no real order to their lives. Achieved goals can for a season, mask the emptiness, cover over the pain of veiled identity and missed purpose. But never can they truly identify you, reveal your purpose, or restore your greatness. Unloving people and hurtful experiences often birth hatred, bitterness, and emptiness in the depths of the human soul. And there is always a moment of reckoning in life where you will have to face the source of your emptiness. If you are in that place, please know that without knowing your true identity you can never know your purpose for being. Without knowing Awesome God who is your destiny, the bowls of identity, purpose and true greatness sit glistening on a shelf in the cabinet of your life. **Empty.**

Me. 1976 was a good business year. Thanks to Mr. Smokey Robinson, I finally had the money to produce, co-write and star in my own movie, "Big Time". As Leon Kennedy, my co-producer, and I worked on the film, I just knew that the bowls of identity, purpose and true greatness would finally start filling up and evict the empty void in my life. "Big Time" opened in 1977, with great fanfare, primarily because of Smokey's music and involvement. In some of the theaters we did a live concert featuring Smokey, prior to screening the film. I appeared on the Mike Douglas show, on Good Morning America, Chicago, with Steve Edwards, many radio stations around the nation, and on the cover of many national magazines. I thought I had it all "going on;" but without a spirit filled life I could not evict the empty void. I was spiraling out of control, totally void of peace, no inner fulfillment, and greatness was locked away in an inaccessible vault. My life was misfiring. I did not feel or experience love. I still felt empty. This was not what I had imagined world success to be.

The Creator of the heavens and the earth modeled and fashioned humanity after Himself. And He mandated that we have dominion over everything upon the earth. In the Garden of Eden when God breathed the breath of life into the nostrils of a lump of dirt which was fashioned in His image, man became a living soul. The breath of life was a vital breath from God and it energized man with greatness, clarified his identity, and caused him to have divine inspiration and intellect. Mankind was greatly loved by it's Creator and man had the fullness of life. The day that I was born anew in Jesus Christ, I also received His vital breath. The human intellect and spirit is undeniably a source of tremendous power and energy, enabling many to rise to phenomenal heights. On the human front we can all draw from the creative energy which resides within. Up to 1976, I had drawn heavily on my human intellect and creative energy; but there was no real order in my life. I did not feel loved, and I was unfulfilled because I was void of my creator, **Awesome God.**

You. To have true love and the fullness of life you, like I, need God's Spirit. For mankind is a triune being. Your form is dirt. Your essence is soul. And the life of you is Spirit. You will never know true love and your purpose for being, or tap into your full potential for greatness until you are in possession of God's Spirit, the life source from whence you came. Your accomplishments in business and your possession of things can no more fill the empty void in your life than they did in mine. Jesus said: **"Watch out! Be on your guard against all kinds of greed; a man's life does not consist in the abundance of his possessions."** (Luke 12:15 NIV)

Me. Having the things of this world without the Holy Spirit was not greatness. I desperately wanted to be loved. I needed definition for my being. God's Spirit and His word defines' mankind and restores greatness. Christmas eve night 1976, in my lonely apartment, I accepted Jesus Christ as my savior. Instantly a weight was lifted and I felt a warm love and peace in the midst of my tears. I had a sense of belonging. I did not know how, but I knew life was going to be different. I had to find my purpose for being. Only the creator of something knows its purpose for being. Without God's Spirit I was a flawed human vehicle, misfiring on the highway of life, void of the love fuel that propels human kind to true greatness. With God's Spirit I am the Rolls Royce of humanity! I can now release my potential to be the best! I am capable of being a high performance luxurious mortal vehicle and I am destined to win the race of life. It had to be sad for my Creator to watch his creation misfire, struggle and breakdown on the highway of life because I suffered from ignorance of identity, purpose, and I lacked supreme love fuel. Without God's Spirit I lacked the proper love fuel that powers my human engine. Now I know that I did not have to break down so frequently on the roadside of life. Neither did I have to keep sputtering along in life due to lack of love and constant misfiring of my engine. Most of us know gasoline comes in different grades of octane. The octane grade or number is used to identify the level of power in the liquid motor fuel. High performance luxury cars cannot successfully run on low grade octane motor fuel. Humanity is God's highest form and crowning jewel of creation.

My life had been misfiring because I did not have the right fuel in my tank. Adam's sin in the garden cost us dearly. Sin ushered in separation from God and caused mankind to be devoid of God's Spirit, God's identity, God's purpose and God's greatness; thus mankind, born after Adam's fall in the garden is initially void of the true likeness of his Creator. Without God's Spirit I, along with all humanity, lacked the capacity for holiness, for truth, for peace, for the fruit and the gifts of the Holy Spirit. Without His Spirit, without these divine attributes from God, we cannot enjoy fellowship with our Creator, nor can we maximize our humanity. I was like an expensive high powered automobile operating with the wrong grade of motor fuel. Now, with God I am special and I have a high grade of love octane to operate at maximum efficiency. Some people, like some automobiles, can get by on a low grade of fuel. Others may need a medium grade, but the very best of high performance cars need the supreme grade of fuel. I now have the supreme, high octane love fuel of the Holy Spirit. The Holy Spirit is the only supreme grade of love fuel that makes it possible for you and me to be God's awesome human beings. God lives in **Awesome Me** and He alone can fuel me to operate at my maximum efficiency. **Without the Holy Spirit there was a shadowy veil over my identity and purpose.**

The presence of God within me unveils my true identity, reveals my purpose and God himself is my destiny. His Spirit is the real love spark of my life. I will never misfire or break down on the highway of life as long as I am filled with and led by the Spirit of the true and living God. Because of sin, my natural birth into this world was only a shadow of who I am and what I could become. Natural birth gave me an outer shell, my body and my soul (plugs, wires, ignition switch), but I was void of God's Spirit, the high octane love fuel that enables me to operate at full capacity. God is love and He so loved the world that He gave us Jesus, His only begotten Son. Natural birth is not enough to make us awesome human beings who can experience the supreme love, life, and power of Almighty God. Sin separated you and me from the power of true life.

"Behold, I was shapen in iniquity; and in sin did my mother conceive me." (Psalm 51:5 KJ)

The brush strokes of sin distorted the true picture of who God originally created you and me to be. Sin contaminated our godly natures. We were not born according to the Creator's original specifications. And separation from God is devastating. **Greatness Lost.**

You. How can you be restored to your Creator? Operating in your own strength and deeds you are powerless to restore yourself to your creator. Human efforts and strategies cannot propel you to the necessary height to regain the greatness that you lost in the garden. Sin brought death and separation from the God of creation and life. And nothing in your humanity can provide a thoroughfare whereby you, a dying man or woman, can be rejoined to the living God. Without Jesus Christ you are lost, operating beneath your creative greatness. You are a constant misfire in life that is condemned and doomed to perish in the eternal wrecking yard of damnation. You desperately need a savior. God's unconditional love has provided you a savior, a bridge whereby you can escape the wrecking yard to be reconnected to Him and crossover to the highway of life to step into your destiny.

"For God so loved the world, that he gave his only begotten Son, that whosoever believeth in him should not perish, but have everlasting life. For God sent not his Son into the world to condemn the world; but that the world through him might be saved" (John 3:16, 17 KJ)

God has great love and compassion for you. He gave His only begotten Son as a propitiation for your sins. The Father provided you with an advocate, a holy mechanic who imputes His righteousness to you, fixes your brokenness, and restores you to the newness of life.

"My little children, these things write I unto you, that ye sin not. And if any man sin, we have an advocate with the Father, Jesus Christ the righteous: And he is the propitiation for our sins: and not for ours only, but also for the sins of the whole world." (1John 2:1, 2 KJ)

Jesus Christ, God incarnate, is the only bridge that you can cross over to the Father. He is the only holy mechanic who can fix you up and reconnect you to the Father. **The shedding of His sinless blood is the only currency that is acceptable to the Father for your sins.** Not only is Jesus your sin offering He is also your advocate. He is your defender before the heavenly tribunal. He successfully defended your case and now sits at the right hand of God making intercessions for you. All courts in heaven are closed to Satan, your accuser. He can no longer defame or deny you access to the Father. **You are free!** He can no longer accuse you before the throne of God. He was defeated by the death and the shedding of the innocent blood of Jesus Christ, your advocate. The day you said "yes" to Jesus, your sins were forgivened and erased. You received a blood covering, shielding you from the storming elements of sin and eternal damnation. You are now **AWESOME YOU!** And you have a new high powered love fuel in your tank. Your body may look the same, but you have a new found power in your engine sparked by the high grade love fuel of the Holy Spirit. The God of love and the shed blood of Jesus Christ has forever liberated you from the accusations of the devil.

"And I heard a loud voice saying in heaven, Now is come salvation, and strength, and the kingdom of our God, and the power of his Christ: for the accuser of our brethren is cast down, which accused them before our God day and

night. And they overcame him by the blood of the Lamb, and by the word of their testimony; and they loved not their lives unto the death." (Revelation 12:10, 11 KJ)

Salvation is a heart and tongue matter. The moment that you believe in your heart, pray and confess with your mouth that Jesus is the Son of God, who died for your sins, and that God raised him from the dead, and invite Him to live in your heart, salvation is yours. Immediately you are reconnected to God, your identity is unveiled, and the door is opened for your purpose to be revealed. You are justified by the power of Jesus' resurrection. **Greatness Restored!**

Salvation has restored greatness and power to you. The Holy Spirit is God. He has taken up residence in you and He empowers you and establishes order in your life. He is the supreme love octane that fuels your engine. Your identity is defined by the Holy Spirit who lives in you and through you. **For He is a great God! Therefore you are great and you have great power!** The world carefully weighs your accomplishments, and if they measure up, then assigns you the title of great. Nevertheless, your accomplishments do not make you great. True greatness is the power within you that enables and empowers you to accomplish great things. Do not permit yourself or others to think of you as anyone less than great. **<u>You are awesome, holy royalty</u>!** And your greatness is not determined by the size of your house down here. Not by the size of your ministry. Nor by your bank account or the car you drive. As cars are created to demonstrate the power of gasoline, you are created to demonstrate the power of God's Spirit. The indwelling of the Holy Spirit is your supreme power source. And you can keep your tank filled by asking and walking in obedience to God's word. You are a member of God's chosen royal family. No wonder there's joy in heaven whenever a sinner repents and receives the salvation of our Lord Jesus Christ.

The kingdom of God is within you. Your identity is further revealed and your purpose completely embraced when you allow the greatness of the Spirit within to control your life. Now that He is resident in you, let Him be president over you. Your lifestyle of royalty is quite different than the common man. And as a babe in

Christ, which you are, regardless of your biological age at salvation, you need to be trained in the customs and manners of royalty. Prince William and Prince Harry of England were born as British royalty, but they are still going through extensive training and disciplines to learn how to live as royalty. There are books on etiquette, protocol, and procedures for them to live by. From their beginning on earth, the world has looked at them through microscopic eyes to see how they represent the kingdom of England and the royal family. And so will the world look at you, God's royal child, to see how you represent your Lord's kingdom. The Bible is the one book that should guide your actions and determine your conduct. Therefore, you need to be filled with the Spirit, you need to study and obey the word so that you walk in holiness and virtue. As a new babe you need a drastic change of lifestyle that is in keeping with your true identity and purpose. Godly change comes by surrendering to the word of God and the greatness within you. Put to death the works of the flesh and be crucified with Christ.

To be crucified with Christ you have to die to self will. The more you die to self, the more you surrender to the will and the word of God, the more Christ will be allowed to live in you and release his greatness through you. **Christ living in you is the victorious life.** He is the real source of your identity and purpose. He is the compass that guides you to your destiny. Jesus Christ is your destiny! If you dare see yourself as a suit of clothes that Jesus lives in, walks in, and works in, then you will release the reins of your will and live by faith in the Son of God, who died for your sins.

God has always communed with his people. Holy Communion is much more than the sacraments of bread and wine. Holy Communion is intimate relations and dialogue with God. Is God not speaking to you, you who are indwelled by the Holy Spirit, living under the covenant of grace in the age of the New Testament Church, as he spoke in times past to his patriarch, the father of faith?

"Now the Lord had said to Abram: Get out of your country, From your family, And from your father's house, to a land that I will show you. I will make you a great

nation: I will bless you. And make your name great; and you shall be a blessing:" (Genesis 12:1, 2 NKJ)

God made a covenant with Abram. He promised to make him a great nation and to make his name great. By this covenant God was establishing Abram's identity for generations to come. But first, God called on Abram to separate himself from that which was familiar to him, his country and his family. Three significant points emerge from God's command. (1) God must be first in terms of your allegiance. (2) God knows that familiarity stifles faith and breeds complacency, so He takes you into unfamiliar territory where you have to totally depend on Him. (3)God, who knows all things, will separate you from anything or anyone that hinders His purpose for you. I cannot emphasize enough that God's presence in you gives clarity to your identity, defines your purpose, promotes your destiny, and He is the source of your greatness. Therefore, to rise up and step into your destiny, God must be first. Your destiny is determined and magnified by your relationship to Jesus and His kingdom. Do not fall into the worldly trap of putting possessions and worldly prestige before Jesus. That's not your true source of fulfillment, nor is it where your true identity lies. You will be better served seeking love, joy, peace and the fruits of fulfillment. Why waste valuable time focusing on stuff, when God wants to give you an abundance of material things needed for this life? Jesus said:

"Therefore take no thought, saying, what shall we <u>eat</u>? Or what shall we <u>drink</u>? Or Wherewithal shall we be <u>clothed</u>? For after all these things do the Gentiles seek; for your heavenly Father <u>knoweth</u> that ye have need of all these things. But seek ye <u>first</u> the kingdom of God, and his righteousness; and <u>all these things</u> shall be added unto you." (Matthew 6:31-33 KJ)

When your priorities are right you shall delight in God's wisdom, walk in His favor, and the things of the world are added to you. True and complete fulfillment comes only from a living relationship with Jesus Christ. A relationship with God empowers you to fulfill your purpose. God is your destiny. And the Holy Spirit, your helper, is the promise of God. Take note of what Jesus said before his death and resurrection.

"And behold, I send the promise of my Father upon you: but tarry ye in the city of Jerusalem, until ye be endued with power from on high." (Luke 24:49)

The promise of the Father was for you to be endued with power from on high. The phrase endued with power means to be clothed with power. You can be filled and clothed with power. The ultimate of greatness is to have power within and without. You are not here by accident or coincidence. You are here by divine design, for purpose and eternal destiny. God is your destiny and He has instilled his greatness in you and clothed your outer shell with His power. God is within you because He desires to have an intimate relationship with you. God, the director of your great human drama, is inviting you to come into His throne room and have intimate fellowship with Him, so that your purpose can be revealed, magnified, and embraced. You can hear God's still small voice in your moments of intimacy with Him. Out of intimacy we experience new births, new favor, new ministries, new businesses, new opportunities, new relationships and a new anointing.

Prayer ushers you into God's throne room where he desires to richly abide with you in intimate fellowship. Divine Father loves intimate fellowship with his human children. In His throne room your true identity is unveiled and the bowls of identity and purpose are taken off the shelf and placed on his counter to be filled with your destiny. Part of your purpose is to take dominion over your affairs and this world's system. How can you take authority over the world's system without first knowing something about it? Is God calling you as the lead character in his human drama to an awareness of life that includes a business savvy that enables you to have dominion in this world? Saint of God, rise up! **GREATNESS IS WITHIN AND UPON YOU! YOU ARE INDWELLED AND CLOTHED BY THE SPIRIT OF GOD. YOU ARE GREAT AND YOU HAVE GREAT POWER!**

And thus from the wrecking yard of past sins and misfires you rise like a phoenix to the clarion call of God. You approach the starting gate of a new spiritual and business race, your human body fit and fueled with the supreme love octane of the Holy Spirit, destined to take the checkered flag of victory! In Him you can rise to every new challenge. God is the personification and true embodiment of your destiny! He is your greatest fortune! He is your brilliant compass and He is the only true source of wisdom! **God is your destiny! RISE UP AWESOME YOU! RISE UP AND STEP INTO YOUR DESTINY!**

CHAPTER TWO

A NEW CREATION IN CHRIST!

The Spiritual You is a New Creation In Christ Jesus. You are born again and the Spirit of the true and living God indwells you. You are a new creature. Your body may look the same, but there is a new Master and a new power in your house. **"Therefore <u>if any man</u> be in Christ, he is a new creature: <u>old things</u> are passed away; behold, <u>all things</u> are become new. And <u>all things</u> are of God, who hath <u>reconciled us</u> to himself by Jesus Christ, and hath <u>given to us</u> the ministry of reconciliation; To wit, that God was in Christ, reconciling the world unto himself, not imputing their trespasses unto them; and hath <u>committed unto us</u> the word of reconciliation. Now then <u>we are ambassadors for Christ</u>, as though God did beseech you by us: we pray you in Christ stead, be ye reconciled to God. For he hath made him to be sin for us, who knew no sin; <u>that</u> we might be made the righteousness of God in him."** (2 Corinthians 5:17-21 KJ)

You. As a new creature in Christ Jesus, you have been reconciled to God. You have been made the righteousness of God in Christ Jesus. You have graduated from just being a creature of God to now being a child of God. **God's Spirit makes you His special child.** You are no longer just a member of the human society; you are now a member of God's royal family. As a new creation in Christ you are destined for Max Life. Max Life is the abundant life on earth and eternal life with God in heaven. Jesus said: **"The thief cometh not,**

but for <u>to steal, and to kill</u> and <u>to destroy</u>: <u>I am come that</u> they might have life, and <u>that</u> they might have it <u>more abundantly</u>. <u>I am</u> the good shepherd: the good shepherd <u>giveth his life</u> for the sheep." (John 10:10, 11 KJ)

Jesus is the good shepherd and He willingly gave his life that your sins could be forgiven and eradicated. **You can now have abundant life on earth and eternal life with God. Max Life is only available to you and other Christians.** Max Life is living supernaturally in a natural world. God, the Holy Spirit, has taken up residence in you to transform you from a natural human being to a supernatural being in human form. Your life is no longer a see saw of emotional reactions to the people, events, and things of life that you are exposed to. Your supernatural life is a faith directed, divinely anointed, boldly empowered, and purpose driven life in Christ Jesus, the Good Shepherd. Shepherds lead; Sheep follow. Shepherds give directions; Sheep obey directions. Therefore, Jesus, your Savior, must also be your Lord. His Lordship over you guarantees you Max Life. Jesus will lead and guide you from a mundane existence to a purpose driven abundant lifestyle. Directions for Max Life are found in God's Holy Bible. His word will guide you from the darkness of despair and defeat, to the light of confidence and victory. **"<u>Thy word</u> is a lamp unto my feet, and a light unto my path."** (Psalms 119:105 KJ)

God's word will reveal Him Self and His ways to you. The good shepherd will never be a mystery to you if you will spend quality time in His word. God's greatest desire for you as His new creation is that you know Him and follow Him. His word is also a source of wisdom and knowledge that will enable you to prevail through trials and overcome any obstacle that impedes you from living the Max Life. To know and live your life in the ways of God brings joy, fulfillment and contentment. His word is always true and will never be ineffective in your life. God's word in your life is comparable to rain in a deserted wasteland. Just as the rain will restore the wasteland and cause it to overflow with fruit and vegetation, God's word will produce fruit and success in your life, transforming you from a wasteland to an oasis of plenty. **The Holy Spirit is not a distant power removed from you. He is God within you**. He desires to be intimate with you and nurture you from glory to glory. You also have the privilege to nurture the Spirit within you. Prayer, Praise, Bible Reading and Bible study are four essentials to nurturing the Spirit of God within. Just as you actively feed your flesh, consistently feed your Spirit and allow God within to lead you by applying His word.

Ask yourself, "Would God, the Creator of the heavens and the earth, recreate you to live the same deficient life that you were living before your salvation?" No! God created you anew to live a Max Life in Him. Therefore, you now have to make some major choices between following God's Spirit and living according to His standards, or allowing the old things of the flesh to guide you in the standards of sin and death. For the old things of the flesh to pass away and all things of the Spirit to become new, you have to choose to obey God's Spirit within you. The Spirit of God will be at war with your corrupt flesh. Old habits, peculiar disciplines, and familiar desires will actively stand in the way of the new you walking in God's path of righteousness. God's Word will guide you and His Spirit will strengthen and enable you to overcome old habits and familiar desires. The Holy Spirit is the new sheriff in town. He will bring godly order and establish righteous rule in your life if you choose to obey Him.

Imagine for a moment, that you just purchased a brand new Rolls Royce, the elite model of automobiles. No doubt you want to go beyond your general knowledge of how to drive and operate a car and truly understand how to get maximum enjoyment from your new Rolls. To do this you must spend some quality time in reading the car manual, studying the various instruments and applications. The car manual is the manufacturer's guide to teach you how to operate your new Rolls for maximum efficiency and enjoyment. Your new creation in Christ Jesus makes you the Rolls Royce of humanity. God created you anew and the Bible is His manual of instructions to teach you how to live life to the maximum. Maximum life equates to blessings in the inner person and blessings on the outer person. Your inner person has been blessed by the Holy Spirit. The fruit of the Spirit and the gifts of the Spirit are an outward manifestation of an inward power.

The fruit of the Spirit is like the engine of your new car. One engine with many parts and all the parts work in harmony to create an efficient, high performance automobile. The fruit of the Spirit is one fruit with nine different ingredients: love, joy, peace, longsuffering, gentleness, goodness, faith, meekness, temperance. They all work together to give you Max Life in Jesus Christ. With the fruit of the Spirit you now have a greater capacity to love, to experience joy, to endure hardship and suffer long, to exercise self control, to bask in peace and walk in the faith of Almighty God. There is inside of you a holy fruit that enables and empowers you to operate on a higher human plain.

As a born again believer you are a member of Christ's' body and you have been given at least one gift of the Holy Spirit. No doubt, like most Christians, you will walk in more than one gift. There are various gifts but one spirit. There are also differences of administrations, but the same Lord. And there are diversities of operations, but all under the control of the same God, Jesus Christ, who is the head of the body of Christ. **"For to one is given by the Spirit the <u>word of wisdom</u>; to another the <u>word of knowledge</u> by the same Spirit. To another <u>faith</u> by the same Spirit; to another the <u>gift of healing</u> by the same Spirit; To another the <u>working of miracles</u>; to another <u>prophecy</u>; to another <u>discerning of spirits</u>; to another <u>divers kinds of tongues</u>; to another <u>interpretation of tongues</u>: But <u>all</u> <u>these</u> worketh that one and the selfsame Spirit, dividing to <u>every man</u> severally as he will."** (1 Corinthians 12:8-11 KJ)

You. Do not hesitate to earnestly seek God for Spiritual gift(s). **He truly desires that you walk and operate in anointed power as His ambassador to establish his kingdom on earth.** In time you will come to know what gifts of the Spirit that you operate in. There will be visible manifestations of your gifts. Your spiritual gifts are not for self aggrandizement, but rather to profit the entire body of Christ and to confirm the Word of God. The manifestation of Spiritual gifts in your life is not a true barometer of growth and spiritual maturity. Therefore; do not think too highly of yourself because God anoints you with gifts of the Spirit. A true barometer of your spiritual growth and maturity is your development in the fruit of the Spirit. Periodically check yourself and see if you extend love and walk in joy and peace in the midst of storms. Do you walk in faith when the tides of life seem to be flowing against you? Do you suffer long and exercise self control during trials and tribulations? Are you good, gentle and kind to those who are unlovely toward you? The true measure of spiritual growth and maturity is your level of operation in the fruit of the Spirit. It is maturity in the fruit of the Spirit that promotes the ministry of reconciliation. As you mature in the fruit of the Spirit your witness and your works for God's kingdom will become more fruitful.

Me. Over the years I have noticed how God has navigated the events of my life to be reconciled to family and friends that I had been separated from. Since my salvation I had started to pray for many of the people who hurt and disappointed me. I know that I was led by the Holy Spirit to do this. As I prayed, I noticed that my hurt, anger, and resentment began to subside. Over time, in many prayers, I was asking God to forgive and bless those who had deeply hurt me. Sometimes the people who are the closest to you will hurt you the worse. Over the years, my prayers have disencumbered me from hurt, anger and resentment. After God freed me from my burden, He started to bring people back into my life that I had not seen in years. Many were family members. God was changing me from the old selfish, hurtful me. And many of my old acquaintances were impacted for good by the new me.

You. As a **New Creation in Christ Jesus,** you can also be above the old hurtful you and be reconciled to family and friends. God wants to impact family, friends, and the world through the new you. On God's canvas of humanity He is painting you anew with colors of greatness. You must cease to see the old you with ordinary brush strokes. God's brush strokes are always extraordinary. Therefore, you must accept the fact that you are forever a cut above ordinary natural humanity. You have not arrived but your inner colors have changed and you are indeed a New Creation in Christ Jesus, destined to live a supernatural lifestyle!

God is absolutely pumped about the new you. He has chosen you as His ambassador to represent Him and His kingdom on earth. As you go and walk in His righteous cause, His favor will bless you beyond measure. He wants to prosper you in every phase of your life. God's prosperity is underneath the skin and prosperity in the material realm. **"Let them shout for joy, and be glad, that favour my righteous cause: yea, <u>let</u> them say continually, Let the Lord be magnified, which hath pleasure in the prosperity of his servant."** (Psalms 35:27 KJ) God delights in prospering you and stroking you with colors of greatness. As His ambassador you walk and operate in His power. Earth is not your home. It is foreign soil where you are stationed to represent your Lord. Ambassadors always represent their home constituency on foreign soil. God's kingdom is not ordinary and it is not of this world. Ordinary people cannot adequately represent an extraordinary God. God has made you extraordinary so that you can effectively represent Him. He has high expectations for you; therefore, enjoy Max Life as His New Creation in Christ Jesus.

Me. It has taken time, prayer and the study of God's word, but I have fully embraced the new me. God has given me insight and inspiration to encourage me on my journey. I have had to let go of some hurtful things, words and people, in order to totally embrace the new me. I have had to fight battles in my own mind about who I really am. One of the ways that I have achieved victory in my inner battles is by speaking God's triumphant words over my inner and outer conflicts. I pray frequently asking God to let this mind be in me which was also in Christ Jesus. I was inspired by God's word. **"<u>Let</u> this mind be in you, which was also in Christ Jesus: Who, being in the form of God, thought it not robbery to be equal with God: But <u>made himself</u> of no reputation, and <u>took</u> upon him the form of a servant, and <u>was made</u> in the likeness of men: And being found in fashion as a man, <u>he humbled himself</u>, and <u>became obedient</u> unto death, even the death of the cross."** (Philippians 2:5-8 KJ)

Jesus was made in the likeness of men for his journey on earth. He willingly chose to be a servant and then humbled himself and became obedient unto the death of the cross. He did this for me so that I could be a new creation in Him. I refuse to be the old me. I refuse to languish in the familiar habits of despair and defeat. I speak and declare victory over my life because I am a New Creation in Christ Jesus!

You. Totally embrace the new you. Read the word, meditate on it, memorize it, apply it and speak the words of God your Creator over your life. For as a man thinks, so is he. **You are A New Creation in Christ Jesus! You are an Awesome Supernatural Saint of Awesome Almighty God! And you are destined to live the Max Life on earth.** And I am confident that one glad morning when this life on earth is over you, along with all the faithful saints of God, shall be presented faultless before our Heavenly Father with exceeding joy

CHAPTER THREE

MENTAL PICTURES, MASTER PHOTO

To embrace all that God has invested in you, you need to see yourself as God sees you. You need to correct the damaged and flawed mental pictures that you have allowed people and the experiences of this world to create in your mind. The world's mental pictures are based primarily on position, possessions and performance. Your worth is greater than your title, your position in life, or your possessions. You are greater than your last performance. You can hinder divine purpose in your life if you don't see yourself as God sees you. You always experience what you believe. If you constantly think or see something in your mind you will soon experience it in your life. The mental pictures that you have of yourself soon become the master photo of your existence.

"For as he thinks within himself, so is he." (Proverbs 23:7a NASB)

To illustrate this point, see your life as a snapshot. Jesus, our Creator, is the Master Photographer. Before natural birth God knew you, he knew your end before you had a beginning. Your life at birth represented a portion of film that was exposed to a small sphere of natural light. God put you on earth in the laboratory of life to go through the development process, so that your true image could be revealed. In the development process all the excess, unexposed film will be removed. Therefore, at some point in your development process, God calls you to be exposed to Spiritual light, because there's more to the photographer's image than what natural light can reveal. Spiritual light allows the film much greater exposure. The Spirit of your Photographer drew you to Himself. And when you responded affirmatively to the drawing of the Holy Spirit, you were born again and you became an **anointed negative.** Your **anointed negative** is a greater exposed image, and it is washed in a variety of development chemicals (love, joy, peace, faith, self control, patience, kindness, goodness, meekness) until your life is transformed into His image. Going through the development process allows you to see and become what the Master Photographer originally saw in his eternal lens. He knew you before he snapped your earthly picture. He has always known you.

"Now <u>the word of the Lord</u> came to me saying, <u>Before</u> I formed you in the womb I knew you, And <u>before</u> you were born I consecrated you; I have appointed you a prophet to the nations." (Jeremiah 1:4, 5 NASB)

The word of God tells Jeremiah that God knew him before he was born on earth. God ordained him as a prophet to the nations. There was identity and purpose for Jeremiah's life before his earthly birth. God also knew you before you were born. And like Jeremiah, you were born for purpose with an identity. Jeremiah could have ignored the voice of God and walked in disobedience and missed his purpose. He could have chosen to only be exposed to natural light; thus forfeiting his true and complete identity. He could have allowed the world to tell him who he was. Listening to the voice of the world could have caused him to miss his destiny. Today, whose voice do you choose to listen to - the voice of Destiny or this world?

Only the Master Photographer knows the complete image he saw in taking the picture; therefore, only the Master Photographer can properly develop the negative. From original creation in the garden, Jesus breathed a spiritual component on mankind's negative. There is so much more to you than natural light can reveal. No human film was ever designed to only be exposed to natural light. Master photos are exposed to human and spiritual light. Two things make the difference in a developed visible image and a master photo - the light that the film is exposed to and who mixes the chemicals in the lab. Regrettably, many live and die without Jesus in their lives - having become only a visible image exposed to natural human light. When you accepted God's love and gave your life to Jesus you became exposed to Spiritual light. **Jesus makes the difference in your life.** He is the spiritual light that gives greater exposure and enlargement to develop your permanently etched image.

As your good shepherd, Jesus will guide you, protect you, correct you, feed you and He will fulfill you. His word guides you through the darkened minefields of life, and gives you spiritual sustenance. He also gives you spiritual gifts, and He personally mixes the right chemical quantities of the fruit of the Spirit to develop you to be a master photo. **From the beginning of your new life in Jesus you are a masterpiece in the making.** No one can guide you through the darkness in the laboratory of this life as Jesus can. He is the light of the world, and the light of your life.

> **"Then Jesus again spoke to them, saying, I am the Light of the world; he who follows Me will not walk in darkness, but will have the Light of life."** (John 8:12 NASB)

Jesus, the Master Photographer, is the living word. He is the logos; the embodiment of the written word of God. The living word is the divine wisdom manifested in the creation and redemption of the world. The Bible is the written word that lights our path. His applied word will always guide your steps to avoid the ditches on the highway of life and to reach your heavenly destination.

Salvation in Jesus does not automatically change your mental pictures. Salvation gives you the power and the word of God gives you the images of and the guidelines to develop new mental pictures. None of us have arrived at new birth; therefore, we are masterpieces in the making. To develop into a master photo you need to read, study, memorize, and know what the word of God says about you and your destiny. God's word will inform you, enlighten you, inspire you, encourage you, enrich you, and motivate you. Whatever you take in is what will come out. A constant diet of the word can change any damaged and flawed mental pictures you may have had at new birth in Christ. Application of the word is essential for victorious living. And when you have a kingdom mentality, and not a church or human mindset, you will embrace God's word in your daily lifestyle. To know the word and not do it, is comparable to living like a pauper when you have a bank account with millions of dollars on deposit. Failure to use the instrument that gets the money from the bank to you will cause you to live beneath your rightful level of prosperity. God's word is the instrument that releases kingdom power in the affairs of your life. It is also a rich resource that clarifies your identity, guides your life, and feeds your spirit. And God wants you to prosper. He takes pleasure in your prosperity. God's prosperity begins underneath the skin. It involves more than an accumulation of money and stuff. However, God's prosperity will also manifest in the material realm. Especially to those who have a kingdom mentality. God desires that you prosper in the spirit, the soul, and the body.

"Beloved, <u>I pray that you may</u> prosper in all things and be in health, just <u>as</u> your soul prospers." (3 John 1:2 NKJ)

"<u>Let</u> them shout for joy, and be glad, that favour my righteous cause: yea, <u>let</u> them say continually, <u>Let</u> the Lord be magnified, which hath pleasure in the prosperity of his servants." (Psalms 35:27 KJ)

"<u>Praise the Lord</u>. <u>Blessed is</u> the man who fears the Lord, who delights greatly in His commandments. His descendants will be mighty on earth: The generation of <u>the upright</u> will be blessed. Wealth and riches will be in his house, and his righteousness endures for ever." (Psalm 112:1-3 NKJ)

God believes in you. He has created you with identity and purpose to rule over this world. Your "ruler ship" begins with your individual world and expands according to God's call on your life.

Your ruler ship of your situations and circumstances is greatly determined by the mental pictures you have of yourself. Your mental pictures will greatly determine how you manage the crisis in your life. Life on earth is an exercise in crisis management. Have your mental pictures been those of frustration, stagnation, procrastination, and defeat? **No more!** You are a new creation in Christ. You are designed and empowered to manage every crisis in your life. So then, how can you bring healing, correction, and change to the damaged, flawed mental pictures that you have of yourself? First, you need to choose to have the mind of Jesus Christ, the anointed one. His mind is not damaged or flawed. His mind created worlds and spoke cosmos out of chaos. Jesus was also the ultimate crisis manager when he lived on earth.

> **"Let this mind be in you, which was also in Christ Jesus: Who being in the form of God, thought it not robbery to be equal with God. But made himself of no reputation, and took upon him the form of a servant, and was made in the likeness of men: And being found in fashion as a man, he humbled himself, and became obedient unto death, even the death of the cross."** (Philippians 2:5-8 KJ)

Do you dare let the mind of God be in you? It is a willful choice that you should make. It is an active choice that requires a diligence on your part to tape the truth of God over the lies of the devil and this world. Today in this fast paced world you probably don't take time to erase information off a cassette or video tape. You simply tape over it. Be active in the study of God's word and allow it to tape truth over lies. Your mind (tape) will record whatever you expose it to. Reading God's word gives you knowledge. Knowing God's word changes your thought life. Doing God's word establishes dominion over your world and brings you victory and prosperity in spirit, soul, and body. Your mind is designed and built to process, retain, and release information. Who, what, and where does your source of information emanate from? You make the choice and you answer the question.

Second, you have to develop a kingdom mentality. A kingdom mentality is choosing to believe and accept God's word as your final authority. A kingdom mentality is not only thinking like God, but also operating like God. A kingdom mentality is having a godly perspective. In Genesis, the Bible says that you are made in God's image and after His likeness. After His likeness means that you are to operate like God. You are to take dominion and rule over your life and your world just as God does. With salvation, you get the Holy Spirit, divine power from on high, and you now have the spirit of truth to teach you all things, thus, equipping you to rule and have dominion.

Without fail, God will orchestrate or allow you to go through some familiar circumstances and crisis that challenged you before your salvation. When this happens you have to willfully choose to ignore the voice of habit. You don't have to respond in the same manner as you did when you were unsaved. When you were unsaved, your emotions guided you. Your responses were based on feelings, what you saw, and thought. When you have lived a life guided by emotions your mental pictures are damaged, distorted, and usually negative. Now you are a New Creation in Christ Jesus. All things have become new. Therefore, you need new mental pictures so that you will have new responses to old and new challenges. Motivated by your faith in God, your new mental pictures and responses will be shaped by God's word and not your emotions or past experiences. It is impossible to have a kingdom mentality without a strong abiding faith in God and His word.

"For we walk by faith, not by sight." (2 Corinthians 5:7 NKJ)

"So then <u>faith comes by</u> hearing, and <u>hearing by</u> the word of God." (Romans 10:17 NKJ)

Faith is always active. We <u>walk by faith</u> and <u>faith cometh by hearing</u>. Faith is never stagnant. You can't use yesterday's faith for today's or tomorrow's challenges. There is no substitute for consistent study of the word to build a sturdy unwavering faith

The fruit of the Spirit is the spiritual chemical that God uses to develop you in the laboratory of life. It is one fruit with nine different ingredients. All ingredients are necessary to produce victorious living, but none greater than love and faith. Throughout your development process love and faith will be the sustaining forces in your life. It was love that caused God to extend his saving grace to you. It was your faith that responded to His grace and ushered you into your salvation experience. When you begin to see yourself through the eyes of faith you see yourself as God sees you. When you have a kingdom mentality you know that you have godly strength within that enables you to defy defeat. You can rise above every obstacle and look at you and your world through spiritual lenses and eyes of faith. Eyes of faith make you peculiar and not ordinary. Eyes of faith and a kingdom mentality give you a conquering mindset that makes you a cut above average. Eyes of faith enable you to successfully manage your crisis because you have a godly perspective that reveals your godly potential for victory and success.

"That he would grant you, according to the riches of his glory, to be strengthened with might through his Spirit in the inner man." (Ephesians 3:16)

"I can do all things through Christ who strengthens me." (Philippians 4:13)

Your faith is built on God's sustaining love and what His word says about you. The word of God is your truth and His word says:

"But <u>you are</u> a chosen generation, a royal priesthood, a holy nation. His own special people, that you may proclaim the praises of Him who called you out of darkness into His marvelous light." (1Peter 2:9)

The fact that God chose you says that you are special. God's word says you are royal, holy, and peculiar. Royals rule over something. Holy people are spirit filled and spirit led people of God. Peculiar people are special people. They do not see themselves nor do they respond to crises and challenges the way that ordinary people do. They have a kingdom mentality and they choose to see victory over defeat and triumph over tragedy! The word of God says:

> **"Who shall separate us from the love of Christ? Shall tribulation, or distress, or persecution, or famines, or nakedness, or peril, or sword? Nay, in all these things <u>we are more than conquerors through him that loved us</u>. For <u>I am persuaded</u>, that neither death, nor life, nor angels, nor principalities, nor powers, nor things present, nor things to come, nor height, nor depth, nor any other creature, <u>shall be able</u> to separate us from the love of God, which is in Christ Jesus our Lord."** (Romans 8:35; 38,39)

You are engaged in a lasting relationship with the Holy Awesome God of creation and nothing can separate you from His love. **God loves you deeply and He wants the best for you.** One of God's great desires is that you see yourself as He does. God sees you as **Awesome You!** He wants you to live your life with a kingdom mentality and fulfill His great plan for your life. God will never leave you nor forsake you. His good thoughts are constantly with you and you will find Him when you seek Him with all your heart. God is not a respecter of persons and His word to Israel also applies to you.

> **"For I know the plans I have for you,' declares the Lord, plans to prosper you and not to harm you, plans to give you hope and a future. Then you will call upon me and come and pray to me, and I will listen to you. You will seek me and find me when you seek me with all your heart."** (Jeremiah 29:11-13 NIV)

When you earnestly seek God in His word, you will discover His presence throughout your life and circumstances. Knowing that God is always with you and that He thinks good thoughts about you, enables you to think good thoughts toward yourself. Hearing and knowing God's word should always be the final authority in your life. You know that God has plans to prosper you, plans to give you a hope and a future. This truth should shape your mental pictures to change and line up with God's word. By his word He spoke a world into existence. His word changed chaos into cosmos, disorder into divine order. Surely he can take whatever chaos you brought into your relationship with Him and change it to cosmos.

Now that you have a kingdom mentality and spiritual light in your life you are well on your way to becoming a master photo. Your relationship with God and an abiding faith in His word makes you more than a conqueror. Studying and applying the word of God, along with a consistent prayer life, will bring healing, correction, and change to your damaged and flawed emotions. Your godly perspective will cause your mental pictures to change, and you will see yourself as the chosen saint that God says you are. And you are more than a conqueror through Jesus Christ, who loves you.

You can develop a kingdom mentality and correct damaged emotions through the vital and practical exercise of daily speaking healing words of truth from God's holy word. Diligently guard against speaking or receiving negative words of death from your tongue or any other tongue.

"Death and life are in the power of the tongue: and they that love it shall eat the fruit thereof." (Proverbs 18:21)

What you say, good or bad, greatly affects the mental pictures you have of yourself. What you say and what you receive from others helps to form your mental pictures. You can choose to eat good/positive or bad/negative fruit. Choose to receive God's word and speak it over your life; thus, taking charge of your appetite, your environment and exercising dominion over your world. Guard against allowing people who do not have a godly perspective and speak words of death to occupy your surroundings.

Be fanatical about the voice you allow to mold and guide you. Choose the voice of your Creator over the voice of people, situations and circumstances. Situations and circumstances usually speak in a negative voice of despair. To overcome negative, distorted mental pictures of you, spend twenty minutes daily, in the privacy of any room that has a mirror in it. Look in the mirror and speak aloud to yourself, God's healing words of affirmation and validation. To be most effective personalize what you say. Let the word of God talk to you. This exercise will also aid in the memorization of the word. God's word tells you exactly how God sees you.

"Yet in all these things we are <u>more than conquerors through Him who loved us</u>." (Romans 8:37)

"I can do all things <u>through</u> Christ who strengthens me." (Philippians 4:13)

"And the Lord will make you the head and not the tail; you shall be above only, and not be beneath, if you heed the commandments of the Lord your God, which I command you today, and are careful to observe them." (Deuteronomy 28:13)

"<u>Thus says the Lord</u>, your Redeemer, the Holy One of Israel: I am the Lord your God, who teaches you to profit, who leads you by the way you should go." (Isaiah 48:17)

"And my God shall supply <u>all your need</u> according to His riches in glory by Christ Jesus." (Philippians 4:19)

Personalize the above Scriptures and speak them over your life: "I am more than a conqueror through Christ Jesus who loves me!" "I can do all things through Christ who strengthens me!" "I am the head and not the tail! I am above only and never beneath! I will listen and pay special attention to the commandments of the Lord my God! I will be careful to do all that He tells me to do!" "My God shall teach me to profit and lead me in the way that I should go!" "My God shall supply all my need according to his riches in glory by Christ Jesus!" Saturate your mind with the word of God. See it, hear it, meditate on it, speak it and do it. God's word will facilitate your life; and bring healing to your mind and body.

"My son, give attention to my words; Incline your ear to my sayings. Do not let them depart from your eyes; Keep them in the midst of your heart. For they are life to those who find them, And health to all their flesh." (Proverbs 4:20-22 NKJ)

This proverb gives you four dynamic principles for a productive life, a strong mind, and a healthy body. (1) Pay attention to God's word for it is the source of abundant living. (2) Hear the word and allow it to influence your decisions and actions. (3) Read the word consistently and let the word paint triumphant pictures of the real you. (4) Keep the word in your heart and walk in it. Meditate on the word as you walk through life and it will promote good health and guard your heart and mind from the evils in the world.

"Keep thy heart with all diligence; for out of it are the issues of life." (Proverbs 4:23)

The issues of life relates to more than the arteries which carry the blood to all parts of the body. It also refers to the evil and good deeds that come from the heart of mankind. God's word is life to you. It can be stored in your heart and never far from you if you make a conscience effort to meditate on it frequently, memorize it often, speak it consistently, and apply it daily. Allow God's word to dictate the issues of your heart.

Me. I believe in and have great respect for medical doctors; but they are never my first, my primary or my last option when my family and I are sick. Very seldom are we sick; but, I have learned to anoint my family and myself with oil, and pray over us. I also saturate us with the word frequently and always during any kind of crisis; whether spiritual, mental, physical, or financial. By faith, I declare blessings over our lives, as I let my petitions and supplications be made known to God, with thanksgiving. Thanksgiving is the language of faith; therefore, I spend a great deal of time thanking God during my prayers and throughout my day. I also declare **God's will, God's leading, God's peace, and God's resources** over our lives in my daily prayers. *"Today, Dear God, I declare your Godly* *will over our lives. Thy will be done in our lives as it is in heaven. Thank you for Your Godly leading in our lives today. Thy word is a lamp unto our feet and a light unto our path. Lord Jesus, You are our Great Shepherd, we are your sheep. You know us and we follow you. Anoint our eyes to see. Anoint our ears to hear. Anoint our minds to think your thoughts. Let this mind be in us which was also in Christ Jesus. Anoint our lips to speak words of life and encouragement. Anoint our hands to touch others with compassion. Anoint our hearts to receive your word. Anoint our wills to obey your word. Thank you for Your Godly peace today. Peace that passes all understanding. Peace that flows like a river in the midst of every storm. Thank you for Your Godly resources. Thank you for the right timing, the right situation and circumstances. Thank you for the right people and projects. Thank you for the right financial deal."* I have decided that God will always have the first and last word in the affairs of our lives.

God gave me the following declaration in celebration of my birthday in 2005. I have committed these words to memory through constant repetition, and I have also taught them to my fourteen year old son, Michael. He and I pray these words over our lives and our family, each morning, before he goes to school. I pray them again later, during my prayer time in God's throne room. *"TODAY, I'M SET FOR VICTORY, SUCCESS, PROSPERITY, HEALTH, PEACE AND GREAT INCREASE! I THANK GOD MY FATHER, FOR HIS AWESOME, FAR BEYOND FAVOR AND HIGH INFLUENCE' OPERATING IN, OVER, AND THROUGH MY LIFE...* (I name other family members). *THANK YOU LORD JESUS! WE ARE BLESSED AND HIGHLY FAVORED WITH YOUR FAR BEYOND FAVOR AND HIGH INFLUENCE, TODAY'! INCREASE! INCREASE! INCREASE!"*

You. To experience the explosive power of God's word you have to own it. To own it, you have to personalize it, speak it repeatedly and do it. The constant personal repetition and implementation of God's word makes it yours. The word of God, working in conjunction with the Holy Spirit, is the dynamite substance of your faith. Doing the word lights the fuse to explode the dynamite power in **AWESOME YOU!** Search the Bible for other Scriptures that will speak healing to your damaged and flawed emotions; thus, changing and correcting your mental pictures. Trust God your Creator, have His mind, speak His truths and allow Him to have the first and last word in the affairs of your life. Do you dare have a godly perspective and see yourself as God does? **GOD SEES AWESOME YOU AS A MASTERPIECE IN THE MAKING!**

CHAPTER FOUR

A MASTERPIECE IN THE MAKING!

As saints of God, who have not arrived yet, we are truly Masterpieces in the Making. We are now under godly construction and the Lord Jesus Christ is the architect and the master builder. Own and embrace these truths. You are a new creation in Christ Jesus and the Holy Spirit and God's word continues to reveal your true identity, correct your mental pictures, and heal your damaged emotions to make you a master photo. Owning and embracing the word of God builds you up and equips you to live as a supernatural being in a natural world. You are Christ workmanship created unto good works.

"For we are His workmanship, created in Christ Jesus for good works, which God prepared beforehand that we should walk in them." (Ephesians 2:10 NKJ)

Jesus Christ is the Master; therefore, those of us who are His workmanship created in Him, we are pieces of the Master. Our God is a God of excellence. As His workmanship created unto good works we must also strive for excellence. We must rise above the crowd of mediocrity and excel as anointed vessels of God. Masterpieces should be a carbon copy of their master. And we honor God by rising above the common ground to excel above mediocrity. God did not create us just to get by. Jesus came as a human, like us, so that humanity could be like Him. He spent time on earth living with humanity, demonstrating His love, His compassion, His passion and His power, so that those of us whose lives are hid in Him could be like Him and live like Him.

You. See the new you from a godly perspective. Shake off the shackles of past fears and mistakes. Embrace God's word; let God's anointing, and your gifts thrive, let fear and weakness die. You are what you perceive yourself to be. Therefore, your new self image should evolve from your master. It is virtually impossible to rise above your perception of yourself. What you think of yourself and how you see yourself is what you will ultimately become. God alone knows your true potential and when He saved you, He empowered you to become a masterpiece. You are His workmanship under godly construction to do good works which He prepared for you before your salvation experience. God has planted in you all that you need to become His masterpiece. God will never abandon you. He will not leave His work in your life undone.

"Being confident of this very thing, that He who has begun a good work in you will complete it until the day of Jesus Christ." (Philippians 1:6 NKJ)

Our God sees each one of us as a diamond in the rough. And diamonds in the rough are nonetheless diamonds. The diamond cutter who cuts, cleans, molds and shapes the diamond is the defining factor that ultimately determines the value and worth of what the diamond will become. Throughout the pages of the Bible we read of God's interactions with His creation. Often He begins a relationship by telling someone what they will become if they obey Him, and follow His directions. And what they become is much greater than what they perceived of themselves to be. Take note of God's call to Jeremiah:

"Then the word of the Lord came to me, saying: "Before I formed you in the womb I knew you; Before you were

born I sanctified you; I ordained you a prophet to the nations." (Jeremiah 1:4, 5 NKJ)

God knows you before you are conceived in your mother's womb. He designed purpose, potential, and perspective for you before you knew Him. Jeremiah questioned God about his youth, thinking that he was too young to speak on behalf of Almighty God. God saw great potential in Jeremiah and spoke these words to him:

"Do not say, I am a youth,' For you shall go to all to whom I send you, And whatever I command you, you shall speak. Do not be afraid of their faces, For I am with you to deliver you," says the Lord." (Jeremiah 1:7, 8 NKJ)

Jeremiah went on to become one of the greatest prophets to the nation of Israel, speaking on behalf of Almighty God. The same God who spoke to Jeremiah speaks to you. Whatever assignment God gives you, He has already anointed and equipped you to do it. Therefore, you must see yourself as God does. Your life is hid in Him and nothing is too hard for your God. The Lord Jesus Christ is the great diamond cutter and He is a master potter. He knows how to clean, cut, shape and mold you into a vessel of honor and excellence. The words that God spoke through Jeremiah, at the potter's house, to the nation of Israel can be a great source of encouragement to you.

"Then the word of the Lord came to me, saying: O house of Israel, can I not do with you as this potter?' Look, as the clay in the potter's hand, so are you in My hand, O house of Israel! The instant I speak concerning a nation and concerning a kingdom, to pluck up, to pull down, and to destroy it, if that nation against whom I have spoken turns from its evil, I will relent of the disaster that I thought to bring upon it. And the instant I speak concerning a nation and concerning a kingdom, to build and to plant it, if it does evil in My sight so that it does not obey My voice, then

I will relent concerning the good with which I said I would benefit it." (Jeremiah 18:5-10 NKJ)

It is clear from God's word that He is in charge of individuals and nations. If you walk in obedience to His word, you will rise to great heights, and walk in the blessings of God. As God's masterpiece, He will do great and mighty things in and through your life. God sees you as A Masterpiece in the Making! If you see yourself otherwise, then you risk missing your purpose and living beneath your godly capacity. Embrace God's word and allow His word to align your perception with His perception of you. God created you and I. He knows what He has deposited in us before we came to know Him.

There was an obvious change in Jeremiah's prospective after God spoke to him. Is God not the potter and we the clay? The potter is the ultimate visionary for a lump of clay. The diamond cutter is the ultimate visionary for the diamond in the rough. God can, and God does birth His vision for our lives into us. Therefore, we need to receive His godly perception of us. For God has anointed us, and He greatly desires to mold us, and shape us into His masterpieces. With a godly perspective, we can successfully do the works of service that were prepared for us beforehand. Do not diminish your value to God by having a negative perception of yourself.

Me. Hurtful words and negative racial activities were a part of my growing up in Texas. My time in the entertainment business continued to reinforce some of the hurtful experiences from childhood. I always worked diligently to overcome and prove myself worthy. I also thought that I could try harder, be smarter, work longer, and outwork the next person to accomplish my goals. My problem was, I had allowed my perception, and my confidence to be attached to my accomplishments and possessions. I did not learn until God began to speak to me in His word, that my value was truly attached to my Creator, and what He says about me. My perception greatly changed when I learned that I had been chosen by God into a holy family of royalty and Jesus had washed me in His blood and made me a king and a priest unto God the Father.

"But you are a chosen generation, a royal priesthood, a holy nation. His own special people, that you may proclaim the praises of Him who called you out of darkness into His marvelous light; who once were not a people but are now the people of God, who had not obtained mercy but now have obtained mercy." (1 Peter 2:9, 10 NKJ)

"As His divine power has given to us all things that pertain to life and godliness, through the knowledge of Him who called us by glory and virtue, by which have been given to us exceedingly great and precious promises, that through these you may be partakers of the divine nature, having escaped the corruption that is in the world through lust." (2 Peter 1:3, 4 NKJ)

"To Him who loved us and washed us from our sins in His own blood, and has made us kings and priests to His God and Father, to Him be glory and dominion forever and ever. Amen" (Revelations 1:5B, 6 NKJ)

These Scriptures clearly define who I am and who you are. The word king in Revelation is a generic word. It also includes queens. I have spent many hours, reading, studying, memorizing, and speaking these words over my life. They have become the seed and root of my being. It did not happen quickly, and it did not come easily, but it did happen. God's word is like seeds planted in the vineyard of our humanity. His seeds are complete but it takes time for growth and development. Like any seed, I had to continue to nurture God's word in my vineyard through praise and prayer. I claimed His promises, knowing that God has given me all things pertaining to life and godliness. I am equipped and empowered in the natural and spiritual realm. I am a partaker of God's divine nature. Through the knowledge of Jesus I have discovered that I am A Masterpiece in the Making!

Over time I have experienced a dramatic change, and received a joyful spirit from reading, studying, memorizing and speaking over my life what God says about me. And His words continue to stimulate a positive change in my perception of myself.

You. Rise above hurtful words and allow God's word to heal your damaged emotions. Embrace the words of your Creator. Agree with God's word and not your emotions. Allow the Holy Spirit and the word of God to affirm and inspire you. When you have a godly perception of yourself you can run with purpose, perspective, and passion. Jesus died that you could become His servants. You are empowered by God to do greater works and establish His kingdom on earth. **You are God's Anointed Masterpiece!**

A great example in the Bible that gives insight and encouragement to become God's masterpiece is the story of Gideon. God saw great potential in Gideon. God partnered with him to accomplish great things for His people and His kingdom on earth. The disobedient children of Israel had done evil in the sight of the Lord, so God delivered them into the hand of the Midianites. The Midianites, the Amalekites and other people of the East came against Israel and destroyed their crops and stole their livestock, leaving them in a destitute condition. Israel cried out to the Lord asking for help. Almighty God chose Gideon, the son of Joash, the Abiezrite to deliver his people from the stranglehold of the Midianites. Gideon threshed wheat in secret by the winepress to hide it from the Midianites. Gideon thought very little of himself, based on his family heritage and their position among the other tribes. He also said that he was the least in his father's house. That was Gideon's perception. Listen to how the Angel of the Lord addressed him and revealed God's perception of him.

"The Lord is with you, you mighty man of valor!" (Judges 6:12 NKJ)

God called Gideon a mighty man of valor! God knew he was brave, strong in mind and spirit. God's perception of Gideon was not based on his family heritage, his present conditions, or his status in the community. God had purpose for Gideon's life. He saw Gideon's potential and His perception of him was totally elevated above Gideon's own perception of himself. God has purpose for you and I, and He also has an elevated perception of you and I. The Creator knows the capabilities of his created beings before He reveals them to us.

Gideon was told that the Lord was with him. Having heard about the great exploits of God, Gideon ask the Angel of the Lord, where are all the miracles that he had heard his father talk about when God brought them up from Egypt? The Angel of the Lord, who was Jesus, came to Gideon, and called him a mighty man of valor, revealing God's perception of him. Then God reveals His purpose for Gideon's life. God's perception of us is always in agreement with God's purpose for us.

"Then the Lord turned to him and said, Go in this might of yours, and you shall save Israel from the hand of the Midianites. Have I not sent you?" (Judges 6:14 NKJ)

When Gideon questioned his abilities and his family connections, God told Gideon that He would be with him, and that he would defeat the Midianites as one man. After the Lord departed from Gideon, his perception of himself changed drastically. He also received a new name, Jerubbaal, which means great, captain, chief, and to contend. His new name was more in line with his new godly perception of himself. Gideon rallied his troops on Mount Gilead and some thirty-two thousand men answered the call. God told Gideon the army was too large for God to give him victory over the Midianites, without them thinking that they had won the battle in their own strength, and deny God his rightful glory. Following God's instructions, Gideon told all those who were fearful and afraid to leave Mt. Gilead at once. Twenty-two thousand of the people left. God said, there were still too many, so he told Gideon how to test the men to see who was fit for battle. Three hundred men passed the test and followed Gideon into battle. God diminished the number of warriors because He was going to deliver the Midianites and Amalekites by His power into the hands of Gideon and Israel. We see an example of A Limited Partnership for Unlimited Success, between God and humanity. God supplies power, resources, guidance and mankind has to do all the work. The Spirit of the Lord was upon Gideon and he, along with three hundred men, defeated Israel's enemies, blowing the trumpets, breaking pitchers and shouting a loud war cry: "The sword of the Lord and of Gideon!"

You. What God did for Gideon He will also do it for you. God delights in elevating His created beings and He specializes in picking up the downcast. God has designed you for purpose. His perception of you, no matter what you thought of yourself at salvation, is greater than your human perception. His perception of you is in agreement with His purpose for your life.

Me. In 1999, I was sitting on my front stoop in Herndon, Virginia. It was a beautiful early evening in late September. As I looked up at the white fluffy clouds slowly dancing across the canopy of tranquil blue sky, I started to whisper, "Lord, thank you... what a masterpiece you have created. You are a master creator." I thanked God for all His provisions. "Thank you for my family. Thank you for your call on my life. Thank you for the fruit and the gifts of the Holy Spirit operating in my life. Thank you, Lord... thank you for your masterpiece..." As I continued to sit and gaze into the sky, I kept saying... "What a masterpiece. What an awesome God you are..." The peace and the joy of the Lord overwhelmed me. Sometime in the midst of my reverie my four year old son, Michael, came and sat beside me on the stoop in front of our townhouse. As he gently leaned against me, putting his hand on my back, I looked down at him. He looked up at me with a gentle smile on his face. As I put my arm around him, both of us looking up into the sky, God spoke to me and said: "He is My Masterpiece. You are My Masterpiece." Immediately, tears began to well up in my eyes. I quickly wiped them away with my free hand and looked down at Michael who was still looking into the sky. As Michael and I sat there, I meditated on God's words about my son and I... "He is My Masterpiece. You are My Masterpiece." I knew that God was not just saying that Michael and I were His masterpieces. I immediately thought of Scriptures that I had committed to memory, telling me that we were God's special people chosen by Him. As His words continued to resonate in my mind God took me on a scriptural journey.

He took me back to Genesis and His creation of mankind in His image and after His likeness. God spoke all life into existence with magnanimous litanies of "Let there be..." But with man, His crowning jewel of creation, He took dirt, shaped and molded it in His image. Then He breathed His breath of divine inspiration, intellect, soul and spirit into man and man became a living being. Man's disobedience to God in the Garden of Eden, an oasis of plenty created by God for man, caused mankind to immediately be disconnected from God spiritually and ultimately to die physically. Mankind forfeited God's divine inspiration and lost His inward presence, ushering death into mankind's scenario. For many years mankind suffered greatly being spiritually separated from God and void of divine inspiration. Jesus, the Son of God, willingly came to earth to die for mankind's sin and provide a path whereby we could once again be reconnected to God the Father. Jesus restored mankind as God's crowning jewel of creation. I began to quietly thank Jesus for saving me, being my bridge back to the Father and sending the Holy Spirit, my teacher and Comforter to richly indwell me.

From that day until now I have taught Michael that he is A Masterpiece in the Making. I wanted to give him a Godly perception of himself before teachers and others in the world planted their seeds into his life. I not only taught Michael, but I also began a consistent regimen to reinforce and retrain myself to accept and embrace God's perception of me. As a child of God I am also A Masterpiece in the Making! I fully embrace and accept what God said to me. My son, my wife and I have not arrived at full maturity. We are still in the making. Our lives on earth are apprenticeships where we are under godly construction. We continue to grow and mature in the Spirit. To this day, if you ask him, Michael will tell you that he is A MASTERPIECE IN THE MAKING.

I know that you, like all Christians, are under godly construction. To have a solid foundation we all have to embrace God's perception of us. The Jesus in us is the Master. We are individually pieces of the Master. Diligently search God's word. He speaks volumes to you and I through His word. You also may have special moments as I described above about Michael and I. However God speaks, embrace His word and faithfully walk in it. Believe what God says about you, and do what God tells you. Walking in His perception of you, and working out His purpose for you will cause you to be a **FANTASTIC SAINT WITH A FANATICAL FAITH!**

CHAPTER FIVE

FANTASTIC SAINT, FANATICAL FAITH!

YOU ARE CHOSEN! YOU ARE ROYAL! YOU ARE HOLY and **YOU ARE PECULIAR! And you have great potential! God literally calls you fantastic!** You are God's fantastic saint, called out of darkness, illuminated and developed by His light to do great works.

> **"For <u>we are</u> His workmanship, created in Christ Jesus <u>for</u> good works, which God prepared beforehand and <u>that</u> we should walk in them."** (Ephesians 2:10)

You are God's handiwork, consecrated unto Him to do good works. You are Destiny's child of purpose. When Jesus walked on earth He repeatedly told His followers and other listeners the purpose for which He had come. And His purpose was much greater than His job as a carpenter.

> **"And He was handed the book of the prophet Isaiah. And when He had opened the book, He found the place where it was written: The Spirit of the Lord is upon Me, Because He has anointed Me To preach the gospel to the poor; He has sent Me to heal the brokenhearted, To proclaim liberty to the captives And recovery of sight to the blind,**

To set at liberty those who are oppressed;To proclaim the acceptable year of the Lord.' Then He closed the book, and gave it back to the attendant and sat down. And the eyes of all who were in the synagogue were fixed on Him. And He began to say to them, Today this Scripture is fulfilled in your hearing.' So all bore witness to Him, and marveled at the gracious words which proceeded out of His mouth. And they said, "Is this not Joseph's son?"(Luke 4:17-22 NKJ)

"Now in the morning, having risen a long while before daylight, He went out and departed to a solitary place; and there He prayed. And Simon and those who were with Him searched for Him. When they found Him, they said to Him, Everyone is looking for You.' But He said to them, Let us go into the next town, that I may preach there also, because for this purpose I have come forth.' And He was preaching in their synagogues throughout all Galilee, and casting out demons." (Mark 1:35-39 NKJ)

Jesus was faithful to fulfill His purpose for being on earth. His life was about much more than building cabinets, tables, benches, etc. Being a carpenter was His job. And even though those in the synagogue identified Him with His earthly father and occupation, He knew it was not His purpose. He had come to preach to the hurting, the lost, to heal the sick, to cast out demons, and to set the captives free. Then He chose twelve men as disciples to walk with Him. He allowed them to see Him at work, so that they would have a model to follow. Peter, Matthew and His other disciples had various jobs as itinerant fishermen and tax collector; but to be His disciples, they had to forsake all and follow Him. They became fishers of men. They used their talents to embrace and fulfill their purpose. God often uses our talents and acquired skills; therefore, He may use your talents and skills to fulfill your purpose.

One of the essential keys to the fulfillment of purpose is to be found faithful. Jesus was a man of faith who was faithful to a life of prayer, Holy Communion with the Father, and dedication to His responsibilities. He rose early before his day of ministry to spend quality time with His Father. His faith was fortified, His strength renewed, and His inspiration rekindle during His prayer time with the Father. Jesus was faithful. And the Holy Scriptures commands every servant of Christ to be faithful.

"Let a man so consider us, as servants of Christ and stewards of the mysteries of God. Moreover it is required in stewards that one be found faithful." (1 Corinthians 4:1, 2 NKJ)

Today, Jesus is still the most perfect and complete model to follow as a human being. He was a great leader who was totally committed to serving humanity. He consistently demonstrated the power of faith in the spoken word. He spoke miracle after miracle in the lives of the people He touched and served. He consistently chided His disciples about having little faith. On a trip from Bethany He saw a fig tree with leaves. Leaves indicated that the tree should have figs on it. When He found no figs He spoke a curse on the tree and it dried up from the roots and died. Peter and the disciples were amazed that his spoken word caused the tree to die overnight.

"And Jesus answering saith unto them, <u>Have faith in God.</u> For verily I say unto you, That whosoever shall say unto this mountain, Be thou removed, and be thou cast into the sea; and <u>shall not doubt in his heart</u>, but <u>shall believe</u> that those things which he saith shall come to pass, <u>he shall have whatsoever he saith</u>. Therefore I say unto you, <u>What things</u> soever ye desire, when ye pray, <u>believe</u> that ye receive them, and <u>ye shall have them</u>. And <u>when ye</u> stand praying, forgive, if ye have ought against any: that your Father also which is in heaven may forgive you your trespasses. <u>But if ye</u> do not forgive, neither will your Father which is in heaven forgive your trespasses." (Mark 11:22-26 KJ)

Jesus tells Peter, the other disciples, you and I, to have a fanatical faith. A fanatical faith is enthusiastic, it's intense, it's excessive, and it's very rewarding. This fanatical faith that the Master commands us to have has four dynamic "d's". Jesus tells us to have faith in God. He commands us to be **decisive.** Faith in God is decisive, it's resolute, and it does not waver because God is the object of our faith. Therefore when we have a decisive faith in God, we will declare a thing and not ask for it. Listen to his words carefully. <u>He did not say what you ask</u>. He said <u>what you say and doubt not</u>. He said <u>what you desire, believe that you receive</u>. Learn the promises of God in his word and make declarations instead of praying interrogative prayers. Yes, we can ask, but ask in agreement with His promises, and not out of curiosity.

The Master also tells us to be **defiant.** Defy the mountains-the obstacles in our way. Do not give up and succumb to our problems. Defy our challenges by declaring the word of God to them. Do not allow problems and challenges to beat you down. Stand in the power of God's might and defy them. God is all powerful. Nothing is too hard for Him. God will move on our behalf when we have had enough to say: **"I'm not putting up with this anymore! MOUNTAIN! BE REMOVED! GET OUT OF MY WAY NOW!"**

Jesus tells us to be **dependent** on God. He says that what we ask the Father in his name we shall have. Once you know his promise you declare a thing in agreement with his word. Be dependent on God when you pray and believe that you have received what you declare in agreement with his promise. **The promises of God are yea and amen. So be it!**

The greatest hindrance to receiving answers and having victory in our prayer life is found in the fourth "d." The Master commands us to be **devoted to forgiveness.** When we pray, we must forgive. Hold no grudge in our hearts for it blocks the airwaves of our prayers reaching the heart of God. He may hear our prayer but it cannot penetrate his heart if we refuse to forgive. Forgiveness is a matter of the heart between you, God, and the person you have been wounded by. Forgiveness is not based on our right and the other persons wrong. That is why it requires devotion on our part. Forgiveness is not a casual, surface response. It is deeply felt and purposefully given. Yes, you are wounded. Maybe you have been wounded by someone close to you who you loved and trusted. Sometimes you will be hurt the worst by the people you love and trust the most. The question is never did they wrong and wound you. The question is, do you have the faith to trust God where you hurt? Can you let go and let God rule in the place of your wounded pain? Being devoted to forgiveness comes from maturity in the faith. **Devotion to forgiveness is our greatest demonstration of exemplifying the love of Christ.** On the cross of Calvary, after having been falsely tried, lied on, beaten, scourged, ridiculed, spat on, and crowned with thorns, Jesus said: "Father forgive them, for they know not what they do." He was devoted to forgiveness. Your purpose, and my purpose, is to be like Christ.

You. Prayer is absolutely essential for you to be a fantastic saint with a fanatical faith. Prayer allows you to dialogue with God. **You talk and God listens. God talks and you listen.** In prayer, God will often reaffirm what He has said in His word. God has made some promises to you in his word. God has said some dynamic truths about you in the Holy Scriptures. Through prayer you can declare what God has said about you and thus have access to divine power for your daily pursuits. **Through prayer you have heavenly treasures for your earthly needs.** Prayer keeps you focused and always dependant on God. You are God's ambassador and you have the power of attorney to act on His behalf. The name of Jesus gives you acceptance in heaven and authority on earth.

> **"And <u>in that day</u> ye shall <u>ask me nothing</u>. Verily, verily, I say unto you, <u>Whatsoever</u> ye shall ask the Father <u>in my name</u>, he will give it you. Hitherto have ye ask nothing in my name: <u>ask</u>, and ye shall receive, <u>that</u> your joy may be full."** (John 16:23, 24 KJ)

Jesus speaks to his disciples and to you and I, His church. He speaks of the time when He will no longer be with us on earth. In that day He commands you to ask the Father in His name, and whatsoever you ask the Father in His name, you shall receive that your joy may be full. Do not hesitate nor be afraid to ask for any spiritual, physical, or material blessing, but always ask in faith. **God will withhold no good thing from you if you walk uprightly.** Faith is the necessary ingredient to receive anything from God. Obedience to God fortifies your faith in God.

Faith without works is dead. Therefore, your faith is constantly tested. Problems and challenges that you could not face and conquer before, now you can in Christ Jesus. And Christ will test your faith at a very early stage and throughout your walk with Him. Jesus tested Peter's faith in the very early stages of their relationship. After using his boat to teach the multitude, the Master commanded Peter to launch out into the deep and let down his nets for a catch. This may not seem like a big deal but it was a great test of faith for Peter and his fishing partners. Peter's first response was a natural reaction based on his feelings and fishing expertise:

"And Simon answering said unto him, Master, we have toiled all the night, and have taken nothing: nevertheless <u>at thy word</u> I will let down the net." (Luke 5:5 KJ)

Peter's fishing experience momentarily guided his thoughts and his reaction. No doubt he thought, "It's noonday and very hot, when the fish swim down at the bottom of the lake. Our nets cannot reach the fish." That is why they would fish at night, when the fish swam near the top of the lake. Also, he had already cleaned his nets and did not want to have to clean them again by dropping them back into the water. Listen to Peter's emotions and experience guiding his thoughts. "Why row back out into the deep? We are tired, we have toiled all night. We just want to go home. We won't catch any fish, it's too hot. We just finished cleaning the nets!" And then his faith kicked in... "nevertheless at thy word I will let down the net." When Peter obeyed the Master and dropped his net, he and his partners caught more fish than the nets could hold. They had a boat load of fish, more than they could handle, so he called to all the fishing buddies on shore to come out and help. And they filled both boats with so many fish that the boats began to sink.

Jesus teaches us volumes through this encounter with Peter and the fishermen. You too can reap the benefits of these principles. **Faith** in God's word should always override emotions and life experiences. Faith is tested in deep water. **You will never reap deep water blessings in shallow water living.** Faith is not tested in shallow water living but in deep water launches. **Trusting in and obeying God's word always brings a bounty for you and others.** God gave Peter a bounty because He wanted to bless the other fisherman who had toiled all night and caught nothing. God never blesses you with just you in mind. His desire is to always meet the needs of others through you. God desires that you be His channel, through whom His blessings will flow into the lives of others. Heaven and earth shall pass away but the word of God shall stand. Always trust God's word and put it into action.

Later in Peter's relationship with the Master, his faith was tested in a greater way and he allowed the conditions around him to erode his faith.

"And in the fourth watch of the night Jesus went unto them, <u>walking on the sea.</u> And when the disciples saw him walking on the sea, they were troubled, saying, It is a spirit; and they cried out for <u>fear'</u>. But straightway Jesus spake unto them, saying, Be of good cheer; it is I; <u>be not afraid</u>. And Peter answered him and said, Lord, if it be thou, bid me come unto thee on the water'. And he said, Come. And when Peter was come down out of the ship, <u>he walked</u> on the water, to go to Jesus. <u>But when he saw the wind boisterous</u>, he was afraid; and beginning to sink, he cried, saying, Lord, save me'. And immediately Jesus stretched forth his hand, and caught him, and said unto him, O thou of <u>little faith</u>, wherefore didst thou <u>doubt</u>"? (Matthew 14:25-31 KJ)

There are times in life when storms are raging and only the voice of God can speak to our fear. God often allows storms to test us. Being tested in a storm is a great challenge that builds fanatical faith. When you obey God's word and not allow the conditions of the storm to erode your faith, you can experience water walking miracles. After Jesus identifies himself, He tells the disciples to not be afraid. Peter, in response, makes a faith request. He asked Jesus to bid him come to him on the water. Peter asked Jesus to let him walk on water. And Jesus response was, "Come! Walk on the water". Take note that Peter's faith propelled him to get out of the boat and walk on water. Peter walked on water until he took his eyes off Jesus and looked at the conditions surrounding him. You can have fanatical faith, especially when you are tested in a storm, if you keep your eyes stayed on Jesus. You can exercise water walking faith if you keep your eyes stayed on Jesus and obey His word. Being focused on Jesus in the midst of a storm builds trust and keeps you in perfect peace.

"Thou wilt keep him in perfect peace, whose mind is stayed on thee: because he trusteth in thee." (Isaiah 26:3 KJ)

More often than not, what breaks down and erodes your faith are the sight factors. What you see, what you hear, what you think, and what you feel are sight factors. Sight factors should never dictate your steps because they usually work against faith.

"For we walk by faith, not by sight." (2 Corinthians 5:7 KJ)

It's not the amount of faith that enables you to stand in the storm, it's more of how do you release the faith you have, and not allow it to be eroded by sight factors. If you are saved, you definitely have faith. Faith was your part in the salvation experience. Grace was God's part. **"For <u>by grace</u> are ye saved <u>through</u> faith; and that <u>not of</u> yourselves: <u>it is</u> the gift of God."** (Ephesians 2:8 KJ) And God has given you a measure of faith. You can increase and strengthened the measure you have through prayer, reading, studying, memorizing, and applying the word of God.

Other components to having a fanatical faith are praise and thanksgiving. Praise elevates faith to a higher level of trusting God. Your praise is a willful act to acknowledge God and trust him in all your tests. There is corporate praise, when a group of saints come together in an assembly to praise and worship. And there is personal praise, where individually, you choose to praise God instead of bowing to your feelings and circumstances. Personal praise, in the midst of a severe storm, assures you of God's favor. And the favor of God enables you to stand strong and overcome any test. God's favor is absolutely necessary for victory and success. When God delights and takes pleasure in you, no obstacle can stand in your way and no enemy can take you down. Listen and memorize these verses from one of my favorite Praise Psalms.

"I will extol You, O Lord; for You have lifted me up, and have not let my foes rejoice over me. O Lord my God, I cried out to You, and You healed me. O Lord, You brought my soul up from the grave: You have kept me alive, that I should not go down to the pit. Sing praise to the Lord, you saints of His, and give thanks at the remembrance of His holy name. For His anger is but for a moment; His favor is for life: Weeping may endure for a night, but joy comes in the morning. Now in my prosperity I said, I shall never be moved. Lord, by Your favor You have made my mountain to stand strong: You hid Your face, and I was troubled." (Psalms 30:1-7 NKJ)

I say these words clapping my hands, giving God my praise clap! I sing them! I shout them! I make them my own. You can make them your personal praise. Personal praise can be as fanatical as your personality dictates. It is between you and God. Personal praise is essential during a test because encouragement is not always forthcoming from others when you are in the midst of a severe storm. Whenever you find yourself in a storm, remember that God has orchestrated, designed or allowed the test to reveal your inner strength and ability. **From God's perspective tests are never designed to show your weakness, but to reveal your strength**. Because God has high expectations of us he allows tests in our lives to reveal our strength. To keep your faith alive and your focus on God, choose to praise him. Your personal praise will encourage you. Personal praise will strengthen you and elevate you to a higher level of God's favor. Personal praise shifts you into the right gear to accelerate your victory during the test. Personal praise will usher you into your increase. Never feel sorry for yourself when you are going through a storm. God still speaks to the storms of your life. He alone can quiet the angry waves and command peace. **So instead of a pity party, engage in a praise party.** Personal praise energizes your faith to bring you out of a storm. Your faith is fed and bred in the word of God. It is nurtured and covered in the cocoon of prayer. It is invigorated and fortified in personal praise. Therefore, release your faith with the fanfare of praise and thanksgiving and it will be most effective in the work arena. Faith is dynamite, and personal praise is the lighted fuse that explodes it! Keep your faith alive!

David had a personal praise. He knew how to encourage himself when he was being tested in a severe storm. After the Amalekites had invaded Ziklag, burned it with fire and taken the wives and children of David and all his men, they wept and cried aloud until they had no more strength to weep. David was greatly distressed and the people spoke of stoning him. In his distress David encouraged himself in the Lord. He was strengthened by his personal praise of his God. Instead of feeling sorry for himself and wallowing in a pity party, he no doubt spent time thanking God for what He had already done for him and then he inquired of God what he should do. **"Shall I pursue?"** And God told him: **"Pursue: for thou shalt surely overtake them, and without fail recover it all."** David obeyed God and recovered everything. It happened because he had the favor of the Lord and he chose to give Almighty God some crazy praise. Crazy praise is when your circumstances tell you it does not make sense to praise God, but enthusiastically, you do it anyhow. Crazy praise activates the fruit of the spirit and the joy of the Lord shakes up your whole being with strength. And the favor of God, along with the joy of the Lord will enable you to stand strong. Remember, the Psalmist told us that God's favor makes our mountain stand strong. And in difficult times we know that the joy of the Lord is our strength. (Read 1 Samuel 30:1-20)

Thanksgiving is the language of faith. Thanksgiving is not something that you give to God after the fact. Thanksgiving is the wrapping, the envelope that you send your request to God in.

"Be careful for nothing; but in everything by prayer and supplication with thanksgiving let your requests be made known unto God." (Philippians 4:6)

Prayers are incomplete without thanksgiving, and the one who prays without thanksgiving is either ungrateful or ignorant of God's bounty in his life. Thanksgiving acknowledges what God has already done and blesses Him for what He is going to do. Thanksgiving should always be given to God the Father for Jesus' life on earth, his death, burial, and resurrection. Because of what Jesus did you can go directly to the throne of God and let your requests be made known with thanksgiving. Praise and thanksgiving are the two essential components that usher you into the presence of God. This is another favorite Psalm of praise.

"Make a joyful noise unto the Lord, all ye lands. Serve the Lord with gladness: come before his presence with singing. Know ye that the Lord he is God: it is he that hath made us, and not we ourselves; we are his people, and the sheep of his pasture. Enter into his gates with thanksgiving, and into his courts with praise: be thankful unto him, and bless his name. For the Lord is good; his mercy is everlasting; and his truth endureth to all generations." (Psalm 100 KJ)

A fanatical faith that is nurtured by personal praise and thanksgiving will always bring victorious results in the midst of storms. God never intended for you and I to continue in a state of victimization to the events, the circumstances, and the prince of this world. You and I are new creations in Christ Jesus and all things have become new. We were chosen by God to be fantastic saints and fanatical people of faith.

God has designed humanity with a nature that makes life dull and boring if not challenged by the unknown. Our greatest sense of accomplishment comes from sailing in uncharted waters and finding ways to navigate and stay adrift. Uncharted waters challenge us to either design new ships or find new ways of sailing. With familiarity we tend to become complacent and bored by the routine. Deep waters are always an adventure. Jesus challenged the disciples to launch out into the deep. **The Psalmist said we see God's wonders performed in the deep.** (Psalms 107:24)

God gave Abram some insight from which we would be wise to learn. Some things and people in our lives are not designed to be a part of our journey. Some people in our lives refuse to leave the shores of safety and navigate in deep waters. If not careful they will anchor us to shore. The design of anchors is they have to be dropped to be effective. When God is calling us to launch out in deep water, we need to drop people who anchor us to shores of safety. To hold on to that which is not a part of our journey can only delay our arrival or cause us to miss our destination. Many gifted and talented men and women never arrived at their destination because their lives are cluttered with the dead weight of people and things that are not true to their purpose. They do not belong. Lot was obviously not intended by God to be a part of Abram's journey. Taking him along only distracted Abram from his purpose and caused him to get off course. It is not difficult to identify people and things that are not suppose to be a part of our lives. Simply examine what and who it is that keeps you from seeking God first. Who and what causes you to take detours on your highway of purpose? Once examined and identified, it takes courage to detach oneself from stumbling blocks. But, rid yourself you must, if you desire to rise up and step into your destiny. Abram's involvement with Lot could have delayed God's additional blessings of land to him.

> **"And the Lord said unto Abram, <u>after that Lot was separated from him</u>, Lift up now thine eyes, and look from the place where thou art northward, and southward, and eastward, and westward: For all the land which thou seest, to thee will I give it, and to thy seed for ever."** (Genesis 13:14, 15 KJ)

Lot became a problem and Abram had to rescue him in the battle of Dan, the only war in which he ever fought. Having the wrong people in our lives can cause problems and waste our resources fighting battles that are not ours. Sin can delay our blessings and cause serious detours and mishaps on the highway of purpose. But God, our Destiny, is always in control. And He is faithful to keep his promises. God came to Abram many years after his original promise to make him a great nation - to reassure him.

> **"After these things the word of the Lord came unto Abram in a vision, saying Fear not, Abram: I am thy shield and thy exceeding great reward. And Abram said, Lord God, what wilt thou give me, seeing I go childless, and the steward of my house is this Eliezer of Damascus? Behold to me thou hast given no seed: and, lo, one born in my house is mine heir. And, behold, the word of the Lord came unto him, saying, This shall not be thine heir; but he that shall come forth out of thine own bowels shall be thine heir. And he brought him forth abroad, and said, Look now toward heaven, and tell the stars, if thou be able to number them: and he said unto him, So shall thy seed be. And he believed in the Lord; and he counted it to him for righteousness."** (Genesis 15:1-6 KJ)

Like Abram, we can get sidetracked on the highway of purpose when things don't happen in our time frame. We must resist all urges and pressures that time and people place on us. Wait on the Lord and be of good courage. When Abram hearkened to the voice of Sarai, his wife, and slept with her handmaid, Hagar, he opened his life, his family, and his legacy to untold hurt and hatred that continues to this day.

Once God has made us a promise, He will orchestrate the events of our lives to fulfill His promise and time cannot eradicate His faithfulness. It was twenty-five years after God's original promise to Abram that Isaac, his son of promise and laughter was born. **God keeps his promises.**

There can be no denial of Jesus' faithfulness. He is a God of promise who was filled with greatness and clothed with power from on high. He has called and sent us to be like Him. And He gave us His identity and His source of greatness. Take note of what

Jesus said before His death and resurrection: **"And, behold, I send the promise of my Father upon you: but tarry ye in the city of Jerusalem, until ye be endued with power from on high."** (Luke 24:49 KJ)

The promise of the Father was for every believer to be clothed with power from on high. After the resurrection Jesus came in the midst: **"Then said Jesus to them again, Peace be unto you; as my Father hath sent me, even so send I you. And when he had said this, he breathed on them, and saith unto them, Receive ye the Holy Ghost."** (John 20:21, 22 KJ)

Therefore, every believer should recognize that we have been sent by Jesus as He was sent by the Father. He was clothed in power and filled with the Holy Spirit to do great miracles upon the earth that the true identity of humanity might be unveiled and mankind would be restored to his Creator. Because our God was faithful to keep His promise to give us the Holy Spirit, we are a great people who have great power. We have greatness within and we are also clothed with greatness. We have God's anointing to do great works. Jesus was raised from the dead on the third day and he told his disciples to wait, for they would receive power to be His witnesses after the Holy Ghost came upon them. After saying these things Jesus left this earth that the Holy Spirit, our Comforter, and Teacher, the Promise of the Father could come. The Apostle Peter, preaching on the day of Pentecost, after they (all believers present) were filled with the Holy Ghost, spoke of the promise of the Holy Ghost to future generations

"This Jesus hath God raised up. whereof we all are witnesses. Therefore being by the right hand of God exalted, and having received of the Father the promise of the Holy Ghost, he hath shed forth this, which ye now see and hear. For the promise is unto you, and to your children, and to all that are afar off, even as many as the Lord our God shall call." (Acts 2:32,33;39 KJ)

The Lord our God has called and equipped you and I to walk as **FANTASTIC SAINTS** with a **FANATICAL FAITH!**

Reconnected and restored to God by the Blood of Jesus!

Identified, Inspired, Informed and Instructed by the Spirit and the Word of God!

Set aside, Sustained and Strengthened for Service to the Kingdom of God!

Endued and enveloped by the Anointed Power of Almighty God!

CHAPTER SIX

STEPS TO DELIVERANCE!

What hinders me from Rising Up, Stepping Into My Destiny and fulfilling my Purpose?

To walk in God, your Destiny, and fulfill your purpose, you have to step out of some familiar patterns, habits, and influences that have become strongholds in your life. All of us come to God with a multitude of sin in our lives. Those sins and habits that so easily beset you and I are strongholds that have become familiar, and we have to work in conjunction with the Holy Spirit and the Word of God to deny their desire, destroy their hold, break their yoke, and be set free from them. Salvation is just the beginning, no matter how dynamic your salvation experience may have been.

Me. Prior to being saved by Jesus, I lived a decadent lifestyle of wine, women, and sex. As a child growing up in Texas, I was often in the limelight because I started out at an early age dancing and singing at local outings and on local television. I was exposed to the places, events, and atmospheres of my peers and a much older group of people. I was introduced to sex and a very decadent life-style at much too young an age. I was having sex with my peers and women who were older and much more experience than me. I lived a demented lifestyle of seeking esteem in beautiful looks, shapes, and relating to women as objects of sexual pleasure. I usually had a deep sense of loneliness that I tried to satisfy and eradicate through illicit sex. In my early adult life, as a successful actor and writer, I knew I had a serious problem when I would be with a beautiful woman and after the sexual activity I still felt empty, lonely, and all alone. There was something missing on the inside that I could not satisfy from outside activities and indulging my sexual desires with women. I later came to understand that my emptiness was caused by a need to know Jesus-my Creator.

At a highpoint in my career in 1976, after having co-written, co-produced, and starred in my own movie, "Big Time," I was at a Christmas Party on Christmas Eve. The party was hosted in the Beverly Hills home of my friend, Smokey Robinson. I remember it well for this was the night I broke down on the highway of life. The engine of my being literally shut down. It broke down and shut off. Sometime after ten o'clock at night, I could not take the music, the laughter, the food, the recognition, or the beautiful ladies fawning over me. Earlier that night I found myself in that familiar place of - toying in my mind as to who I might take home with me to have breakfast with on Christmas day. One beautiful lady in particular had invited herself over to my place; but for some unknown reason I had not accepted her invitation. Nothing was working for me, I had to leave. When I told my friend, he questioned me as to what was wrong. I could not specify any particular thing. I just knew I was frustrated, confused, out of sorts, and I had to leave. I left with a feeling of desperation, knowing that I needed help.

Later that night in the living room of my lonely apartment, I started reading a little book entitled "Good News for The Modern Man." As I read I reflected back on some Bible studies where I had heard testimonies about some people's first encounter with Jesus. I had heard them speak of how they had seen a bright light in their room, some had seen a vision. Others said they heard a voice. Something deep inside of me yearned to know, to see, and hear Jesus. Instantly, I thought about how I had sat on this same couch, begging God, some nine months earlier to give me the money to produce my film. I even promised God that I would give Him my life. When I made that promise to God, it was nothing more than a begging plea from a desperate man. I was totally void of sincerity.

I also remembered, later in July, just before we started filming "Big Time," my producing partner, Leon Kennedy and I stood in this same room, praying, begging God to cover our mistakes, and help us complete the film at a greatly reduced budget than what we originally started with. At ten minutes before midnight on the eve of Christmas, I looked up at the clock. My vision quickly became blurred by the tears welling up in my eyes. Suddenly my mind went into a rewind mode, and I traveled back through some experiences during the filming of the movie. At each incident where we had made a mistake that should have shut down the movie and cost us dearly, I knew that God had been there with us and He had carried us on His back to victory. It was like the picture - "Footprints in The Sand," where the only footprints in the sand were those of Jesus who was carrying the person in need on His back. I started crying out, "Lord Jesus, save me! Save me, Lord... Jesus, please come into my life!" An overwhelming peace engulfed me. A quiet stillness pervaded the room. I did not feel empty, void, and alone. I looked up at the clock again and it was twelve minutes after midnight. It was Christmas day and I instantly knew that I had received the greatest Christmas gift that I could ever receive.

My salvation experience is very special to me. I have heard other salvation testimonies that were so much more dramatic than mine. Regardless of the degree of drama in our salvation experience, salvation does not instantly deliver us from the strongholds in our lives. Our relationship with God changes immediately. At new birth we are all babes in Christ who need to be trained up in the way that we should go. We need time to learn, to develop disciplines and mature in Christ. Maturity comes through obedience to the Holy Spirit and walking in the word of God.

For years I struggled to be totally free of sexual sin-my greatest stronghold. Even after God had called me to preach His gospel, I struggled with sexual sin and desperately needed to be delivered. After six months of running from God's call to be His evangelist, saying to myself, "God can't use anyone as wretched as me:" I finally surrendered to God's will to preach the gospel. I was more determined than ever that I would overcome my addiction. Over time I became stronger through much prayer, counseling, the study of the word, and a sincere desire to please God. During a long period of celibacy I would feel my flesh on fire in the solitary presence of a beautiful sister. After living as a celibate man, with my stubborn determination for eighteen months, I was ensnared by the stronghold of sexual sin on a Sunday night, after preaching under God's anointing in three different services that day. In the midst of the sexual act I felt ashamed, empty, disappointed, and dirty. In desperation I stopped and got out of bed! I got down on my knees, begging God to forgive me and I cried out repeatedly to God... "Please do not take your Holy Spirit from me." I had made the mistake of thinking that I could walk uprightly before God through my own strong will and determination. God spoke to me in a still quiet voice and told me: "But by My grace you are what you are. It's not by your power, nor your might, but by My Spirit!" **I WAS FED UP!** I knew I could not go on this way.

You. Whatever sin and familiar habit that has become a stronghold to you, unless you are delivered, the stronghold will constantly break your fellowship with God, hinder the work of the Holy Spirit in your life and abort or destroy your purpose. There are four dynamic steps to being delivered.

Through the sharing of various testimonies and the spirit led study of biblical characters you will discover that the first step is always the same for everyone. When you become sick and tired of someone or something that is troubling you, change is imminent. **You have to get fed up with the stronghold in order to be delivered from it.** When Moses got fed up with the Egyptians treatment of his people, Israel, he chose to do something about the situation. He chose his purpose over popularity by refusing to be called the son of Pharaoh's daughter and suffered afflictions with the people of God rather than enjoy the pleasures of sin for a season. When Esther got fed up with Haman and his deceptive ways to destroy Mordecai and all the Jews, she did something about it. She decided to go see the king which was not according to law. She determined to intercede on behalf of Mordecai and her people, even if she perished. When the late Rosa Parks got fed up with segregated seating on public transportation, she took an adamant stand and refused to give up her seat. Her public stance brought about changes in racial segregation in public transportation and facilities. Candy Lightner, the mother who started MADD was fed up with drunk drivers killing innocent people. When a drunk driver, a repeat offender, killed her daughter she started a national organization that has helped to change laws and create a vehement atmosphere against people driving while drunk.

A great case study in the Holy Scriptures with the steps to deliverance is found in the life of Elijah and his confrontation with wicked King Ahab, and his wife Jezebel, who had led the nation of Israel into idolatrous worship. Wicked King Ahab was more devious than all the kings before him. He led the people into idolatry. He set up altars and built a temple in Samaria for Baal worship. The nation of Israel followed him in Baal worship until Elijah got tired of it. When he got fed up he obeyed the voice of God and went to Samaria to confront Ahab and the nation of Israel, at the risk of losing his life.

On his way to meet Ahab Elijah encountered Obadiah who was in charge of Ahab's house. Obadiah feared the Lord and he had hid and fed some of God's prophets when Jezebel was massacring them. Listen to Elijah's tone as he speaks to Obadiah. "Go! Tell your master, Elijah is here." Later Elijah said to Obadiah: "As the LORD of hosts lives, before whom I stand, I will surely present myself to Ahab today." Elijah's tone of voice and choice of words truly indicates that he is fed up with Ahab and Jezebel's mess. He is ticked off and today, right now, some changes are going to be made.

To experience deliverance from strongholds and walk in victory you have to get sick and tired of the devil robbing you of your joy, ripping off your blessings, stealing your prosperity and influencing you through familiar habits and actions that forfeit the promises of God in your life. You have to be fed up with hearing about miracles in the lives of other saints, but in your life, it's like pass over. Victimized by the strongholds of your familiar thoughts, words, habits, fears and actions; therefore, you experience no miracles, no victory, no prosperity, just scratching out a living from payday to payday. You experience no joy, no peace or favor from God. All the blessings of God have passed you by. Enough is enough! **ARE YOU FED UP?!**

When Elijah became fed up, he demanded a showdown with King Ahab and his eight hundred and fifty false prophets on Mount

Carmel. He was not overwhelmed or intimidated by the number of false prophets who stood against him. When you are fed up like Elijah, you will stand against any odds. Elijah knew that the strongholds of idolatry and idol worship was troubling and controlling the nation of Israel. The people had turned from the word of God to please their flesh and the world. So he demanded that King Ahab call all Israel to him on Mt. Carmel, along with the four hundred and fifty prophets of Baal, and the four hundred prophets of Asherah, who ate at Jezebel's table.

The people were broken down, demoralized and controlled by idolatrous Baal worship. They did not even realize how greatly ensnared they had become or how far away they were from walking in the commandments of Jehovah, the God who had delivered them. Strongholds do not have to be visible and active at all times. They can lie dormant for a season, but until they have been rooted out they can rise up and control you when you least expect it. Baal worship had become a way of life for Israel and this stronghold was destroying them from within. Elijah was fed up. He did not waste time doubting or having a pity party. Doubt and pity are exercises in futility. To overcome false gods and destroy the stronghold of idolatrous worship he called the people to repentance. **REPAIR THROUGH REPENTANCE!**

The second step to deliverance is true repentance. Ask God to forgive you. Confess your strongholds of sin and turn from them. Turning from strongholds is a personal determination, but you need the power of God to achieve your goal. The altar of your heart can only be repaired through repenting, asking God to forgive you, and turning away from the sin that doth so easily beset you. Familiar thoughts, habits, and actions should never sit on the throne of your life. Don't feed and nurture bad habits and familiar spirits through bad choices. You can't continue to frequent the clubs, nightspots, parties and events that promote the lifestyle you have chosen to walk away from. Do not indulge music, television or movies that feed and promote your bad habits and strongholds. True repentance requires you to turn away from that which so easily ensnares you.

I have not ceased to be amazed, over the years, at people who have expressed a sincere desire to be free of drugs, drinking, sex and abuse. And yet, many continue to inhabit the places, socialize with the people and participate in the activities that promote their illicit behavior. **Shut it out! Cut it off!** Even if everybody you know is doing it. As a new creation in Christ Jesus you can and you should acquire some new friends and associates whose lives are guided by the word of God. God's word is true and the word of God will always accomplish whatever God sends it forth to do. His word will comfort you, correct you, instruct you, inspire you, revive you, and restore you. **HIS WORD WILL GUIDE YOU AND LIGHT YOUR PATH!** (Psalms 119:105)

God's word is the solid foundation that allows you, as God's temple, to build strong walls of light that expose and shut out the penetrating darkness in the world. Take firm steps on a solid foundation and walk as a child of light. Do not allow darkness, evil and fleshly desires to dominate your life. Obey God by walking in His word. For God always backs up His word and His blessings overflow in the lives of His obedient saints. God hears the prayers of a repented saint and He will show Himself mighty on your behalf. To set your life in order, escape the debilitating darkness of this world, and walk in victory choose to obey the word of God.

The word will strengthen you to gird your mind, and guard your heart. With a girded mind, and a guarded heart you will not continue to return to old familiar habits, and former lusts that so easily ensnared you in times past.

> **"Therefore gird up the lions of your mind, be sober, and rest your hope fully upon the grace that is to be brought to you at the revelation of Jesus Christ: as obedient children, not conforming yourselves to the former lusts, as in your ignorance; but as He who called you is holy, you also be holy in all your conduct, because it is written, Be holy, for I am holy."** (1 Peter 1:13-16 NKJ)

God's word enables you to have the mind of Christ. His word is absolutely essential for your repentance in overcoming sinful habits, and living in harmony with the Spirit of God within you. Elijah understood this in his day and he challenged the nation of Israel on Mount Carmel.

Elijah cried out to the God of Abraham, Isaac, and Israel, asking Him to make Himself known! To call the people to repentance, Elijah let the people know that he had come to confront Ahab, the prophets of Asherah, the prophets of Baal, and the lies, and darkness of Baal worship that Israel was caught up in. He did not hesitate to stand against overwhelming odds because he knew that his God was the true and living God, and that Jehovah honors His word above His name.

"I will worship toward thy holy temple, and praise thy name for thy loving kindness and for thy truth: <u>for thou hast magnified thy word above all thy name.</u>" (Psalms 138:2 KJ)

Elijah came to all the people to call them to repentance and to prove who the true and living God was. **"How long will you falter between two opinions? If the LORD is God, follow Him; but if Baal, follow him."** (1 Kings 18:21) The question that Elijah posed to Israel allows you to see that one of the primary purposes of a stronghold is to create doubt in Almighty God and destroy your fellowship. Israel knew God as deliverer, provider, and sustainer; and yet they doubted and turned away from God to follow a wicked king in worshiping a false idol. Doubting God became a severe stronghold which led them into the bondage of idolatry. The stronghold of doubt destroyed their fellowship with and tore down the altar of praise and worship to the true and living God. The stronghold of doubt seeded unbelief and halting between various opinions. To believe God for salvation and then doubt and turn from Him in your daily lifestyle is tantamount to living a defeated sinful life in a world of dark despair. And the lack of daily fellowship will delay or abort your purpose. It will minimize your peace and maximize your fear and turmoil. Elijah was fed up! He knew that to call the people of Israel to true repentance he had to prove that the God of their deliverance was the true and living God. Only the true and living God could send down fire from heaven to consume the sacrifice and lick up the water in the trench.

The third step to deliverance from a stronghold is to reestablish fellowship with God through praise and worship. **PREPARE THE ALTAR FOR PRAISE AND WORSHIP!** Elijah knew that the people needed to reestablish fellowship with the true and living God, so he told the people to come near to him. When all came near to him, he repaired the altar of the Lord which was broken down. The true altar of worship for you and every New Testament believer is your heart. It is very difficult to fellowship with God on a consistent basis with a cold, fearful, broken down heart. How do you repair and prepare the altar? Praise and worship invigorates your heart and enables you to capture God's perspective and power. Praise and worship rekindles the flame of God's fire that smolders in the deep recesses of your heart. Praise and worship causes the Spirit of God to flow out of your belly like rivers of living waters. You can either burn or drown the demons that have become strongholds in your life. Flames of fire and rivers of living water are types of spiritual anointings. God can, and He will restore your soul and lead you in paths of righteousness. Deliverance is never just about overcoming in the natural. Strongholds are manifested in the flesh but they are not relegated only to the flesh. There are always strong spiritual roots to every stronghold; therefore, spiritual connection, heart repair, praise, worship, word application, and God's anointing are necessary to destroy the stronghold.

"And it shall come to pass in that day, that his burden shall be taken away from off thy shoulder, and his yoke from off thy neck, and the yoke shall be destroyed because of the anointing." (Isaiah 10:27 KJ)

Me. Today, by the grace of God, **I am free** of sexual addiction. My body is no longer an instrument of sin. I maintain my freedom through consistent prayer, praise, worship, reading, study and application of the word. My praise and worship keeps a constant flow of God's Spiritual waters stirred up and overflowing in my life. The emptiness, loneliness, and disappointment is gone, replaced by peace, love, and joy, derived from my intimate relationship with God my Father through Jesus Christ. I am blessed by God to have a beautiful spirit filled wife and son sharing my daily existence. Walking intimately with God has birthed new appetites that are prompted by my spirit and not my flesh. What God has done for me and others, He will surely do for you. Will you trust Him and seek His deliverance from your strongholds? Your victory is always in Christ Jesus. His anointing will destroy every stronghold.

You. God not only saved you, he has freed you from the bondages of sin. He has also anointed you for His service. God's anointing destroys the yoke of strongholds. **Praise and worship releases God's anointing in your life.** In the midst of your tears, your fears, your pain and your discouragement, make up your mind to worship God and walk in obedience to His word. Praise Him with thanksgiving for saving you and for every other blessing that comes to your mind. Strongholds may cause you to momentarily put God's blessings on the back burner of your consciousness; but you cannot be saved and experience any level of fellowship with God without having been blessed by God. You are blessed to be a child of God with your name written down in the Lamb's book of life. You are blessed to call Jesus savior and know that you can cast all your cares upon Him for He cares for you. You are blessed to delight yourself in the Lord, knowing that He will give you the desires of your heart. You are blessed because when you give to the work of God, He will supply all of your needs according to His riches in glory by Christ Jesus. Instead of allowing your fleshly feelings of fear and despair to dictate your actions, follow the example of King David, who encouraged himself in the Lord, and rose above his painful discouragement. Just for a moment let's revisit the story.

After returning from battle and finding that the Amalekites had burned Ziklag and taken his family and the families of his men captive, King David was greatly distressed and disheartened. King David and his men lifted up their voices and wept until they had no more strength to weep. David was further distressed when his men spoke of stoning him. David refused to engage in an exercise of futility by doubting God and having a pity party. Instead, he prayed and encouraged himself in the LORD his God. His praise and worship energized his heart, overcame his fear and misery and helped him to articulate God's sovereignty in his life. (Read 1 Samuel 30)

Like King David, know that Jesus is your good shepherd and you shall not want. Therefore, set your heart and fix your mind on thanking God for His corrections and directions. You don't thank God for the calamity but thank Him in the calamity. For God is always your source of deliverance and His will is that you give thanks and rejoice in all things.

"Rejoice always, pray without ceasing, in everything give thanks; for this is the will of God in Christ Jesus for you." (1 Thessalonians 5:16-18 NKJ)

God inhabits the praises of His people. When God inhabits your praise, shackles are broken, strongholds are destroyed and deliverance will take place. The strongholds may have sapped your energy and broken down your altar of prayer, praise, and thanksgiving. **Repent and repair by encouraging yourself in the Lord!** Praising God enables you to take back the throne of your heart.

Elijah cried out to the God of heaven in the midst of Israel, King Ahab, and the false prophets of Baal and Asherah. **"Hear me, O Lord, hear me, that this people may know that thou art the Lord God, and that thou hast turned their heart back again. Then the fire of the Lord fell, and consumed the burnt sacrifice, and the wood, and the stones, and the dust, and licked up the water that was in the trench. And when all the people saw it, they fell on their faces: and they said, The LORD, he is the GOD; the LORD, he is the GOD."** (1 Kings 18:37-39 KJ)

The fourth step to deliverance from a stronghold is confessing the deity of God. It is not enough to just believe in your heart that God is. **CONFESS HIM AS GOD!** After God sent down fire and proved that He was the true and living God, all the people lay prostrate and cried out: "The LORD - he is GOD!" After Israel witnessed the miracle of fire from heaven they believed in and confessed Jehovah as God. Their confession was an outward demonstration of their inward belief. Confessing God enabled Israel to cast out the stronghold of fear and doubt. Confessing God is even necessary for our salvation.

"That if you confess with thy mouth the Lord Jesus and believe in your heart that God has raised Him from the dead, you will be saved. For with the heart one believes unto righteousness, and with the mouth confession is made unto salavation." (Romans 10:9, 10 NKJ)

Many years ago on television a very popular comedian named Flip Wilson would do skits and comedy routines where his character would do something wrong, mean, hurtful, or stupid, and his character would say: "The devil made me do it!" Although it was a comedy skit, he had heard that phrase used in society and it is still used by some today. People confess the devil, while others damn the name of God in a profane way. Confessions of faith and the spoken word have tremendous power, regardless of who speaks them. For God honors his word above His name.

In whatever situation, circumstance or need that presents itself in your life, confess God and His word. There is miracle working power in confessing the word of God. You will quickly learn in life's experiences that speaking the word of God and not your circumstances will bring you victory and success. It will eradicate doubt and fear. It's important to acknowledge needs and problems, but don't continue to confess them. Continual confession of needs and problems will breed doubt and fear. Continual confession will make the need or the problem greater than God in your mind. Once acknowledged, begin to confess God and speak His word over the need or the problem.

Do not allow the need or problem to become a stronghold by continually saying it or talking to others about it. God is bigger than any problem or need that you will ever have. The more you confess God and speak His word, the quicker your need is met and the smaller your problem becomes. Nothing is too hard for our God.

Me. In September, 2000, God told me that my season was over to live in and operate my ministry out of Virginia. Living by faith with total trust in God to meet my every need, I began to make preparations to leave Virginia, even though I had no idea where I was going at the time. After I shared with my wife, KJoy, I also informed our pastor and started looking into what we would need to do to sell our townhouse. My family and I did not have a lot of money to move so we needed to get as much as we could from the sale of our home. On October 13, 2000, during my prayer and devotion, I was reading "My Utmost for His Highest," by Oswald Chambers. As I read about God's encounter with Moses, I instantly knew that God was saying to me that I had to go back to Southern California where He had birthed my purpose and His call for my life. Had God asked me where I would like to go, California would not have been in the top fifty places of my choosing. God spoke and I wrote at the top of the page: "Moses had to go back to Egypt, where God birthed his purpose for being. Christipher, go back to where God birthed His promise and His purpose in you."

Even though I now knew where we were going, I still asked my wife to keep silent and not discuss our move with anyone. I did not want a lot of people asking me questions that I did not have answers to. I did not want to hear their comments or their opinions. I knew from my earlier move from California to Herndon, Virginia, the perils of talking to people and seeking validation about a move of faith. When God had told me to go to the east coast in 1989, and that He would tie up all the loose ends of my life, I shared the news, thinking that relatives and Christian friends would be excited for me. Quite the contrary, I was accused of leaving my post of duty at my home church. I was constantly questioned as to whether I was truly hearing from God, and why He would send me to a place where I had no ministry support, no family, and knew very few people. Many well meaning people in my inner circle said: "Watch it! You are leaving your post! You are going off on some wild goose chase!" Continual discussions, negative confessions, and hurtful comments plunged me into a stronghold of doubt and fear. For a while I was traumatized by fear and doubt. Even as I moved forward in my preparation to leave California, I was hesitant, second guessing every decision. My fear and doubt prohibited me from hearing from God. I felt isolated, confused, and afraid. I continued moving forward because I knew I had initially heard God tell me to go; however, every decision, every step forward, I had to wrestle and fight to be freed of the stronghold of doubt and fear.

As I reflected on the blessings of God and how He had kept me, raised me up, and expanded my ministry of evangelism. I knew that only God could have opened doors and sustained me and my family in a full time ministry where I have never charged for my services. I had a track record with the God of heaven and He had faithfully proven Himself to me many times. I was determined that I would obey God and move from the east back to the west coast. I refused to talk to people about the move and quietly prepared to move back to California.

I trusted God because of His unyielding faithfulness to me. It was in Virginia, where I met Karen. After speaking in a four day revival at Christ Fellowship, the then pastor, my friend, Enoch Butler, asked Karen to bless the congregation with a song. I had seen her in the crowd each night and she had come by and thanked me for the words of encouragement that I had spoken. She truly blessed us with her anointed singing. That night after service during the fellowship, she slipped me a note that left a lasting impression on me. I was unmarried at the time and I was constantly inundated with bold messages from single sisters in congregations everywhere, that God had told them that I was supposed to be their husband. When this first started occurring I was a little embarrassed and I did not quite know how to respond without being blunt and offensive. Later, God gave me the wisdom to respond with these words: "I will pray about it. And when God tells me what He told you, we will talk." Unlike some others she had decided not to fawn all over me each night after service; however, she wanted to ask me a question about an exhortation that I had given to the people about starting a convalescent ministry. How to set up ministries in assisted living facilities and sharing the good news of the gospel. I have a passion for the work of God and I try to encourage other saints to vacate the cushion pews and air conditioned buildings for ministry in the hedges and highways of life.

I later called Karen from Florida and shared some particulars on how I had started many other convalescent ministries. I knew she was a special lady. I even tested her in the area of giving by asking her to monthly support a child through a Christian organization. She did that faithfully for almost a year until we were married. Later, I took over the responsibility and increased our support to two children. We continue to support our other two children.

After I had settled in Virginia, God told me that Karen was to be my wife. We were married November 18, 1989, and given a beautiful wedding by Christ Fellowship Church which became our home church in Virginia. KJoy later received a prophetic word from my surrogate daughter Shani, who was in law school in Virginia. She said that God was going to bless us with a child. Michael Joseph was God's gift to us in 1995. At Michael's birth I was fifty-five years old. I remember sitting in our living room, after the initial joy and euphoria of being told that KJoy was pregnant. I thought to myself that I was having an Abraham experience.

During my time in Virginia, God truly blessed me and tied up some ends that I had not realize were loose. This time I was determined to make this move totally trusting in the Lord, and leaning not unto my own or other people's understanding. I knew that it would be a challenge, a major test for my family and me, but I was determined to trust God with all my heart and allow Him to direct our paths. I made a willful decision to walk in the peace of God and not be caught up in the stronghold of doubt and fear. I knew that God had some blessings for us and it was necessary for us to relocate so that we would be at the right place to receive His blessings.

There are times in life when God sends blessings to the place where He has instructed us to be; however, because we are not where God told us to be, our blessings are "returned to sender," with a note saying - not at this address. God's anointing in our lives had destroyed the stronghold of doubt and fear. We were freed and filled by the Holy Spirit. KJoy, Michael, and I prayed. We knew that this was a major test, but together with God we could handle and pass this test. I was very excited as I prepared to move back to the west coast. I knew that God had great things in store for my family and me. **I knew that there would be a blessing in our testing!**

CHAPTER SEVEN

BLESSED IN THE TEST!

Me. In mid May, 2001, nearing the end of the school year we started to paint, do minor repairs and fix up our townhouse in Virginia. After much prayer and seeking God's favor, we had been led to sell our home without using a realtor. In four days after putting the house on the market we had a buyer willing to pay our asking price. Throughout June, 2001, before my family and I left Virginia, I spent considerable time in God's throne room (my prayer closet), seeking His favor for a safe, smooth transition, and a new home to move into right away. Along with Sean, my grown middle son, and Lenny, a good friend, I would be driving across country in a large rental truck containing our household belongings and one of our vehicles on a trailer behind it. One of us would also be driving our other vehicle. We definitely needed God's favor for a safe and smooth drive that would take us almost three days. While asking God for favor, I began to thank him and confess that we would have a safe timely trip without incident or accident.

I also begged God and thanked Him for giving me favor to get a home loan with a seven percent interest rate, which is what I was paying on our townhouse in Virginia. At the time I was praying, the lowest interest rates available on a thirty year fixed mortgage was seven and a half percent. I thanked God, praised Him, and confessed that I had received a seven percent rate. Over the years, living by faith in God, I had learned to totally embrace Holy Scriptures that had made such great impact in my life. **"Be careful (anxious) for nothing; <u>but in every thing by prayer and supplication with thanksgiving let your requests be made known unto God. And the peace of God, which passeth all understanding, shall keep your hearts and minds through Christ Jesus."</u>** (Philippians 4:6, 7) I truly believe that thanksgiving is the language of faith and the root of peace. I had matured in the faith over the years. I had learned to thank God and give Him praise when I was asking Him for a blessing. Although this was a major test and an awesome challenge before us, I repeatedly told my family and close friends this was a move of trust. I trusted God with all my heart; hence, I had a peace that surpassed my human understanding and I was ready to leave.

When I arrived safely and timely in California I put our belongings in storage and moved in with my oldest son Terry, in Los Angeles. KJoy and Michael were in Philadelphia, staying temporarily with her mother and sister. I cried out to God, thanking Him again, seeking His favor to purchase a nice house in a safe, children friendly neighborhood in the Inland Empire area of California, which was approximately ninety minutes from my son's apartment in Los Angeles. I also ask God to make it all happen in time for Michael to enroll in his new school. Over the years I had learned to ask God for, believe God for, and thank God for many things at once. There was buoyancy in my faith and a peace in my spirit when I finally sat down with Yvonne Williams, my realtor, who I had met by phone while living in Virginia. She was a blessing sent from God. Her primary concern was my family's welfare in getting a house. She educated me in the many nuances and strategies of buying a house. Some strategies I will share later in this book.

The first three lenders I spoke to were excited about our excellent credit rating and they quoted me the lowest current interest rate of eight and one quarter percent. I would not budge. I kept confessing the seven percent rate and thanking God for it. In mid July I was still looking for both a house and a lender who would give me my desired interest rate. My wife and I had previously traveled to Southern California and chosen the Inland Empire area as our resident location. Also, we had decided that we wanted a house with an adjacent RV parking space to allow extra secured playing space for Michael.

I continued to look and pray. By faith I enrolled Michael in a private Christian school in the Inland Empire area and paid for his books and testing. I took bold steps of faith because I knew that God had told me to relocate back to California. I continued to look at houses even though I had not secured financing at my desired rate. Yvonne never wavered in her commitment to helping me find a house; however, she told me that the rate I was being offered was a very good rate. As we continued to look, I kept saying: "My Father owns the cattle on a thousand hills, all the silver and gold is His. The world and all that dwell therein. He has a house for my family and I." I did not know how, but I knew that God would make a way somehow. On Wednesday, a week before I was schedule to leave California for Virginia, I looked at a house that met all of our needs. On Friday, I drove back up the street to the house repeatedly during the early evening hours to check out the neighborhood. Adults were cutting lawns and children were outside playing. Many others, including parents, children, joggers, and teenage basketball players, were in the park just down the street from the house. A police sub-station and fire station is located next to the park. I knew that this was our new neighborhood. God would make it happen. I asked Yvonne to make a counter offer to the seller, offering a few thousand less than what he was asking.

I had been invited by Pastor Decker Tapscott, a faithful and supportive friend, to return to Warrenton, Virginia, to speak at his camp meeting at Faith Christian Church in August. My family and I agreed that we would meet in Virginia, and we would all fly back to California to complete our relocation, even though we did not own a house as yet. I was scheduled to speak on a Friday evening. When I arrived I asked Pastor Tapscott, who has a strong prophetic anointing on him, if God had given him a word for me? He asked me to stay over to Saturday Evening for the close of the meeting. Because he knew about my past and the relocation, he wanted to see if God would send a prophetic word through Pastor Brooks, another minister at the church, who also had a strong prophetic anointing. Pastor Brooks and I had not met. Pastor Tapscott invited my family and I to stay through the weekend and the church would cover our hotel expense.

It was great being back together after a seven week separation. Being separated from my family and not having a place to call home was a real test for me. I drew strength and a source of peace from reflecting on how Jesus had chosen to leave His home in glory and dwell on earth, separated from His Father for thirty-three years to make it possible for you, me, and so many others to become members of the family of God. I confessed aloud repeatedly... **"I'm blessed in this test!"**

The Spirit of the Lord was truly upon me as I spoke on Friday night. At my ministry table Michael and KJoy assisted me in serving the people. A friend, Marketia Collins, from our home church congregation blessed me with an offering check for $100. She thanked me for the word and also purchased a series of tapes. Later, at the hotel, KJoy, Michael and I rejoiced over the sweet spirit, good food, and rich fellowship we had experienced at the church. We were also extremely grateful for the monetary blessing of a thousand dollar honorarium for speaking that night. KJoy, Michael and I talked about the house that I had found and the different things that we could do with this extra money toward my ministry housing allowance. We prayed together, thanking God for His faithfulness and our new house. In our peaceful excitement we later drifted off to sleep. The next morning we awoke with a spirit of expectation and thanksgiving. Even though we did not have a locked agreement and financing on the house in California, we were still excited, expecting God to do something great on our behalf. Throughout the day we had great fellowship, spending time with old friends. Whenever someone asked if we had a house yet, I would answer, "Yes we do! I just don't know the address yet!"

When we arrived at the camp meeting on Saturday night, I was pumped up with an exciting spirit of great expectation! I knew God had a word for us. After walking in and being told that Diane Palmer, a prophetess was the speaker for the evening, I could hardly contain myself. This was not a coincidence. Pastor Tapscott had wisely asked us to come back at a time when a prophetic anointing would be flowing. I had a broad smile on my face when I sat, knowing that the night I came expecting to hear a word from the Lord, a prophetess was the anointed vessel that God had chosen to speak to

His people. Part of the uniqueness of Diane's ministry is she sings her prophecy. In the melodiously prophetic words that flowed from God's anointed vessel, she told how she had driven by this beautiful house for years and thought of it as her dream house. After a few years of sacrifice and savings, she had amassed ten thousand dollars toward the purchase of her first home. One night God challenged Diane by asking: "Do you trust me?" Diane replied "Yes Lord!" God asked her again and she replied, "Lord, you know I trust you!" For the third time God ask - "Diane, do you trust me?" In tears she replied, "Yes Lord! I trust you." God pointed out a lady with three children across the room from her and instructed Diane to give the ten thousand dollars that she had saved to this lady, who was a single mother with children, who would never be able to save that kind of money to buy a house. Obediently Diane trusted and obeyed God, giving the lady her ten thousand dollar savings.

Her anointing and her excitement went to another level as she told us how God, in a matter of days, had touched an organization and they sent her a check for one hundred thousand dollars. Later, while driving by her dream house, God told Diane to stop and knock on the door. There was no "for sale" sign on the property so she continued to drive until God spoke to her the second time, telling her to go back and knock on the door. She obeyed, turned her car around, went back and knocked on the door. The man who owned the house came to the door and told Diane that he and his wife had just decided the night before to sell their house. Diane got her dream house. I got excited because I knew God was setting us up for a blessing. For a while the presence of God was so strong that people were weeping, shouting, walking, falling on the floor, and the steps leading up to the pulpit. In the midst of it all I heard God ask me: "Christipher, do you trust me?" With tears flowing down my cheeks, I said – "Yes Lord! You know I trust you. Yes Lord!" God told me in that moment to give back to the church all that I had received in the offering. I sat for a moment quietly saying, "Yes Lord... yes Lord! Yes Lord... yes Lord!"

Finally, I turned to KJoy and told her what God had directed me to do. One of the many things that I love most about my wife is her willingness to give. She has never hesitated or questioned me about giving to others when we had a great need in our lives. She asked me if I had any temporary checks from our California bank. I shook my head and said: "I wrote the last check and put a hundred dollars in the offering last night. After a few moments of silence she asked me if I could sign my honorarium check and give it back to the church. I nodded yes. Moments later a prophetic word was spoken over us by Diane Palmer, Pastor Brooks, and Pastor Tapscott. I was prostrate on the floor, weeping and thanking God for an anointed word from Him. They all had spoken prophetic words of encouragement but God anointed Pastor Brooks with specific insights about issues in my past life that only God and I knew about. I received further insight as to why God was sending me back to the place where He had birthed His purpose in my life. Later, at the beginning of raising the offering, I got up, rushed outside to the car, retrieve the honorarium check from my briefcase and came back inside. I sat down next to Yvette, the church finance administrator, and told her what God had told me to do, asking her if I could sign the check back over to the church. After a brief pause and an inquisitive look of "are you sure," she nodded yes.

When we went back to the hotel that night I knew that we had just been tested by God. And I had learned, from previous events in my life and the study of Joseph's life and many other Biblical characters in the Holy Scriptures, that **the seeds of our blessings are always planted in the soil of our testing**! God had a blessing for us in this test!

You. To live in this world and accomplish God's purpose for your life will require you to pass some tests. See your tests from God's perspective, as revelations for preparation. God allows His people to be tested. One of the primary reasons that God will allow you to be tested is to reveal your character, your strength, your faith, your stamina, your intestinal fortitude, and your anointed ability to endure hardship and overcome trials. God's testing and His revelations are preparations for you to be promoted and step up to another level of His glory in your life. God is preparing you for a higher call on your life and a greater role in His kingdom. Most of us would agree that tests are usually associated with promotions in our lives. In school we are tested to be promoted to the next grade level. On the job we are tested for promotion and advancement. We would never know our capacity to move up without being tested. We would never know our ability to endure hardship as good soldiers and become mighty victors without being tested. In the spirit and natural realms of life our promotions are linked to us passing some tests. Therefore, we need to look at our tests from a different perspective. From a godly perspective our tests are always for our benefit, because the seeds of our blessings are planted in the soil of our testing. Take note of Jesus words: **"These things I have spoken to you, that in Me you may have peace. In the world you will have tribulation: <u>but be of good cheer</u>; I have overcome the world."** (John 16:33 NKJ)

The same Spirit that empowered Jesus to overcome the world lives in you. Gods' testing is never designed to destroy you and disrupt your peace. In Christ you can have peace in the midst of the stormy test. And you can do all things through Christ, who strengthens you. Tests should never be a surprise because Jesus tells us that we will have tribulation in this world. The second primary reason we have tribulation is because we are out of sync with this world. To live holy and walk in the peace of God you have to live by godly principles and standards that many in this world do not embrace or uphold. In following God you will make decisions that do not sit well in the realm of earthly reasoning. Often times in your decision making you will have to choose between purpose and popularity. **You must never allow your inward security to be based on your outward appearance or popularity.** Never abort your purpose seeking approval from others. Do not place your emotional well being in the hands of another. And do not expect others to meet the needs in your life that only God can meet. Choose God's purpose for your life! Trust God! Obey Him and walk in your promotion for you will be blessed in your tests!

Always know that God wants to keep raising you up to another level of glory in Him. To go from glory to glory you have to endure hardship and pass tests in this life. One of the key reasons that we have the Holy Bible is to inform and inspire us through the lives of others. Daniel had been promoted as ruler over the whole province of Babylon. After he petitioned King Nebuchadnezzar, the king promoted three Hebrews, Shadrach, Meshach and Abed-Nego over the affairs of the province of Babylon. Later, the king built an image of gold and commanded that all the people of Babylon had to bow down and worship his false god. All those who refused to worship would be thrown into a burning fiery furnace. The jealous Chaldeans resented the promotion of the three Hebrews and accused them before the king. **"There are certain Jews whom you have set over the affairs of the province of Babylon: Shadrach, Meshach, and Abed-Nego; these men, O King, have not paid due regard to you. They do not serve your gods or worship the gold image which you have set up."** (Daniel 3:12 NKJ)

The king, in a furious rage sent for the three Hebrews. They refused to bow to a false god in the face of a raging king who threatened their lives. **"If that is the case, our God whom we serve is able to deliver us from the burning fiery furnace, and He will deliver us from your hand, O king. But if not, let it be known to you, O king, that we do not serve your gods, nor will we worship the gold image which you have set up."** (Daniel 3:17 NKJ) The king had the three Hebrews bound and tied up in their own clothing. Sometimes the test you face will be very severe, it may even be life threatening. Do you dare trust in the God you serve to deliver you? Can you believe that God is in control of all your tests? The three Hebrews trusted God and believed that He was able to deliver them. King Nebuchadnezzar had the furnace heated so hot that it killed the men who threw the three Hebrews into the furnace. **"Then King Nebuchadnezzar was astonished; and he rose in haste and spoke, saying to his counselors, Did we not cast three men bound into the midst of the fire?' They answered and said to the king, True, O king.' Look!' he answered, I see four men loose, walking in the midst of the fire; and they are not hurt, and the form of the fourth is like the Son of God."** (Daniel 3:24, 25 NKJ)

Jesus, the Son of God, was in the fiery furnace beforehand. He shielded the three Hebrews from the burning fire. They did not even have the smell of smoke on them. The hot furnace was the place of their testing. Jesus is always the seed of our blessings. He was in the fiery furnace, the soil of their testing, when they were thrown in. God is in control of your life; therefore, have a godly perspective in the midst of your tests. Your godly perspective and your attitude that enables you to stand in a test can lead others to worship the true and living God whom you serve. Nebuchadnezzar was greatly impacted by the godly perspective and strong stand of the three Hebrews **"Nebuchadnezzare spoke, saying, Blessed be the God of Shadrach, Meshach, and Abed-Nego, who sent His Angel and delivered His servants who trusted in Him, and they have frustrated the king's word, and yielded their bodies, that they should not serve nor worship any god except their own God! Therefore I make a decree that any people, nation, or language which speaks anything amiss against the God of Shadrach, Meshach, and Abed-Nego shall be cut in pieces, and their houses shall be made an ash heap; because there is no other God who can deliver like this. Then the king promoted Shadrach, Meshach and Abed-Nego in the province of Babylon."** (Daniel 3:28-30 NKJ)

The three Hebrews received another promotion from the king after they passed the test of the fiery furnace. Jesus, the seed of their blessings, was planted in the soil of their testing beforehand, to deliver them and bless them with promotion.

Me. On a very high note I caught an airplane and flew back to California on Monday morning. I purposely booked myself on an earlier flight so that I could make sure everything was in order when I picked my family up from the airport later that night. As soon as I entered my son Terry's apartment he greeted me and told me I had a slew of messages. He especially drew my attention to one man who had called numerous times on Monday looking for me. When I looked at the name and number I recognized it as one of the original lenders that I had spoken to several weeks ago. When I called him by telephone he asked me if I had purchased a house. I told him no. He then said he thought that his company could work with me. I told him to cut through the chase and tell me how much interest they would charge us. He said that they could get us in at seven percent. I said we can do business. Within a few days KJoy and I had an acceptable agreement on a four bedroom, three bath house with a RV parking space in Rialto, California. The house was unoccupied so we were blessed to get a quick escrow that was scheduled to close on September 11, 2001. The events of nine eleven put off our closing until Friday, the fourteenth of September, when the interest rates were dropped to lower than seven percent. I had asked God for seven percent. I confessed it and thanked Him for seven percent. We got exactly what we asked, thanked and believed God for. God even gave us favor to stay temporarily with Norman and Daz Patterson, some friends who lived in the same city that we were moving into. This enabled us to get Michael to school without having to drive ninety minutes twice a day. All things truly worked together for our good and the seeds of our blessings were definitely imbedded in the soil of our testing. What enabled us to have faith and walk in peace during the test? An abiding trust in God based on past experiences and some valuable principles we learned from the life of Joseph.

A close examination of Joseph's life and other biblical characters, as well as many of my own experiences have led me to believe that all of our tests are designed, promoted and orchestrated by God's divine providence. God the divine is always in control. Providence comes from a Greek word that means to consider in advance; to look out for beforehand; to provide for; oversight and care. God considers us before our tests. He looks out for us beforehand. He designs, orchestrates or promotes our tests to accomplish His desired end for our lives. Before we get in a test God has already provided beforehand what we need to make it through. God plants seeds of blessings in the ground of our circumstances, the soil of our situations, before we get involved in the various tests. If we will faithful work the land of our circumstances and situations, our seeds will be cultivated to bear much fruit in our lives. With that understanding it is not difficult to embrace and walk in the word that God gives us through the Apostle James:

> **"My brethren, count it all joy when you fall into various trials, knowing that the testing of your faith produces patience. But let patience have its perfect work, that you may be perfect and complete, lacking nothing."** (James 1:3, 4 NKJ)

You. In the beginning of your relationship with God, you will not have the faith, the trust or the maturity to fully embrace and walk in the anointed words of Apostle James. It is very important that you don't condemn yourself or allow other well meaning religious people to condemn you because you struggle and falter during some tests in your early Christian walk. **"There is therefore now no condemnation to those who are in Christ Jesus, who do not walk according to the flesh, but according to the Spirit."** (Romans 8:1) Your life is hid in Christ Jesus! You have a relationship with Him that is more powerful than any religion. It takes time and numerous experiences with God to mature to the place where you count it all joy when you are being tested. Also know that God will take you at His pace; therefore, do not allow negative words, actions and reactions from others to pressure you into trying to meet their expectations or thinking that you can't do what God is asking of you. **Never place your emotional health in the hands of another person.** Yes, you have a part to play, but God is in the test with you, and He will empower you if you give Him your undivided attention, have a good attitude, be accountable and guard your actions. Don't waste time having a pity party. And do not take the path of least resistance by wallowing in a familiar sin or habit that so easily besets you.

I have just shared four dynamic "A's," that I call the A-Train. On the track of testing let's take the A-Train to the Joy Station! In our brief examination of Joseph we shall see these four "A's" lived out in his life. **ATTENTION! ATTITUDE! ACCOUNTABILITY! ACTIONS!** It is apparent from life's experiences and the study of Biblical characters that God allows tests in our lives to get our undivided attention and change our focus. A serious test can change our focus, put us in gear and drive us to our prayer closets like nothing else. A severe test can cause a wandering mind to cease from wandering and **focus undivided attention on God.** Tests have a way of slowing us down and drawing our attention to prayer and the word of God. Over the years I have matured to the place where some of my greatest moments of peace are in the midst of a severe test when I am totally focused on Christ. **"Thou wilt keep him in perfect peace, whose mind is stayed on thee: because he trusteth in thee. Trust ye in the Lord forever: for in the Lord Jehovah is everlasting strength."** (Isaiah 26:3, 4 KJ)

Where is your trust today? What and who are you focused on? Does God have your undivided attention? When the Angel of the

Lord appeared to Moses in a flame of fire in the midst of a burning bush, He did not speak to Moses until Moses turned aside from all distractions to focus his undivided attention on the Lord in the flame of fire. **"And <u>when the Lord saw that he turned aside to see,</u> God called <u>unto him</u> out of the midst of the bush, and said, Moses, Moses. And he said, Here am I."** (Exodus 3:4 KJ) You will not usually hear God when you are caught up and distracted by people, events, and the affairs of life. To develop a hearing ear and have intimacy with God, you must set aside a place and a time to meet God on a consistent basis. The Holy Scriptures teach us to pray without ceasing, meaning that you should always be in a prayerful mode, have an attitude of prayer.

Me. Riding alone in my car I will often pray silently and aloud. At the gym during my workout I have incorporated prayer and thanksgiving into my different routines. Prayer is a consistent and prominent part of my life; however, I have a prayer closet (God's throne room) and a certain time, Monday through Friday, that I enter in to spend quality uninterrupted time with God. When I am away from home for ministry or personal reasons I will still spend quality time with God in prayer. Wherever God meets me is holy ground and it is His throne room. And in His presence I receive instructions and directions. In His presence I have peace, joy, intimacy and fullness of the Holy Spirit.

You. Established a place and a time that you agree to meet God on a consistent basis. I assure you that God will always be in that place at the time you promised to show up. This is the place and the time that you give God your undivided attention. You have to put family and friends on notice that you are not to be disturbed in that place during your time with God. Intimacy with God is strongly enhanced by your obedience to God and giving Him your undivided attention. You will also develop a hearing ear to know the voice of God. It is not necessarily an audible voice but God has a voice. Jesus said: **"My sheep hear my voice, and I know them, and they follow me."** (John 10:27) The same way your ear and your emotions are trained to recognize the voice of your earthly parents, your spiritual ear and your faith can be trained to recognize the voice of your Heavenly Father.

God has different ways to speak to us, but through an intimate, obedient relationship we learn to recognize His voice and accept the different ways He speaks to us. Many times God will speak directly to you through the Holy Scriptures. Other times He may speak through prophecy or dreams. He may speak through another person, and not just a preacher. I have personally found some janitors, cooks, faithful mothers, and other praying saints in the church to be more anointed than some preachers. By all means, give respect to whoever is due respect; however, don't be impressed by position or title, but seek one who is anointed by God. God may also speak through your circumstances. However God speaks, it is most important that He has your attention so that you don't miss hearing Him and forfeit His blessings and directions for your life.

In Joseph's life God spoke to him through dreams. At age seventeen God got Joseph's attention through a series of dreams that would profoundly shape the rest of his life. Joseph constantly heard God in each dream. God had Joseph's attention. Because of his youth, informing his father of the evil actions of his brothers and the special love shown to him by his father Jacob, Joseph's brothers hated and despised him. In Joseph's dreams, God told him that he would one day reign over his brothers and family. Because of their hate and envy, his brothers plotted to kill him. His older brother Reuben intervened and persuaded his brothers not to kill him. Later Joseph was sold to a company of Midianites merchants who took Joseph to Egypt and sold him to Potiphar, an officer of Pharaoh and captain of the guard.

Joseph was greatly tested when he was taken away from his family, brought down to Egypt, and sold as a slave to Potiphar. However, Joseph was blessed in his test because the Lord was with him. **"And <u>the Lord was with Joseph</u>, and he was a prosperous man; and he was in the house of his master the Egyptian. And his master saw that <u>the Lord was with him</u>, and that the Lord made all that he did to prosper in his hand."** (Genesis 39:2, 3 KJ)

How did Potiphar see that the Lord was with Joseph? He saw it in Joseph's character, his demeanor, his activities and his **attitude**. Because God had gotten Joseph's attention through a series of dreams, Joseph did not fall apart when he was taken from his family. He did not have a vengeful, hateful attitude. He knew what God had told him in the dreams. He chose to allow his attitude to be shaped by the promises of God and not his immediate situation. In Joseph's case, and most times in our situations, God may tell us what He's going to do and where we may end up; but, He does not tell us how He is going to do it or what we have to go through to get to our destination. God told Joseph that he would one day rule in the palace; however, He did not tell Joseph that he had to be thrown in a pit, sold into slavery and spend years in prison in order to get to the palace. Throughout Joseph's testing he never has a vengeful, hateful attitude toward anyone.

When God orchestrates or allows us to go through some difficult tests, some life changing stuff, some take the wind out of your sail situations, He is testing us to reveal and develop our character. **God alone knows what He has put in us and what He has equipped us to do.** I have discovered two dynamic truths about Godly designed tests. One, they are always bigger than what we think we are capable of handling. Two, they are individualized, designed by God, specifically for the person going through the test. Whether designed, orchestrated or allowed by God, He is always in control of our tests. Therefore, we would do well to check our attitude when we are being tested. Jesus told us not to fear, but be of good cheer when we have tribulation.

You. What does God see in you when you are knee deep in the soil of your tests? Does God see fear or faith? Does God see frowning or smiling? Does God hear moaning and groaning, or praise and worship? What attitude does God see in you when you are being tested? Know that God always checks you out when you are being tested. He watches carefully your attitude. Does He see you tripping about problems or trusting in Him? A negative, bad attitude can kill the seeds of your blessings. A negative bad attitude can prolong your time in the soil of testing. A negative bad attitude usually results in you having to repeat the same test at another time.

At no time in the biblical account of Joseph's life do we see him with a negative bad attitude. There is no evidence of him being vengeful and vindictive toward those who wronged him. He was able to keep his attitude in check because he knew that he was in the place of God, and that the Lord who had spoken to him in dreams was with him. **"So Joseph found favor in his sight, and served him. Then he made him overseer of his house, and all that he had he put under his authority. So it was, from the time that he had made him overseer of his house and all that he had, that the LORD blessed the Egyptian's house for Joseph's sake; and the blessing of the LORD was on all that he had in the house and in the field."** (Genesis 39:4, 5 NKJ)

The same God who was with Joseph will also be with you and me during our tests. And if God is with us then we also shall prosper. The Holy Scriptures tell us to count it all joy when we are in a test. Why? Because the soil of our testing is the place of God and our God has planted seeds of blessings in the soil of our tests! A good attitude is nurtured by God's presence and it enables us to know that we are blessed in the test! A good attitude in a test will allow others to see God in us. And many others can be blessed and encouraged on account of our attitude in a test. Potiphar and his entire household were blessed on account of Joseph, during his season of testing. Joseph was without malice and a vindictive attitude because he viewed his testing from God's perspective for his life.

Zuleekha, Potiphar's wife, constantly tried to seduce Joseph. But he refused her advances. Joseph never lost sight of his **accountability** to God and those in authority over him. He could have rationalized his situation and tried to justify wrong actions because he had been treated unjustly. A young man, separated from his family, sold into slavery, not permitted to marry and constantly being seduced by his master's wife. **"But he refused and said to his master's wife, Look, my master does not know what is with me in the house, and he has committed all that he has to my hand. There is no one greater in this house than I, nor has he kept back anything from me but you, because you are his wife. How then can I do this great wickedness, and sin against God?"** (Genesis 39:8 NKJ) Joseph was accountable to God and Potiphar. He was faithful to God and chose to live godly in an ungodly situation. Accountability is doing what you know to be right, even in a wrong situation with ungodly people.

You. Who are you accountable to when all hell breaks loose in your life? What rules, what standards, govern your decisions and behavior when you are being tested? God blesses obedience; therefore, you will always be blessed in your test when you walk in obedience. If you love God, you are commanded to obey Him. Loving God and being accountable to Him is not just reserved for the good times, when your ship is sailing on smooth waters. You will face many tests and temptations in life, but God will always make a way of escape for you. Stay faithful and accountable to God-no matter what. Allow God's Spirit to strengthen you in the season of your testing.

After becoming second in command to the Pharaoh, Joseph had the authority and power to destroy Zuleekha, who had lied on him and caused him to be thrown into prison. Joseph never indulged a negative attitude or lack of accountability to God and those in authority over him, to sway him from the course that God had revealed to him in a series of dreams. His attitude in his tests and his accountability to God greatly shaped and colored his **actions** toward his brothers and all those who mistreated him.

The Pharaoh of Egypt dreamed some dreams that none of his magicians could interpret. The chief butler, who had forgotten Joseph, finally remembered his fault, and told the Pharaoh about Joseph and his ability to interpret dreams. The Pharaoh sent for Joseph and he was taken out of the prison dungeon, cleaned up and brought before the Pharaoh. Even though Joseph wanted to be free from prison, he would not take personal credit for the interpretation. **"So Joseph answered Pharaoh, saying, It is not in me; God will give Pharaoh an answer of peace."** (Genesis 41:16 NKJ) God used dreams to reveal to Joseph his purpose, and now God uses dreams to elevate Joseph to a position of high authority in Egypt. Again, during his test, God caused Joseph to be promoted. **"And Pharaoh said to his servants, 'Can we find such a one as this, a man in whom is the Spirit of God?' Then Pharaoh said to Joseph, Inasmuch as God has shown you all this, there is no one as discerning and wise as you. You shall be over my house, and all my people shall be ruled according to your word; only in regard to the throne will I**

be greater than you.' And Pharaoh said to Joseph, See, I have set you over all the land of Egypt.'' (Genesis 41:38-41 NKJ)

Joseph was thirty years old when he was promoted by Pharaoh to rule over the nation of Egypt. Joseph was also given a wife who bore him two sons. His attitude and accountability to God is reflected in the names he chose for his sons. The first son he named Manasseh: "For God has made me forget all my toil and all my fathers' house." He named the second son, Ephraim: "For God has caused me to be fruitful in the land of my affliction."

During the seven years of plenty Joseph wisely stored away grain that he would use to feed the multitudes during the seven years of famine that would follow. After the severe famine began, Jacob sent his sons to Egypt to get grain for food so that they could all live and not die. Joseph was now governor over the land of Egypt and he was in charge. His brothers came and bowed down to him, not recognizing that he was the brother that they had betrayed. Joseph recognized his brothers and remembered the dreams that God had given him about them. Through a series of questions he determined that his father, well up in age, was still alive and well. When his brothers were brought back to Joseph, he could no longer restrain himself. He broke down and wept over them. **"And Joseph said to his brothers, Please come near to me." So they came near. Then he said: I am Joseph your brother, whom you sold into Egypt. But now, do not therefore be grieved or angry with yourselves because you sold me here; for God sent me before you to preserve life. For these two years the famine has been in the land, and there are still five years in which there will be neither plowing nor harvesting. And God sent me before you to preserve a posterity for you in the earth, and to save your lives by a great deliverance. So now it was not you who sent me here, but God; and He has made me a father to Pharaoh, and lord of all his house, and a ruler throughout all the land of Egypt."** (Gen 45:4-8 NKJ)

Throughout Joseph's testing, he never lost sight of God's purpose for his life and he maintained an excellent attitude because he knew that God was in control of his situation. He told his brothers that they, their families, and all their livestock, would dwell in Goshen and be near to him. He would provide for all of them during the remaining five years of the famine. He asks his brothers to quickly go and tell his father about his glory and stature in Egypt. He also told them to quickly bring his father up to Egypt. Before they left, Joseph demonstrated his love for all of his brothers by kissing them and weeping over them. Joseph's actions toward those who had wronged him were motivated by love and forgiveness. His actions caused even the Pharaoh to be well pleased and tender hearted toward his family. He told Joseph to bring his father and all his family to him and he would give them the best of all the land of Egypt.

Later, Joseph counseled his brothers on how to present themselves as shepherds and then he introduced them to the Pharaoh. All of his actions toward his family, including the brothers who had betrayed him, were pleasing to God because they were actions of love. God's foremost actions toward all his human creation are primarily actions of love. For God so loved the world that He gave his only begotten son, Jesus Christ. Jesus has planted seeds of blessings in the soil of our testing. People may come against us and do harm to us; however, we would do well to follow Joseph's example and respond to the people who wrong us with actions of love. And then throughout our testing we can give God our undivided attention, keep a good attitude, be accountable to God and those in authority over us, and respond with actions of love. Then our testimony can be the same as Joseph's: **"Joseph said to them, Do not be afraid, for I am in the place of God? But as for you, you meant evil against me: but God meant it for good, in order to bring it about as it is this day, to save many people alive."** (Genesis 50:19, 20 NKJ)

Me. Over the last ten years, as I have climbed up on the sixty rungs on the senior ladder of life, I have been reunited with many people from my early life, including close family members. By God's grace and His biblical teachings, I have experienced a level of maturity in the areas of forgiving, letting go, and loving those who had mistreated me.

God has allowed many of the people back into my life, for whom I had been praying. My level of maturity in learning how to forgive and engage in the ministry of reconciliation was facilitated by the inward working of the Holy Spirit embracing God's word within me. The love of God permeated my being, eradicating old scars and emotional wounds. I am free. I am whole. I am at peace. I am greatly blessed to have every old acquaintance and family member back into my life. They are essential to my life and blessings.

You. It is easy to be bitter, angry and resentful toward people who wrong you. A resentful, vindictive attitude will always cause you to respond in an ungodly manner; thus, forfeiting the blessings of God during your test. Fight the good fight of faith! Give God your undivided attention, and strive to allow your attitude, your accountability and your actions to be motivated by the love of God and not your hurtful emotions. When you constantly yield to hurtful emotions they become permanently damaged and scarred. When you walk in faith, putting your trust in God, He will always make a good way out for you. The wrongs that people do toward you can only do permanent damage when you allow them to root in your heart, breeding an unforgiving spirit that controls your behavior. Rise above the stings of painful words and actions by diligently working the soil of your testing where God has beforehand planted seeds of blessings. For God will cause all things to work together for your good, even the tests you go through. Giving God your undivided attention, maintaining a good healthy attitude, being accountable to God and others, walking in and promoting actions of love will cause you to be **BLESSED IN THE TEST!**

CHAPTER EIGHT

WE ARE ANOINTED
FOR VICTORY!

Amajor difference in Jesus' life, while on earth, was His anointing. His name was Jesus; they called him the Christ, meaning the anointed one. Jesus Christ is the anointed one. What made the difference in Moses' life, Joshua's life, Joseph's life and all the people of the Bible that God used in a great way, was the anointing. There are three absolutes for you and me as children of God: (1) God loves us. (2) God will always be with us. (3) God will empower us to do what He calls us to do. His anointing is our power source. His anointing is the high octane in our generator that propels us to do great and mighty things. God wants you and me, his saints, to recognize, to know, to accept and to walk in this dynamic truth: **WE ARE ANOINTED FOR VICTORY!**

Regardless of situations and circumstances, it is imperative that we develop a kingdom mentality that dictates to us that We Are Anointed for Victory! To be a victor we have to overcome and conquer some things. We have to rise above the mundane and live a supernatural life in a very natural world. We have to stretch beyond our comfort zones and operate outside the paradigms of conventional means. We dare not allow God's purpose and vision for us to be clouded or distorted by the difficult situations and circumstances of life. Without doubt, God is calling His people, to embrace their purpose, walk in His promises and take appropriate actions to achieve victory.

When Joshua was facing what appeared to be an insurmountable wall, God did not direct him to see the difficult problem before him. God directed Joshua to see His promise. **"See! I have given Jericho into your hand, its king, and the mighty men of valor."** (Joshua 6:2 NKJ) God directed Joshua to focus on his purpose and walk in God's promise; then, He tells Joshua how to achieve victory. **We can truly walk in our anointed victories when we learn to look through eyes of faith to see the promises of God.** The Apostle Paul gives us insight into the promises of God. **"For all the promises of God in Him are Yes, and in Him Amen, to the glory of God through us. Now He who establishes us with you in Christ and has anointed us is God, who also has sealed us and given us the Spirit in our hearts as a guarantee."** (2 Corinthians 1:20-22 NKJ)

Just as the Holy Spirit dwelling in our hearts, is a guarantee of our salvation, it is also a guarantee of our ability to be rooted, established, and anointed by God. And God does not anoint us for failure. We can achieve failure and despair operating in our own power. In fact, the greatest source of despair of people in church is walking in disobedience, outside the promises of God, in their own power and strategies. God not only anointed Joshua for victory, He also gave him the strategies for the victory. God's ways are not our ways, so walking in our own strategies and power will always lead to defeat and despair.

Throughout the anointed triumphant reign of King David, he always sought God for direction and strategies in going up against his enemies. His numerous victories in battle were not luck, not coincidence, nor by mere happenstance. His victories were a direct result of God's anointing on his life and his diligence to seek direction and strategies from the God who sits high and looks low. David knew that his greatness was directly attributable to God's anointed presence in his life, and God's directions and strategies for his battles. After he and four hundred of his men had followed God's directions, pursued and defeated the Amalekites, took back their families and a large bounty, some wicked men in their midst wanted to keep all the bounty for themselves and not share with the two hundred men who had stayed behind to protect their supplies. **"But David said, My brethren, you shall not do so <u>with what the LORD has given us, who has preserved us and delivered into our hand</u> the troop that came against us."** (1 Samuel 30:23)

The earlier Scriptures in 2 Corinthians established four dynamic truths that will bless and inspire us to walk as sons and daughters of God. (1) God establishes us in Christ Jesus. (2) He anoints us. And his anointing is not just reserved for the preacher or officers in the church. His anointing is for every born again believer. (3) He seals us with the stamp of His ownership. (4) God gives us his Spirit. We are the sons and daughters of Almighty God. These four dynamic truths are promises of God. And the promises of God in Jesus Christ are yea and Amen! And they are given for God's glory that is revealed through us. God's presence in our lives and his anointing on our lives is God's glory operating through us, enabling us to fulfill God's purpose for our lives and walk in victory on this earth.

Me. During the early stages of traveling as a full time evangelist I was often amazed and awestruck at the move of the Holy Spirit in worship services that I was ministering in. I would often stand to speak at the pulpit after praise and worship, with my notes meticulous prepared, and I began flowing in God's anointing. Often times I knew that God was honoring my earlier prayer: "Holy Spirit I decrease now that you might increase to bless your people and my people. Have your own way, Lord. Use your humble servant." Somehow I would cease following my notes and the Holy Spirit would take over. I would be quoting and explaining Scriptures that I had not worked on for this particular message. The word came forth with power and conviction! People got saved. Some were healed and others delivered from bondage. People would be on the floor weeping, others on their feet, walking, jumping, dancing, shouting! I would always experience this unusual surge of power within me. It was beyond my human comprehension. When I would later listen to recordings of my messages, I would weep uncontrollably, thanking God for speaking through me. It was God's anointing upon me. I was clothed with His power.

In 1980, in Austin, Texas, my hometown, I was speaking during a Vacation Bible School Revival at The New Testament Church. There was a great move of God's Spirit in the house as the word came forth with power and clarity. Some came down the aisle to accept Jesus as their savior. I prayed with them. After service I always stood at the front door, with the late Pastor Bill Jones, greeting the people as they exited the building. On my way to the front I was stopped by a very gentle, serene lady named Sister Imogene Dixon. She asked if I would pray for her. I told her that I would be happy to pray for her, and then asked her if she could wait a few minutes until I had greeted the people so that I could give her my undivided attention. Quietly, she took a seat away from the crowd in the section where the deacons sat during worship service. After greeting the people I went over to Sister Dixon. She asked me to pray for God's healing in her body. She wanted God's will for her life, even if that meant going home to be with him. She told me that she was not afraid of dying; however, because of a previous very painful illness, she did not want to suffer.

During the prayer, God spoke to me and told me to tell her to thank Him, morning and evening, for the next ten days. No matter how she felt, believe God and thank Him for her healing. He also told me to tell her that the devil would try to discourage her during that time, but no matter what or how she felt, she must continue to believe God and thank Him for her healing. Later, during a medical checkup, her doctor was baffled as he told her that he could not find any trace of the cancer in her body.

Years later, I received a letter dated July 31, 1985, from Sister Dixon, celebrating her five years of being cancer free. She was truly praising God for a threefold blessing in her life. God had healed her of the physical cancer. He blessed her family and gave her the gift of songs. She started writing songs of praise. Today, she is still a graceful serene lady of faith, living victoriously and totally free of cancer. She knows that God has anointed her for victory and she walks in it.

God's anointing on my life has enabled me to overcome some major obstacles and achieve victory in what appeared to be imminent defeat. Shortly after I had been called by God to the ministry of evangelism, where God told me that I would be traveling around the world preaching the gospel, I was diagnosed with a disease called sarcoidosis. This disease attacked my lung functions and caused me to have shortness of breath and other breathing abnormalities. I later thought, isn't it interesting that in all the years I was in the world promoting my own agenda, living like a heathen, and doing my own ungodly thing, I never had any difficulty breathing or talking. And yet, shortly after God calls me to represent Him and speak His word, I have difficulty breathing and talking.

The different doctors and specialists prescribed medical treatment that included taking a steroid called prednisone. While prednisone may have been treating my disease, it was also causing me to have unusual mood swings and temper problems. I was faithful to follow the doctor's instructions. I did the quarterly breathing tests and continued in my weekly exercise routine. I quickly became aware of other people around me who suffered with the same disease. Many of them were bloated and overweight. Many of them were taking much higher doses of medication than I was. Within a short frame of time, two people suffering with the disease died of complications of the disease, the medication, and the excess weight.

I was reminded of Sister Dixon and was prompted by God's Spirit within me to deal with my disease by asking, believing, and thanking God to heal me. I was still traveling and preaching the gospel with strong fervor and enthusiasm. God's anointing was powerful on my life and my ministry. I began to search the Scriptures for words of encouragement. In dealing with my illness the following Scriptures became the foundation of my faith and permeated my thoughts. **"Then Jesus went about all the cities and villages, teaching in their synagogues, preaching the gospel of the kingdom, and healing every sickness and every disease among the people. But when He saw the multitudes, He was moved with compassion for them, because they were weary and scattered, like sheep having no shepherd. Then He said to His disciples, 'The harvest truly is plentiful, but the laborers are few. Therefore pray the Lord of the harvest to send out laborers into His harvest."** (Matthew 9:35-38 NKJ) **"And when He had called His twelve disciples to Him, He gave them power over unclean spirits, to cast them out, and to heal all kinds of sickness and all kinds of disease."** (Matthew 10:1 NKJ)

I knew that I was God's laborer and since God is not a respecter of persons, I also knew that He had given me power to heal the disease that was attacking my body. Shortly after this I started confessing my healing and thanking God for it. I went to my doctor, one of the leading specialists in the treatment of sarcoidosis, and told him that God had healed me. I also told him that I no longer wanted to take the medication. He wanted to trust his science, but I insisted that God had healed me. Seeing that I was adamant about God's healing me, he asked me if I would agree to allow him to wean me off the medication and not abruptly stop taking it. I agreed to take it for another few weeks. After approximately four to six weeks, I stopped taking the medication. Months later I went to the doctor for new x-rays. After careful study of my old and new x-rays, he concluded that the disease had been arrested and was no longer active in my body. He also told me that I had lost some twenty percent of my lung capacity. God was true to His word. He arrested and stopped the disease that was attacking my body. Today, with God's anointing, continuous weekly exercise, and a good diet, I continue to travel throughout the width and breadth of this world teaching and preaching the gospel of Jesus Christ. God's anointing has given me victory in my spiritual life, my physical life and my business life. And under God's anointing I am still blessed and privilege to see others overcome great obstacles and live a victorious life in Christ Jesus.

Over the years I had learned to pray and speak victory over my life. I believed so strongly in God's anointing on my life, no matter how I felt, I would always thank Him for a body not racked with pain and void of all disease. I would also thank God for the in-filling of His Holy Spirit and His anointing within and upon me.

Another Scripture that gives evidence and confirmation of God's anointing for victory is found in the epistles of Peter. **"As his divine power has given to us all things that pertain to life** (our natural existence) **and godliness** (our spiritual existence), **through the knowledge of Him** (Jesus) **who called us by glory and virtue, by which have been given to us exceedingly great and precious promises, that through these you may be partakers of the divine nature, having escaped the corruption that is in the world through lust."** (2 Peter 1:3, 4 NKJ)

God's divine power has given to every saint of the Lord Jesus Christ, all things pertaining to life and godliness. The above Scripture says "Jesus <u>called us</u> by glory and virtue, and He has <u>given to us</u> exceeding great and precious promises..." This includes me and it includes you. God has given us some exceedingly great and precious promises, that we might be partakers of His divine nature. The Holy Spirit lives within us and He is our anointing for victory. Take note that all the promises of God come through the knowledge of Jesus. On earth Jesus was the living word. In the Bible He is the written word. **"In the beginning was the Word, and the Word was with God, and the Word was God. He was in the beginning with God. All things were made through Him, and without Him nothing was made that was made. In Him was life, and the life was the light of men."** (John 1:1-4 NKJ)

Jesus is the Word. As He was preparing to leave earth to return to His home in glory, He told the disciples and those of us who follow him today: **"Nevertheless I tell you the truth. It is to your advantage that I go away; for if I do not go away, the Helper will not come to you; but if I depart, I will send Him to you."** (John 16:7 NKJ) The Holy Spirit is the Helper. He is our Divine Teacher. He is our Mighty Counselor. He is our Comforter and He is our Anointing. As saints of God we are **anointed for victory!** To live a victorious lives there are four essential things that we must do. (1)We have to recognize our anointing. (2)We have to have knowledge of our anointing. (3)We have to accept our anointing. (4)We have to walk in our anointing.

You. As a born again saint of God you must have a kingdom mentality and recognize that God has anointed you with a power that exceeds the natural realm. You live in the world but you are not of the world. Therefore, you must know and accept the fact that God's anointing has made **AWESOME YOU** a cut above those living only in the natural realm. Your focus must be more attuned to the Word and the spiritual things of God. Earnestly desire to live holy before God in an unholy world. God lives in you and your life is hid in God. **"Since, then, you have been raised with Christ, set your hearts on things above, where Christ is seated at the right hand of God. Set your minds on things above, not on earthly**

things. For you died, and your life in now hidden with Christ in God." (Colossians 3:1-3 NIV)

In Christ Jesus you must willfully choose to die to the things of this world. **"Put to death, therefore, whatever belongs to your earthly nature: sexual immorality, impurity, lust, evil desires and greed, which is idolatry. Because of these, the wrath of God is coming. You used to walk in these ways, in the life you once lived. But now you must rid yourselves of all such things as these: anger, rage, malice, slander, and filthy language from your lips."** (Colossians 3:5-8 NIV) You cannot accomplish putting the earthly nature to death operating in your own strength and willpower. You can only accomplish this by yielding to and trusting in the Christ in you. You are a new creation in Christ Jesus, and over time you will walk in victory, if you yield to and trust in His Spirit in you and obey His word for you. God will guide you and empower you to overcome your earthly nature. Your life is hid with Christ in God; therefore, you are living in two different worlds at the same time.

Also, know that because you are hid with Christ in God and living in two different worlds at the same time, you have a privilege that non-believers do not enjoy. In Jesus name you have authority on earth and acceptance in heaven. You can ask the Father for help to meet your needs, overcome your problems, and heal your diseases-in the name of Jesus. **"In that day you will no longer ask me anything. I tell you the truth, my Father will give you whatever you ask in my name. Until now you have not asked for anything in my name. Ask and you will receive, and your joy will be complete."** (John 16:23, 24 NIV) Ask according to God's will and God will hear you and grant the petitions that you request.

Beloved, as a new creation in Christ Jesus, operating with a kingdom mentality, you will be able to step into God's dimensions of glory and take dominion over your life. You are anointed for victory but you have to step into God's sovereign dominion for your life. **Do not be a spectator, be a participator and a leader.** Do not sit in the bleachers or on the sideline, get in the relay race and run your lap. Life is like a relay race where we all have a lap to run. And it is very important that we run our lap so that we can hand the baton off to the next runner, as we run for the gold. The Apostle Paul,

Peter, John, Timothy, James, Mary, Martha, Priscilla and others ran their lap, then handed off the baton to those who came after them. The baton has been handed down to us from the generations of our grandparents and parents. It's our time to run the Christian race. And we have been anointed to win the gold. Do not allow past mistakes or worldly status to discourage and cripple you.

There was a sick cripple man who had an infirmity for thirty-eight years. He sat in the midst of a multitude of sick people at a pool called Bethesda, waiting for the moving of the water. Whoever stepped into the water, after the angel had stirred it, was healed of whatever infirmity they had. Jesus came along one day and asked the sick man if he wanted to be made well? The man did not answer in the affirmative. He allowed his past to shape his response. **"The sick man answered him, Sir, I have no man to put me into the pool when the water is stirred up; but while I am coming, another steps down before me.' Jesus said to him, Rise, take up your bed and walk.' And immediately the man was made well, took up his bed, and walked."** (John 5:7-9 NKJ)

When God saved you, He immediately healed you of your sin infirmity. Before salvation we were all spiritual cripples. God's grace and our faith and confession in Christ Jesus made us whole and enabled us to take dominion over life. Dominion means to rule, to reign, to subdue and bring under control. You are no longer a victim of your sinful flesh, carnal habits or past mistakes. Sins and mistakes of the past are washed away by the blood of Jesus. You are truly a new creation in Christ Jesus designed by God to lead. In the original creation process God handed leadership of the earth over to humanity.

"Then God said, Let Us make man in Our image, according to Our likeness: let them have dominion over the fish of the sea, over the birds of the air, and over the cattle, over all the earth and over every creeping thing that creeps on the earth.' So God created man in His own image; in the image of God He created him; male and female He created them. Then God blessed them, and God said to them, Be fruitful and multiply; fill the earth and subdue it; have dominion over the fish of the sea, over the birds

of the air, and over every living thing that moves on the earth."
(Genesis 1:26-28 NKJ)

God is a leader and He created you to lead and have dominion.
He made you in His image and after His likeness. He wants you to
operate just like He does. God indwells you by His Spirit and anoints
you for victory. Therefore, step into your leadership role. For God
has anointed you to step into the stirred waters of His dimensions for
your life. Do not just go to church and celebrate with a shout! Step
into the move of God's Spirit and engage in ministry as a witness
for Christ. **Stand on God's promises! Don't just sit on the prem-
ises!** Go into the hedges and highways of life compelling men and
women to know this Jesus who healed you of your sin infirmity.
**God wants you and I to step into His anointing, step into His
glory, step into His kingdom work, step into His joy, step into
His peace, step into His healing, step into His deliverance, step
into His promotion and step into His victory!**

Beloved, you and I will not step into and operate in a power
that we do not recognize, know and accept. To be aware of and
operate in God's anointing, we have to recognize that we have
this unique power from God. We also must study the Scriptures to
learn how to operate in God's power. The Bible teaches us that we
have been clothed with God's divine power. **"And, behold, I send
the promise of my Father upon you: but tarry ye in the city of
Jerusalem, until ye be endued with power from on high."** (Luke
24:49 KJ) The word endued means to be clothed; arrayed; to put
on. At salvation we received the Holy Spirit within, which causes
an inner transformation where we received God's divine nature.
And then God clothes us with an outer power, His anointing. What
makes Christians a cut above all humanity is our divine nature and
godly anointing. We are partakers of God's divine nature and we are
anointed by God to lead. This is precisely what it means to be Aborn
again." Walk in God's anointing, step into your leadership role and
live the victorious life that God has designed for you. **YOU ARE
ANOINTED FOR VICTORY!**

CHAPTER NINE

GREAT POTENTIAL AND HIGH EXPECTATIONS!

God has high expectations for His chosen saints. His anointing on us and His presence in us gives us great potential. He is the treasure in our earthen vessels. And His power working in us represents our true potential. God's presence in our natural beings is the supreme power that enables us to do supernatural things. God expects us to walk in the supernatural. Therefore, we need to tap into our great potential as God's Masterpieces. Regardless of our past mistakes, lifestyles, lack of education and training, we have great potential in Christ Jesus. Ideally, it would be great if we all came from an excellent background, with a quality education and/or special training in some field of endeavor. It would be ideal if we all came to God with worldly influence and connections. Our God is a visionary and He has high expectations for each of us. Jesus does not look at who we are and where we are. He looks at who we shall become and where we are going. And by His divine providence, He will navigate our journey. Biblical and world history teaches us that Jesus takes what we have and uses it to His glory. The resources that we have at salvation can be an asset for God's kingdom. He often uses us in the way that He finds us. And the kingdom of God within us is the source of our great potential. We may come to God with a zero on our hearts and a two on our foreheads, but the moment Jesus takes up residence in us, He puts a ten over our hearts and on our foreheads. God has high expectations for each of His saints. He sees in us the great potential that He saw in those He called while living on the earth.

The Lord Jesus saw great potential and had high expectations for each of the disciples that He beckoned to follow him. He also sees great value and potential in you and me. Our past is a stepping stone, not a stumbling block. God has rolled away the shame of our past mistakes. He has rolled away the reproach of our past lifestyles. The Lord Jesus sees you and me totally different than people in the world see us. Often times, people in the world tend to look at us and assess our value through the lenses of our past mistakes, where we came from, what we did, where we are, and what we have. Jesus always looks at our potential and sees what we can become. **The potential that He sees in us causes Him to have high expectations of us.** Remember we are His glittering diamonds in the rough who need to be molded and shaped into beautiful valuable stones of jewelry in His glorious crown. And He is the consummate jeweler, molding and shaping us to His divine perfection.

Me. When God first called me to preach the gospel, I ran and denied the call for over six months. I could not see myself as a preacher of the gospel. I had no background as a preacher. Preachers were not a part of my inner or outer circle. I knew that I had come from a lifestyle of being a three hundred and sixty degree black belt sinner. While in denial, I thought to myself, "what do I know about preaching?" Little did I know, at the time, that Jesus would use the various gifts and training that I had acquired in the world to lift up His name and advance God's kingdom on earth. Over the years I have been greatly encouraged by reading and studying the lives of many of the people that God used to His glory. His high expectations are always obvious. Earlier, I told you about Moses and how the story of his life greatly impacted mine. Moses had a speech impediment. He stammered, and yet God chose him to be His spokesman. You can't talk without stumbling over your words, and God calls you to be His spokesman? That's high expectation! David was a shepherd boy, but God chose him to be the greatest king of Israel. Mary Magdalene was a prostitute who Jesus converted and used to herald His resurrection. Paul, a highly educated man, was a persecutor and murderer of the early church. Jesus redeemed him on the Damascus Road and called him to be one of the great Apostles, whose prolific writings to the early church still edify and bless us today. The Lord Jesus had high expectations for each of them; thus, He looked beyond all of their past imperfections, their present encumbrances and saw their great potential.

Peter's life experiences and those of the early disciples teach volumes to us today. They were not the elite of their society. They were not the learned men of the synagogue. They were itinerant fisherman, tax collectors and the like. **"So it was, as the multitude pressed about Him to hear the word of God, that He stood by the lake of Gennesaret, and saw two boats standing by the lake; but the fishermen had gone from them and were washing their nets. Then He got into one of the boats, which was Simon's, and asked him to put out a little from the land. And He sat down and taught the multitudes from the boat. When He had stopped speaking, He said to Simon, Launch out into the deep and let down your nets for a catch.' But Simon answered and said to Him, Master, we have toiled all night and caught nothing; nevertheless at Your word I will let down the net.' And when they had done this, they caught a great number of fish, and their net was breaking. So they signaled to their partners in the other boat to come and help them. And they came and filled both the boats, so that they began to sink. When Simon Peter saw it, he fell down at Jesus' knees, saying, Depart from me, for I am a sinful man, O Lord!' For he and all who were with him were astonished at the catch of fish which they had taken; and so also were James and John, the sons of Zebedee, who were partners with Simon. And Jesus said to Simon, Do not be afraid. From now on you will catch men.' So when they had brought their boats to land, they forsook all and followed Him."** (Luke 5:1-11 NKJ)

Jesus initially chose a group of itinerant fisherman to follow him. On the world's totem pole of importance and significance these men were at the bottom. The Lord had high expectations, so He looked beyond their present status. He saw their great potential. He also allowed them to see His potential and to know that He had high expectations for them. Peter chose to override all of his fishing expertise and obey Jesus; thus, they were astonished at the greatest catch of fish that they had ever experience. Not only did their nets break, but both boats were sinking because of so many fish. Peter immediately recognized their catch as a supernatural feat. He bowed before Jesus and acknowledged him as Lord. Take note that Jesus did not reject him and cast him overboard when he said he was a sinful man. He was not looking at Peter's present condition and place in life. Jesus was a visionary who had high expectations and purpose for Peter and his partners. He told them: **From now on you will catch men.**

You. No matter where you were when Jesus saved you, and no matter what your past may have been, God is your great potential and He has high expectations for you. Will you dare to see your past and the place where you are when God saved you as a tool and a place of beginning, to serve His kingdom? Your past is of value to God because He often uses our past to define our ministry; however, His high expectations of you are not based on your past or your present condition. They are based on His great potential that is within you. The most effective Christian witnesses to drug dealers and abusers are ex-dealers and ex-abusers. The most sensitive witnesses to pimps and prostitutes are ex-pimps and ex-prostitutes. The most informed witnesses who understand the mentality of thieves and gangsters are ex-thieves and ex-gangsters. Do not be afraid. God is not condemning your past faults or your present status. He knows of His great potential within you and He has high expectations for your future. Like Peter and his partners, you will not stop fishing, you will just change your bait and the object of your catch.

Later when Jesus went out and saw a tax collector named Levi, sitting at a tax office, He beckoned Levi to follow Him. Levi left all and followed Jesus. Levi gave Jesus a great feast in his home and invited other tax collectors. Levi's first witness was to his fellow tax collectors. God uses us where He finds us. In time you will grow and expand, but God will start using you where He finds you.

The great potential that these men had was not immediately known, nor was it visible to them. God was their potential and He had high expectations for them. To release their great potential and reach His high expectations, they had to spend years walking with Jesus. They saw how He operated in the spirit. They learned to start with what they had and trusted God to expand it to what they needed. They saw His compassion in feeding the multitude with two fish and five loaves; in casting out demons and healing the sick of their infirmities. They observed His close relationship with the Father, and how He would steal away to pray, after ministering all day to the multitudes. They saw how significant prayer was in His life and ministry. They watched Him go to the mountains and pray all night to God the Father. They listened to His anointed teaching as He gave them understanding of the things that He spoke to the crowds in parables. They saw His faith in action as He boldly performed miracle after miracle. Through it all Jesus was setting a standard and revealing the glory that they could walk in. He saw great things in them and He also sees great things in you and me. He wants you and me to know that the Holy Spirit, the same great potential that indwelled them, also indwells us. They were able to impact the world for God's kingdom, and so can we.

He later called them together and gave them power and authority over all demons, and to cure all diseases. He sent them out to preach the kingdom of God and to heal the sick. His power and authority did not end with the twelve disciples. His power and the great potential that He saw in them, He also sees in you and me. By God's Divine Providence we can change the world and establish God's kingdom on earth. President Abraham Lincoln, a great leader, a devout Christian, and a praying man, once wrote these words to his friend, Byron Sutherland: "I believe we are all agents and instruments of Divine Providence. I hold myself in my present position and with the authority invested in me, as an instrument of Providence." You and I must also recognized that the Lord Jesus has given us authority and power to be leaders and go into all the world, to save the lost, heal the sick, and set the captives free.

You & Me. God has a divine plan for this world. And His divine plan includes you and me. For us to participate and operate in His divine plan, He gave us His divine nature. You and I have a new divine nature that equips and empowers us to do great things for the kingdom of God. The Holy Spirit inspired Peter, after sitting under

Jesus' leadership and teaching for three years, to write these words: **"Coming to Him as to a living stone, rejected indeed by men, but chosen by God and precious, you also, as living stones, are being built up a spiritual house, a holy priesthood, to offer up spiritual sacrifices acceptable to God through Jesus Christ."** (1 Peter 2:4, 5 NKJ)

We are God's lively stones, His spiritual house with His divine nature, and His divine power. And God has given to us all things that pertain to life (natural needs) and godliness (spiritual needs). And through God's precious promises we have become partakers of His divine nature. He has called us and He is building us up as His spiritual house. Because God has given us His divine nature He has high expectations of us. We are very special to God; thus, we have a very significant role to play in His divine plan. It is important that we spend quality time in prayer and in the word, so that we can know the promises of God and release this great potential that Jesus invested in us. The indwelling Holy Spirit, our great potential, is for the building of God's kingdom and not for personal gratification and self recognition.

Find a way to begin your day in God's throne room with prayer and quality time in the word. God has saved us, designed us, and equipped us to do great things. The only way that we can be "after His likeness," is by learning His voice, knowing His promises, and following His directions. We can't operate like God if we don't know how He operates. We also need to know what God's promises are. He promised us more than eternal life. He promised us that if we suffer with Him we shall also reign with Him. He promised those of us who love him and withstand temptation, the crown of life. He has promised those of us who love His appearing, a crown of righteousness. He promised to strengthen by His grace, those of us who endure hardship as good soldiers. He promised to resurrect all of us, who die in Christ, from the dead. He promised that He would keep us in perfect peace if we keep our minds focused on Him. There are many other promises that God has made known in His word. Spending time in His word draws us close to God and reveals His power and His promises. Knowing the promises of God and having

His divine nature will birth in us a new attitude and gives us a godly perspective.

God desires intimacy with us. It is during our times of intimacy that God will birth in us a new attitude and we gain new perspectives. A godly point of view enables us to tap into and release our great potential. A godly perspective will transform us from shepherd boys and girls to kings and queens in the kingdom of God. With new attitudes and a godly perspective we can slay the giants in the land and embrace God's vision for our lives. We need to walk with a new attitude and have new godly perspectives because we are new creations approaching a brand new future. **We were chosen for a purpose. We are holy for a cause. We are royalty to rule and we are God's special people and thus we are no longer natural beings. We are supernatural beings.**

God has high expectations for us supernatural beings; therefore, He will allow us to go through some storms, face overwhelming odds, overcome some trials, and slay some giants. Like Joseph, we may also have a pit experience, a bondage experience, and a prison experience as part of our preparation to rule in the palace. The great potential that God has imbedded in us will enable us to handle the trials of life, impact the world for Him, and reach the level of His high expectations for us.

God has a divine goal for you and me. To reach our goal and God's high expectations, we need to maintain a godly perspective so that we can endure hardship as good soldiers for God's kingdom. God has given us the authority and He has anointed us with power to reach His goals and high expectations.

God will also strategically place people in our lives to help us develop our potential, enhance our talents, skills and fulfill our purpose. We dare not take for granted people that God places in our lives. Whether teaching us who to avoid and what not to do, or giving us valuable insights and strategies on how to reach our goals and meet God's high expectations, they all play a positive role in our lives.

You. Many of the most influential people that God will place in your life will be members of your church family. God can and will bless you greatly through your church congregation. You are not saved to be a lone ranger. Jesus called a group of people together, in the original twelve disciples and later in the seventy disciples that He sent out in groups and two by two. It is absolutely imperative that you belong to a Bible believing and Bible teaching church. Your home church becomes your extended family. In some cases they can be the family that you never had. You are accountable to your extended family and they are accountable to you. Your pastor is God's under shepherd who, along with other seasoned saints, will teach you and train you up in the way that you should go. Your home church should be a congregation of awesome individuals coming together for the collective purpose of learning and knowing God, as you work out your salvation. And together you will take the world for Christ. As part of God's team, you will come to discern and recognize your individual anointed spiritual gifts. Carefully and prayerfully seek a church family that models the disciples and the early church. People who come from all walks of life, coming together for the sole purpose of being the family of God, encouraging, edifying one another and taking the gospel into the whole world. Be Spirit led and wisely choose a church where you can be nurtured, prepared and launched into ministry.

Me. Over the years my church families have played a very significant part in my life and ministry. Many years ago, while in the entertainment business, I met two beautiful, caring, and anointed saints named Frank and Bunny Wilson. Frank Wilson was a very successful song writer and record producer. Frank was one of the top producers at Motown Records when I first met him. Frank and Bunny had a very unique ministry that was tailored to meet the needs of high profile entertainers and sports celebrities. I would often go to their home for Bible Study. During one of the Bible studies I met and connected with Chuck Singleton, an anointed teacher of God's word. Chuck was a pastor but he also had a ministry that addressed the special needs of celebrities. At one time, he was the chaplain of professional sports teams in the Los Angeles area.

Frank and Bunny then introduced me to my first home church, Mt. Zion Missionary Baptist Church, in Los Angeles, California. Dr. Edward V. Hill became my pastor in 1977. The late Dr. Hill, an anointed man of God, was also a great preacher model for me and many other preachers who are presently impacting this world for Jesus Christ. Some of the other strong role models and anointed teachers at Mt. Zion, who greatly influenced my life, were Dr. Edward Bass, the assistant pastor and his lovely wife, Sister Gwen Bass. Currently, their son Ogden, my close friend, who is an anointed preacher, director and editor, supports financially and supplies all the electronic recording equipment and cell phone for my ministry. Associate Pastors DeArmon Crayton, a great teacher of the word, along with Teddy Hart, and Nathan Nolen were excellent leaders and role models. Deacons Woodrow Marshall and Cleveland Ashley, chairman of the Deacons, were strong role models and mentors who treated all the new members like sons and daughters. Ronald and Willie O'Guinn, Michael and Carolyn Spotsville and Fred Lawson were close friends and strong supporters. First Lady, Sister Jane Edna Hill, along with Minister Charles Walker, a fellow actor and friend, headed up the high school department of Sunday School, where I was first assigned to teach the word. They nurtured and guided me to become a good teacher and strong role model to many high school students, who have now become outstanding men and women in their communities.

At Mt. Zion, I also met Clay and Tammy Drayton. Clay, a successful song writer and musician, later became a dynamic gospel preacher. Tammy is an anointed praise dancer and singer. Clay was the person that God used to help me understand His call on my life to the ministry of evangelism. Often times we would leave our secular job and drive to distant places where Clay was invited to preach. On a few occasions, during some financial struggles, Clay would stop by my apartment and put a check in my hand, telling me that God had told him to bless me. I also had the privilege to grow in the faith with Dr. Ronn Elmore, a noted author and dynamic speaker, and his anointed wife and singer, Aladrian Elmore. Later I befriended Clifton Davis, who became an anointed evangelist and television host. These, and many other Mt. Zion church members, sowed into my life and became my family away from home. A very talented friend that I met through Frank and Bunny was Mario DuCre. He helped me to publish my first book and print all my ministry materials. All of the previously mentioned people were the spiritual giants that Jesus used to replicate Himself in my life while I lived in California.

When I lived in Herndon, Virginia, Christ Fellowship was my home church. I was greatly blessed with mentors who model Christian examples, and encouraged me on the way. Pastor Enoch and First Lady LaGretta Butler, allowed me to stay in their home when I first arrived in Virginia. Their support made my transition to the east coast, smooth and tranquil. Anointed teachers and role models like Elder Rudy and Mary Wiggins, Elder Joseph and Theresa Jackson, Emma Coles, the late Grandma Kitty, Sylvia Taylor, Pastor Rick and Evelyn Washington, Deacon John and Jean Warren, Deacon Cecil and Mattie Grantham, Elder Alfred and Barbara Jackson, Deacon George and Angie Parrish, Deacon Bryan and Gwendolyn Holoman, Roberta Ford, Pastor Alvin Thomas, Minister John and Pamela Hughes, Pastor Vincent and Sallie Williams, Dr. Chauncey and Sherry Stokes were faithful supporters and good friends. Dr. Stokes is a very successful OB GYN medical doctor and anointed preacher of the gospel. His wife Sherry is a very successful business woman. Their gifted daughter Briana is a creative writer and artist. God also yoked me with Dr. Frank Fisher, an anointed teacher of the word and a very successful businessman, and his gracious wife, Mrs. Sandra Turner Bond Fisher, a successful corporate executive. The Fisher's, Washington, Warren, Hughes, Parrish, Jackson and Stokes families hosted me in their homes over the years as I traveled in ministry. John "Rickey" Hughes would help me drive to meetings in Texas.

While at Christ Fellowship, God blessed my family and I, by placing John and Ginger Finney in our lives. John designed my website and continues to this day to assist me with keeping the ministry website up to date. Anthony and Artrelle Frost, Art and Desiree Monk, Monte and Yvette Coleman, were friends who God used many times as sources of encouragement with their kind words and timely financial blessings. Art, a recent hall of fame inductee, Monte and Charles Mann were strong men of excellence on the NFL gridiron as star players for the Washington Redskins football team. All of them were mighty men of valor on and off the football field. Charles and Tyrena

138

Mann, along with the Monks and Colemans are strong leaders in their families, their communities, and God's church.

Later, Pastor Enoch and First Lady LaGretta, answered God's call to go to Africa to set up ministries and schools to address the needs there. My long time friends, Pastor Walter and First Lady Marva Hamilton, became the first family of Christ Fellowship. Marva taught me what to do, and then handed over the reins of the Food Bank Ministry to me. Pastor Joe and Theresa Jackson started a church in Alpharetta, Georgia. They have always been very strong supporters of my ministry. Theresa taught me, and helped me to disseminate ministry information over the internet. Another long time friend, Pastor Ralph Duke, assisted me in conducting a monthly ministry at the men's correctional facility in Staunton, VA. We would drive over three hours each first Thursday of the month, to go and preach at the prison. God honored Ralph's faithfulness and called him to pastor Beacon Hill Baptist Church many years ago. He and first Lady Pamela Duke are faithful servants to God's kingdom. Today, Pastors Duke, Hamilton and Washington, along with faithful saints from Christ Fellowship and Beacon Hill, still conduct the food bank and prison ministries. Eddie Nichols and Brian Smith helped me with home repairs.

God also used anointed saints outside of my home church to help me to launch my worldwide evangelism ministry. Anointed Evangelist Manuel Scott, Jr., counseled me in how to set up my ministry and sowed the first seed into it. Pastor John and Marie Peyton, hosted me in their home and introduced my ministry to the Northern Virginia and Jacksonville, Florida areas. The late Bishop Lawrence Callahan and First Lady Delores Callahan, hosted me, and introduced my ministry to various churches throughout the state of Florida. My long time friend and board member, Pastor Jimmie Flakes and First Lady Dorothy Flakes, hosted me in their home, and introduced my ministry throughout the state of Texas. Pastor Flakes, Minister L.M. Rivers and Minister/Attorney Ashton Cumberbatch, Jr., helped me to incorporate my nonprofit ministry. Ashton's wife, Jennifer, an anointed minister and artist, has always been a source of inspiration. Mrs. Willie Mae "Ain't Ankie" Kirk, Leon "Dad" and Dorothy "Mom" Anderson opened their homes, and their hearts to support me. I had the privilege to lead their son, Leon, Jr, to Christ. He is my faithful armor bearer whenever I am in Austin. Deacon Donnie and Sister Mary Scott allow me to use their car, when I am in Texas. Pastor Billy Walker, Deacon Bud Rogers, Minister Arthur and Myrtle Shaw and the saints of The New Testament Church are strong supporters, along with Sisters Deborah Batts and Patricia Cannon. Attorney Clay and Sharon Barton, anointed teachers of God's word and good friends, have faithfully supported me with their prayers, wise counsel, and finances. James Walker, a computer genius and successful business man, gave me wise counsel on investing and sowed a large seed to bless my family and me. He also set up my website, purchased my domain name and donated a computer and printer to LCEM. His wife Rhonda is a health/fitness expert.

In the mid-nineties when I did a study on Biblical Ethnicity, Minnie Taylor, a dear friend in the publishing business, discovered and sent me a copy of "The Doorway Papers," by noted Christian Anthropologist Dr. Arthur C. Custance. His papers were a source of great blessings. The inspirational informative teaching of Dr. Clarence Walker, a friend and biblical scholar, was also a tremendous tool in helping me to learn of our Biblical heritage. Dr. Ja'Ola Walker, his wife, is also an anointed writer and teacher of the word.

Pastor Harry Griffin, for many years, helped me drive from Texas to California to preach. He and his wife Gail host me in their home in Stockton. God announced a great life changing blessing in my life through my surrogate daughter, Shani, who I met at the Open Door House of Prayer. Pastor Amelia Adams, her mother, Pastor Griffin, and the saints of Open Door are faithful friends and supporters. Shani gave KJoy a prophetic word, during a Thanksgiving visit in 1994. We learned from her that God was going to bless us with a child. I rejoiced weeks later, when my wife told me that we were expecting our first child. Elder Troy Moss greatly blesses my ministry with his CD duplications, wise counsel and financial support. Pastor Ronnie Walton introduced my ministry to Northern California. He and his wife, Dorothy, along with Deacon Leon and LaVern Horne, have hosted me in their homes over the years. LaVern, before retiring from state government, was responsible for getting California State Resolutions, recognizing the work of LCEM.

God has greatly blessed me, and encouraged me through the faithful support of many kind saints in various locations. Always be thankful for the people that God places in your life. He connects us to a variety of anointed people to bless us and mold us into the vessels He has designed us to be.

Today, Chuck Singleton is my pastor and friend. Loveland Church is my new church family. Along with Pastor Chuck, God has placed a new group of anointed saints in my life; Pastors Willie Lewis, Terry Starks, Billy Bauer, Emile Allen, Raymond Turner, Rob Banks and Julius West. Pastor Lewis is an excellent teacher of the word. Pastor Draymond Crawford and Mrs. Estelle Crawford (Papa "C" & Mama "C") hosted me in their home and are faithful god-parents to my son Michael. Anointed minister Mom Marie Brewington gives helpful advice. My friend, Gordon Hannon, a teacher and writer helps me to edit my manuscripts. Paul McZeal, an estate planner, assisted my family and me in setting up our Living Trust. He also gives me beautiful wrist watches. His wife, Anita, is an inspiring teacher of the word. Mom Rose and Brother Henry Long are faithful prayer warriors. Deacons Saul Miller, Myron Hester and Carl House are strong men of valor and financial supporters. Deacon Harold Patton is my friend and tax consultant. Deacon William Curry, a faithful friend and liberal giver, and his wife Marsha, supports my family and me in many ways. Also, Brother Hooks, Deacon Joe Hines and the faithful workers of Jubilee Pantry. The late Cassandra "Chosen One" Jackson assisted me in booking my travel. Awesome Minnie Anderson assists me in my ministry table and CD duplication.

Years ago, before Pastor Chuck became my under shepherd, he often encouraged me, and gave me wise counsel. Pastor Chuck saw the hand of God on me and the gifts of God operating in my life. During a time of emotional frustration and pain, I was fasting and praying, and God directed me to contact Chuck. He helped me to launch my evangelism ministry when he recommend me to two pastors, his dad, Dr. Isaac Singleton, who invited me to preach at his church, in Joliet, Illinois; and Dr. I.V. Hilliard of Houston, Texas.

Over the years I have maintained the relationships with Frank, Bunny, Dr. Isaac and Mom Pearl Singleton, an anointed woman of God. Frank recently earned his doctorate and now pastors a thriving church called New Dawn Christian Village in Los Angeles. Dr. Frank, along with Bunny, a successful writer and prolific speaker, continue to nurture, teach and encourage many young saints, some in the entertainment industry, who are members of the New Dawn congregation.

Pastor Chuck and First Lady Charlyn Singleton, an anointed preacher of the gospel, continue to sow into my life and the lives of many others throughout the world. Pastors Frank Stallworth, James Crawford, Lynol Phillips, Clarence Fomby, Vernard Williams, Arlene McCall, Dianne Jamerson, Ruby Benjamin, Marlon Jackson, Hugh Hairston, Paul Gilkes, Eddie Williams, Gordon Laine, Mom Beckey Davis, Gretta Parks, Esther and Gus Alexander, Mary Ann Williams, Vangie Lewis, Nita Hill, the Pattersons, Holmes, Daniels, Tampkins and Moore families are anointed encouragers, along with anointed Reyna Banks, Linda Davis and the VIP dancers. Robb Cook, Valerie Singleton, Bobby Bryant and the Loveland choir, praise team and male chorus. My Loveland family is an anointed blessing to my family and me. Your church family is absolutely necessary for your growth and support. Together, you can walk in anointed power and revolutionize the world.

Jesus is the supreme model. He not only modeled what the disciples should and could be, He also modeled their power and potential. He, along with the disciples, serviced the needs of others with great compassion. He did not act alone. After ministering to the needs of the people, He would spend personal time teaching His disciples that they could and should do what He was doing. **"I am the vine, you are the branches. He who abides in Me, and I in him, bears much fruit; for without Me you can do nothing. If you abide in Me, and My words abide in you, you will ask what you desire, and it shall be done for you. By this My Father is glorified, that you bear much fruit: so you will be My disciples."** (John 15:5;7 NKJ)

Today, Jesus is still the true vine and you and I are the branches. If we abide in Him and His words abide in us, we can ask what we desire and it shall be done for us. The Father is glorified when we release this great potential within us to bear much fruit for His kingdom. As branches of the true vine we are pieces and parts of

Jesus, who is the Master. **We are Masterpieces in the making! Therefore we need to partner with our God in the ministry that He has anointed and appointed us to do.**

You. Whatever level of ministry that God is calling you to, His desire is to partner with you. He wants to walk in your body, love with your heart, see with your eyes, hear with your ears, touch with your hands and talk with your mouth. He is the source of great power residing within you. Jesus Christ is the same yesterday, today and forever. So what He did and how He worked through faithful men and women in Biblical days, He desires to do the same through you today. God always provides the resources. His resources consist of His power, His provisions and His directions. You, along with God, will have unlimited success as you walk in faith, follow His directions and obey His word. Get involved and have a living relationship with God. Don't stop at church affiliation and be satisfied with occupying pew space on Sunday and midweek. Walk with God and go wherever He sends you! Do whatever He tells you! Stir up the passion and release the great potential within you! **Have faith in God! He has great expectations for you and He is the source of the great potential that now resides in you! Focus on the Christ in you, who is the hope of Glory!**

There is a heavenly calling on your life! Therefore, seek to fulfill the call of God on your life. Allow these words of Apostle Paul to enlighten, encourage, and speak for you. **"Brethren, I count not myself to have apprehended; but this one thing I do, forgetting those things which are behind, and reaching forth unto those things which are before, I press toward the mark for the prize of the high calling of God in Christ Jesus."** (Philippians 3:13, 14 KJ) Stand firm in your faith, stir up the fire and passion of God's Spirit within you and press toward the mark for the prize of the high calling of God in Christ Jesus. Do not allow yourself or others to shackle you with your past. Use the things of your past that can help build your ministry; however, do not linger on the mistakes or rehearse the shame of your past. The past is behind you. The passion and the potential are within you. Stir them up and fan the flames through prayer and the study of God's word. Let the mind of Christ be in you! Seek His face daily in the word. Study God's word to show yourself a workman, approved unto God. Pray unceasingly. Develop intimacy with Almighty God through a consistent prayer life. He resides in you to be intimate with you. **By virtue of God's presence dwelling inside of you, you have great potential and God has high expectations of you! He desires to partner with you in A Limited Partnership for Unlimited Success!**

CHAPTER TEN

A LIMITED PARTNERSHIP FOR UNLIMITED SUCCESS!

Throughout the preceding chapters we have looked at characters from God's magnificent drama chronicled in the Holy Scriptures, and personal life experiences, and testimonies from others, including myself. An emerging emphatic truth has been revealed in God's relationship with His creation. Beloved, **Awesome You** and **Awesome Me** are in A Limited Partnership for Unlimited Success with **AWESOME ALMIGHTY GOD!** We actually see the blueprint for this partnership in God's creative process in the book of Genesis. Let's walk together down the corridors of God's Holy Writ, and get some insight into A Limited Partnership for Unlimited Success.

In the midst of the magnanimous litanies of "Let there be...," God the Father, God the Son, and God the Holy Spirit did something very unique. The Triune Godhead said **"Let Us make man in Our image and after Our likeness; let them have dominion over the fish of the sea, over the birds of the air, and over the cattle, over all the earth and over every creeping thing that creeps on the earth."** (Genesis 1:26 NKJ) God made mankind, male and female, in His image and after His likeness. Then God blessed them and said to them: **"Be fruitful and multiply; fill the earth and subdue it; have dominion over the fish of the sea, over the birds of the air, and over every living thing that moves on the earth."**

(Genesis 1:28 NKJ) God goes on to describe His creative process of making man. **"And the LORD GOD formed man of the dust of the ground, and breathed into his nostrils the breath of life; and man became a living being."** (Genesis 2:7 NKJ)

God planted a garden eastward in Eden. In the midst of the garden there was the tree of life, and the tree of the knowledge of good and evil. Later God put man in the Garden of Eden to tend (dress) it, and keep it. God brought every animal that He had made to Adam and Adam gave them names. Recognizing that it was not good for man to be alone, God decided to make Adam a helper comparable to him. God caused Adam to fall into a deep sleep; and He took a rib from Adam, and made a woman. When God presented the woman to Adam he said: **"This is now bone of my bones and flesh of my flesh; She shall be called Woman, because she was taken out of Man."** (Genesis 2:23 NKJ)

Careful Biblical examination of the creative process clearly reveals three primary reasons why **Awesome God** created mankind. The **Awesome Triune God** has a threefold purpose for our earthly existence. The first purpose is for **<u>Fellowship</u>**. God spoke and made all other living creatures; but only man was made in God's image and after His likeness. God formed the animals from the dirt as well as man; but God only breathed His breath into man. Why did God breathe His pneuma (Spirit) into man? So that mankind could fellowship with Him. Mankind is the crowning glory of God's creation. We alone are made in His image, and after His likeness. God made mankind to communicate and fellowship with Him. Being made in the likeness of God enables us to think and operate like God. Throughout the history of humanity on this earth, we all have had the blessed privilege to fellowship, and have intimate communication with God our Creator. God wants to be intimate with every living being. He wants to reveal Himself and shower us with His unceasing love, joy, peace, and power. He desires intimacy with us so that He can birth new blessings in our lives. Remember, out of intimacy comes new births, new beginnings, new ministries, new strategies, and new triumphs. An active prayer life where we talk to, and listen to God is fellowship, and intimate communication. Reading, studying, memorizing, and walking in the word of God causes us to be in fellowship and intimate communication with God. Private praise and worship, as well as collective worship in our church assemblies, is also fellowship with God. **Saints of God we must sincerely engage in intimate communication and fellowship with our Creator. The Lord Jesus Christ came, and died for each of us that we might be restored to a position whereby we can have intimate fellowship with the Father, through the indwelling presence of the Holy Spirit. Without God's presence within us we could not communicate or fellowship with Him.**

Adam had intimate communication and fellowship with God. God repeatedly told Adam that He had given him everything that He made on the earth. God created humanity to be His family on earth. Today, many choose to live as creatures of God rather than as children of God. Without confessing and receiving Jesus Christ as Savior, human beings are void of the indwelling presence of the Holy Spirit. Without the indwelling presence of the Holy Spirit, human beings cannot fellowship with God, and enjoy family relationship. Our lives are hid in Jesus, guaranteeing us the right of family relationship, and the privilege to communicate, and have fellowship with the Father through the Holy Spirit.

Throughout the creative process in the book of Genesis, God repeatedly introduces us to the second primary reason why we were created. We were created for **Leadership.** God told us to take dominion and subdue the earth after He created us. When God tells us to take dominion and subdue the earth, to be fruitful, multiply, and fill the earth, He is giving human kind supreme authority to lead and supervise all His creation. God created us for leadership. God is the ultimate leader, and He made us in His image, and after His likeness. God told Adam about the tree of life, and the tree of the knowledge of good and evil. He commanded Adam not to eat of the fruit of the tree of the knowledge of good and evil. Please note and learn from Adam, leadership is always internal before it can effectively be external. His wife, Eve, had a conversation with the serpent as Adam stood by. God had brought all the animals to Adam for him to name. Adam knew the purpose, the function, and the makeup of every animal. When the serpent spoke contrary to what God had said he should have exercised leadership by rebuking and destroying the serpent. The Bible says that Adam was with Eve when she had the conversation with Satan in the garden. Adam was in charge. God had given him the authority and the responsibility to take care of the garden and protect it. Adam's failure to exercise leadership and protect the garden caused the downfall of all humanity.

When we fail to give leadership in our homes, our churches, our communities, and our government, we also allow Satan, the prince of darkness to wreck havoc, and disaster over that which God told us to take dominion over.

Adam was in fellowship with God and knew that God had put him in charge. God had spoken clearly to Adam about the tree of life, and the tree of the knowledge of good and evil. Adam was God's leader over the garden; and yet he failed miserably in his leadership role when he did not step up, take authority and correct Eve when she spoke incorrectly about what God had said. God told Adam they could not eat the fruit. He never said they could not touch it. Obviously Adam had not effectively communicated God's command. Effective communication is essential for good leadership. Eve had no business talking to a foreigner in their homeland. But Adam allowed her to usurp his authority, and carry on a conversation with the serpent. When Eve touched the fruit, and nothing happened, she was encouraged to go a step further and eat it. Take note, Adam followed his wife rather than God. When he ate, both of their eyes were opened, and they died spiritually. They led humanity into a sinful state causing separation from the God of their creation and ushered spiritual and physical death into the earthly existence of humankind.

Brothers, when we don't step up and exercise leadership in our homes with our families, the consequences are severe and lasting. If we abdicate our leadership roles we put undue pressure on our wives, and children, causing the family to plunge into an unnatural state of chaos and confusion. Often times our children pay the severe price for the lack of male leadership in the home. When a mother and father choose to not stay together, why abandon your children, causing them to be scarred and emotionally damaged? **BROTHERS! IF WE STAY OUR CHILDREN WON'T STRAY!** We must maintain a godly perspective and be a **Faithful Attentive**

Teacher Helper, Encouraging our children as Resourceful responsible role models. Be a father because the lack of male leadership causes too many children to suffer severe consequences. Breath and britches can make a baby, but it takes a father to stay for the long haul. It takes a man with a godly perspective to provide love, caring, and leadership for his children and family. **STEP UP MEN! IT IS TIME FOR US TO LEAD WITH A GODLY PERSPECTIVE!**

The third primary reason that God created humanity is for **Partnership**. God wants to partner with every created being in A Limited Partnership for Unlimited Success. We get insight from the following verses of Scriptures: **"And God said, See, I have given you every herb that yields seed which is on the face of all the earth, and every tree whose fruit yields seed; to you it shall be for food. Also, to every beast of the earth, to every bird of the air, and to everything that creeps on the earth, in which there is life, I have given every green herb for food'; and it was so."** (Genesis 1:29, 30 NKJ) **"This is the history of the heavens and the earth when they were created, in the day that the LORD God made the earth and the heavens, before any plant of the field was in the earth and before any herb of the field had grown. For the LORD God had not caused it to rain on the earth, and there was no man to till the ground; but a mist went up from the earth and watered the whole face of the ground. And the LORD God formed man of the dust of the ground, and breathed into his nostrils the breath of life; and man became a living being."** (Genesis 2:4-7 NKJ) **"Then the LORD God took the man and put him in the Garden of Eden to tend and keep it."** (Genesis 2:15 NKJ) The preceding scriptures clearly reveal a Limit Partnership between God and His created beings.

A Limited Partnership has a General Partner, and a Limited Partner. The partnership is only limited in the designation of the roles of responsibility. Because our God is Awesome, any partnership with Him is guaranteed to have unlimited success. God, the Limited Partner, supplies all the resources, the power, and the guidance. As the General Partners we have to do all the work. God gave us a world. He continues to supply us with power and guidance. Our partnership will always flourish with great abundance if we will faithfully do the work that is required to produce unlimited success. In God's historical description of the creation of the heavens, and the earth, the Bible says that the LORD God had not caused it to rain on the earth, and there was no man to till the ground. God did not send rain upon the earth before creating man, because He knew that rain would cause everything to grow in great abundance. So, God caused a mist to water the ground, enough moisture to keep everything alive. Once man was created, and started working the ground, God sent the rain, and caused everything to grow in great abundance.

As awesome saints of God, we should never be satisfied with just the mist of life. God did not design us to just get by. He did not design us to eke out a living, struggling to survive from payday to payday. If our names are written in the Lamb's Book of Life, we are God's children. Our Father owns the cattle on a thousand hills, all the silver and gold is His; therefore, we should not be satisfied with settling for the crumbs of life, and living beneath our kingdom status. We are kings, queens and priests unto our God by virtue of the fact that we have been washed in the blood of Jesus.

"To Him who loved us and washed us from our sins in His own blood, and has made us kings and priests to His God and Father, to Him be glory and dominion forever and ever, Amen." (Revelation 1:6 NKJ) The word king is generic, it also includes queens.

ME. I thank God for my father, Maurice, who spent quality time teaching me business principles when I was a child growing up in Austin, Texas. Although he was not a formerly educated man, my Dad was a giant in the business world. He instilled in me a strong work ethic, and taught me that hard work was honorable, and it pays off. As a child I had different odd jobs. During a rite of passage, my Dad took me shopping, and bought me a nice suit, dress slacks, shirts, shoes, and all the accessories. Because my Dad dressed nicely, I always wanted to wear nice clothes. I did not like the customary blue jeans that most of my peers wore, but I was not allowed to wear my dress clothes except for special occasions, and going to church. One day, at approximately twelve years of age, I proposed an arrangement to my father. I ask Daddy if I could wear dress clothes, and khaki pants when I wanted to, if I worked to earn the money to buy them? With a broad smile on his face, he patted me on my head and said: "Midgit, if you pay for them you can wear them whenever you want."

Later in life I had the privilege, after achieving a measure of success and fame in the entertainment industry, to enter into a Limited Partnership with Mr. William "Smokey" Robinson. Smokey provided the resources for making the movie, "Big Time." He gave us the money to finance the movie. As executive producer Smokey, chose to create the music and also made other important decisions that guided the project. Leon Kennedy and I, along with a few others, had to do all the work. There were problems along the way and we made mistakes that did not allow the movie to achieve the success that we all had hoped it would. We could have greatly benefitted from having a strong source of wisdom and guidance from our Heavenly Father during the various stages of making the movie. We had limited resources, and we worked diligently, but we did not always have the proper guidance to achieve unlimited success with the film.

Looking back, I know that God had a greater plan for each of our lives. Through our film partnership we all came to the saving grace knowledge of Jesus Christ. Today, Smokey, Leon and I are still friends and we all have anointed ministries, faithfully serving God's kingdom in A Limited Partnership for Unlimited Success.

The beauty of being in A Limited Partnership with Almighty God is God not only provides adequate resources, and the power, He also guides us throughout the work process. When we fellowship with Him, He will give us insights and directions to keep us on track to reach our goals. Our God sits high and looks low. Nothing is hid from Him. He knows the end before there is a beginning. Our Awesome God is the only one who announces His victories before the battles begin. Power and resources without guidance will not guarantee unlimited success. That's why we should walk in A Limited Partnership For Unlimited Success with Almighty God.

YOU. God created you to fellowship with Him, and take dominion by giving leadership in the day to day affairs of your life on earth. There are no limits to your success levels when you partner with God in a Limited Partnership. God is always faithful to provide the resources, the power, and the guidance. Unlimited success is inevitable when you diligently do the work.

"Commit your works to the Lord, and your thoughts will be established." (Proverbs 16:3 NKJ)

The above Proverb strongly suggests a partnership with God. Once our works are committed to the Lord our thoughts, and our dreams will be established. We do the work and trust God to establish our success through His favor, power, resources, and guidance.

We get further insight and understanding of A Limited Partnership For Unlimited Success with Awesome God as we briefly examine the lives of Moses and Joshua. God had miraculous orchestrated the events of Moses life to bring him to a divine encounter in the desert at Horeb, the mountain of God. Moses saw a burning bush that continued to burn. When Moses turned aside to see why the bush was not consumed by the fire, God spoke to him from the midst of the burning bush. Take note, God did not speak until Moses gave God his undivided attention. Listen carefully as God proposes A Limited Partnership For Unlimited Success. **"I have surely seen the oppression of My people who are in Egypt, and have heard their cry because of their taskmasters, for I know their sorrows. So I have come down to deliver them out of the hand of the Egyptians, and to bring them up from that land to a good and large land, to a land flowing with milk and honey, to the place of the Canaanites and the Hittites and the Amorites and the Perizzites and the Hivites and the Jebusites. Come now, therefore, and I will send you to Pharaoh that you may bring My people, the children of Israel, out of Egypt."** (Exodus 3:7, 8; 10 NKJ)

God tells Moses that He has seen Israel's oppression, He has heard their cry, and He knows their sorrow. God also tells Moses that He has come down to deliver Israel out of Egyptian bondage. Then He proposes a Limited Partnership. God tells Moses that He will send him to Pharaoh to bring the children of Israel out of Egypt. When God tells Moses, I have come down to deliver My people, He is saying I will be the Limited Partner. I will supply the power, the resources and the guidance. You go and bring Israel out of Egypt.

Moses, you are the General Partner, you will do the work of speaking to Pharaoh, leading the people out of Egypt and marching to the good and large land that I am providing.

Often times we make the same mistake that Moses made. We don't understand the roles in a Limited Partnership; and thus, we offer God lame excuses. When Moses offered up a multitude of excuses, God told him that He would certainly be with him. God was defining their roles in the partnership. When God said I will certainly be with you, He was telling Moses that He did not need his ability, He needed Moses' availability. God would supply the power, the resources and He would guide them to the good land flowing with milk and honey. He just needed Moses to do the work of speaking to the Pharaoh and walking the people out of Egypt to the Promised Land. It was God's power that caused the plagues, parted the Red Sea, destroyed Pharaoh's army, and protected the children of Israel. He also guided Moses and Israel by a pillar of cloud by day, and a pillar of fire by night.

When we are in A Limited Partnership for Unlimited Success with Awesome God, He brings us out of our problems so that He can bring us into His promises. Egypt was a problem for Israel. God brought them out of Egypt. He promised them a good land flowing with milk and honey. Their journey was delayed, and many who started the journey never reached the promise land because of their disobedience, but ultimately God brought the children of Israel into Canaan, the land of promise.

After Moses died, God called Joshua into A Limited Partnership for Unlimited Success. **"Moses My servant is dead. Now therefore, arise, go over this Jordan, you and all this people, to the land which I am giving to them-the children of Israel. No man shall be able to stand before you all the days of your life; as I was with Moses, so I will be with you. I will not leave you nor forsake you. Be strong and of good courage, for to this people you shall divide as an inheritance the land which I swore to their fathers to give them."** (Joshua 1:2; 5, 6 NKJ)

Joshua and Caleb, two of the spies who came back with a favorable report, wanted to obey God and go in and take possession of the land flowing with milk and honey. Joshua and Caleb were in the minority. The other ten spies, and the entire camp of Israel, cowered in fear rather than to face the giants in the land. God calls Joshua to be the General Partner and take the children of Israel to the land that God was giving them. On the way they also encountered enemies and obstacles, but God was faithful to supply the power, the resources, and the guidance to bring them into the good land flowing with milk and honey. When Joshua and the children of Israel came up against Jericho, a city secured behind a wall, God spoke to him, and reaffirmed their partnership. **"See! I have given Jericho into your hand, its king, and the mighty men of valor. You shall march around the city, all you men of war; you shall go all around the city once. This you shall do six days. And seven priests shall bear seven trumpets of rams' horns before the ark. But the seventh day you shall march around the city seven times, and the priests shall blow the trumpets. It shall come to pass, when they make a long blast with the ram's horn, and when you hear the sound of the trumpet, that all the people shall shout with a great shout; then the wall of the city will fall down flat. And the people shall go up every man straight before him."** (Joshua 6:2-5 NKJ)

Joshua, the priests, the men of war, and the children of Israel walked around the wall, blew rams horns, and shouted! It was God's power that brought down the wall of Jericho. And then Joshua and the people had to go in and take possession of the city.

Throughout the Bible, and world history, including current day events, we see God interacting with His creation in A Limited Partnership for Unlimited Success! God always supplies the power, the resources, and the guidance. Mankind has to do all the work. Today, throughout the world, we see a very decadent and immoral society. Like never before we need the guidance of God. You and I can rise above the depraved conditions that sorely afflict mankind, if we will be intimate with God and devoted to Him. He will guide us, and birth new blessings in our lives in the midst of a decaying world in severe drought. He will make us like a watered garden whose waters fail not. **"The Lord will guide you continually, And satisfy your soul in drought, and strengthen your bones; You shall be like a watered garden, And like a spring of water, whose waters do not fail."** (Isaiah 58:11 NKJ)

God has called you and I to lead. We are chosen by God to give godly leadership to an ungodly world. It is time that we take dominion over this world. And our success is guaranteed if we partner with God in A Limited Partnership for Unlimited Success. Our God sits high and He looks low. He stands outside of time to control all things in time.

He chooses to bless all creation through His chosen and anointed vessels. **We are fearfully and wonderfully made in God's image and after His likeness.** Let us take full advantage of our privilege to fellowship with God by spending quality time in His throne room in prayer, praise, and worship. We are created to step up and step out in leadership. As we faithfully consecrate ourselves unto God and walk in His anointing, we shall lead this wayward society by engaging in kingdom works that glorify our Lord. **The beauty of our Lord is upon us and He shall establish the work of our hands.**

Beloved, **AWESOME GOD** is calling **Awesome You,** and **Awesome Me,** into A Limited Partnership for Unlimited Success. If we will faithfully partner with God, and follow His lead, God will always bring us out of our problems to take us into His promises. Jesus died for each of us that we might have the right to enter into A Limited Partnership for Unlimited Success with the Triune Godhead. There are no limits to our success when God supplies the power, the resources, and leads us on the journey. God desires that we have Max Life with no limits and no bounds. If we will faithfully do the work, God will continue to take us from glory to glory.

Sanctified in the Spirit and the Word of God!

Triumphant in Partnership with God!

Enlarged by the Power, Resources and Guidance of God!

Passion for the Work of God!

CHAPTER ELEVEN

THE PHYSICAL YOU:

FEARFULLY AND WONDERFULLY MADE!

During a time of praise and adoration of Almighty God, his Creator, King David said: **"<u>I will</u> praise thee; <u>for</u> I am fearfully and wonderfully made: marvelous are thy works; and that my soul knoweth right well."** (Psalms 139:14 KJ)

The human body is fearfully and wonderfully made. It consists of various chemicals such as iron, sugar, salt, carbon, iodine, phosphorus, lime, calcium and other ingredients. The body also has some 263 bones, 600 muscles, 970 miles of blood vessels, 10,000,000 nerves and branches, 3,500 sweat tubes to each square inch of skin, 600,000,000 air cells to the lungs that inhale 2,400 gallons of air daily, and a communication (telephone) system that relates to the brain instantly any known sound, taste, touch, smell or sight. The hearbeats 4,200 times an hour and pumps 12 tons of blood daily. Without doubt the physical you is much more intricate than the outer body form and composition that you see.

Originally, before sin entered the human scenario, the physical body was designed to live forever. The sin of mankind ushered humanity into instant spiritual death, separation from God; and ultimately physical death. Physical death is a daily ongoing process.

"**For which cause we faint not; but though our <u>outward man</u> perish, yet the <u>inward man</u> is renewed day by day.**" (2 Corinthians 4:16) The outward man, the physical you is dying daily, but the inward man, the spiritual you is renewed daily. Does this mean that you should just ignore the physical you and make no effort to take care of your body? ABSOLUTELY NOT! The word of God gives us some instructions about the body. "**What? <u>know ye not</u> that your body is the temple of the Holy Ghost which is in you, which ye have of God, and ye are not your own? For ye are <u>bought with a price</u>: therefore glorify God in your <u>body</u>, and in your <u>spirit</u>, which are God's.**" (1 Corinthians 6:19, 20)

You. You can glorify God in the physical you. As God's temple you should live obedient to God's word. This may require you to alter your lifestyle and make radical changes in some very familiar habits. It is disobedient to have sex with someone outside of marriage. Having sex with a friend is an acceptable practice in the world but it is unacceptable to God. Sexual sin is sin against your own body. "**Flee fornication. Every sin that a man doeth is without the body; but he that committeth fornication sinneth against his own body.** (1 Corinthians 6:18). Having sex outside of marriage is fornication. This sin is against your entire constitution, body, soul and spirit. It will destroy you. Many people inside and outside the church who practice this sin suffer ailments of cancer, sexually transmitted diseases and other serious maladies.

Many men and women make the same mistake that I did, becoming entangled in casual sexual encounters, thinking that it is an escape from loneliness. Brothers, God our creator truly understands us. For He said, after making man from the dust, "**it is not good that man should be alone; I will make him a helper comparable to him.**" Immediately after God made woman from Adam's rib, He brought her unto him and they became man and wife. "**Therefore a man shall leave his father and mother and be joined to his wife and they shall become one flesh.**"(Genesis 2:18; 24 NKJ) I understand your loneliness brothers, but casual sex outside of holy matrimony has a scent of intimacy, but it is void of that deep binding love that enjoins two people together. It is void, because it does not have God's presence or His covering. Relationships with a scent of intimacy, lacking God's presence and binding, will never eradicate loneliness, emptiness, and pain. However, casual sex relationships will destroy the soul and the body.

If you seriously look at your body as God's temple, there will be other things you deem are not appropriate. Keep God's temple clean on the inside and the outside. Drinking alcoholic beverages and smoking cigarettes will not keep you from going to heaven. However, alcohol alters your state of mind, causing you to make unwise decisions and have some serious problems. Smoking cigarettes is a slow form of suicide. The poisons in nicotine are the same found in insect spray. No one in their right mind would deliberately take insect spray and spray it down their throat five or six times a day. And yet, smokers who light up five or six times a day are doing exactly that. Alcohol and nicotine alters the bodie's chemistry and destroys vital tissues. How can destroying what God fearfully and wonderfully made glorify Him? It cannot.

Some of the practical ways that you can glorify God in your body is to purposefully feed it with the proper foods, nutriments, and vitamins. You can also keep your body tuned and trained with a disciplined exercise regimen. A properly fed and well tuned human body can do marvelous things and live healthy and productively for many years. Having a body that glorifies God is also having a body that serves you well; and it allows you to be available to God for His service.

I have discovered that what you eat makes your beat. Life is lived by different beats. Some people live life with a brisk, vigorous, and energetic beat of wellness. Others live life with a lethargic, painful beat of physical and emotional challenges. What we eat, how we exercise and care for our bodies determines our beat. Every human body has language beats. Listen to your beats. Proper diet and exercise are essential to living a Max Life.

Me. In my late twenties I found myself in a hospital under going surgery for a form of hemorrhoids. I had just recently co-starred in an original Hollywood play, called "The Bathtub Bandicoot." A friend and fellow co-star, who was a vegetarian, visited me in the hospital. In a very adamant, but loving way, she told me that I had to change my diet immediately and start taking care of my body. She told me how I needed to change my diet to include more fiber, nuts, grains, fruits, vegetables, and stop eating pork, red meat, and fast foods. I had for many years eaten a hearty breakfast consisting of pancakes, French toast, egg and cheese omelets, Canadian bacon, and ham, etc. And yet I was always sluggish during the early part of my day, even when I went to the gym. She was incensed at hearing about my breakfast regimen. Her impassioned threat to take a bat to my head was not taken lightly by me. She also talked to me about knowing my body and listening to my body language. Over the next few days I made some mental decisions to change my lifestyle.

Today, I understand my body language. I know that a heavy breakfast of fatty, starchy foods slows me down and it is counter productive to my being energized and alert. To combat inherited high cholesterol, promote cardiovascular health, and maintain good spiritual and physical stamina, I have developed a daily health regimen. Because I desire wellness in my spirit, soul and body, my wellness program addresses my whole man. My daily routine includes prayer time with my family between 6AM and 7 AM, before they leave home for their school and work activities. Monday through Friday, my personal prayer time in God's throne room is between 8AM-10AM. I also read and meditate on three to five chapters in the Bible. Today, my breakfast consist of oatmeal, whole grain cereal or low fat yogurt with seasonal fruits, cashews and half a bagel, with juice. My normal gym exercise routine is approximately thirty minutes on Monday, Tuesday, Thursday and Friday. My workout includes cardiovascular exercises, running on the treadmill, climbing the stair steps, and riding the bicycle. My workout also includes stomach crunches, chest expansion, back extension, and pectoral exercises. I usually fast on Wednesdays, spending extra time with the Lord in prayer and the Word. I have also learned that my body does not require three meals a day. And I always try to eat my dinner meal before 6 PM. If I snack after dinner it is usually fruit, Trek Mix (almonds, cashews & dried cranberries) or Smart Pop (94% Fat Free) popcorn and juice. I drink water throughout my day and night. I strongly believe in the preventive approach to wellness instead of the reactive; therefore, I take dietary supplements including, GNC Mega Men 50 plus Dietary Supplement, which includes Omega-3 fatty acid. I also take 81mg Aspirin and Papaya Complete to help in my digestion and to release the vital nutrients from the foods I eat. Additionally, to help keep my inherited high cholesterol in check and prevent health related problems I take GNC Cholesterol Formula, Garlique caplets, Vitamin C, Red Yeast rice(1200mg), Omega 3 Fish Oil(1200mg) and Cholest Off. I feel great, my energy and endurance level is high and I very seldom get sick.

I am also blessed to have some spirit filled Christian friends who worked as special and primary fitness trainers. Rhonda Walker and Susan Lewis, have done research and training in the various ways to promote health and wellness in the Physical You. They are both strong motivators in helping people to have fit bodies and live healthy lives, with an emphasis on eating nutritious foods, taking vitamins and supplements, along with a consistent regimen of physical exercise. Vitamins and supplements help us to build and strengthen our immune system while promoting healthy body functions. Rhonda and Susan, through intense study and research, have broken down health, fitness and wellness into three major categories of nutritious foods, vitamins and supplements, and exercise regimen. I was inspired by them to do additional research.

NUTRITIOUS FOODS

Just as many of the foods have different colors, they also have different chemistry product and benefits to our body. A healthy nutritious diet is one that includes all the colors. ORANGE COLORED FOODS, such as carrots, sweet potatoes, mangos, apricots, cantaloupe and peaches are an excellent source of Beta-Carotene. A strong antioxidant can boosts our immunity, reduce the risk of heart attacks and helps to maintain good vision. Also in the orange colored family, oranges, tangerines, nectarines, grapefruit, papaya and lemons. These Bioflavonoids are powerful antioxidants that work with vitamin C. They help reduce the risk of a heart attack. They also help to maintain strong bones and teeth, good vision and healthy skin. RED COLORED FOODS, such as watermelon, pink grapefruit, tomato, tomato based products and guava, are a great source of Lycopene, which reduces the risk of prostate cancer, heart attacks, breast and skin cancer. Also in the red colored family of Anthocyanins are cherries, strawberries, red raspberries, cranberries, beets, red cabbage, red onion, kidney beans and red beans; which are strong antioxidants that reduce the risk of heart attack and Alzheimer's disease. They also help to control high blood pressure. BLUE & PURPLE COLORED FOODS, such as purple grapes, black currants, blueberries, blackberries are also Anthocyanins, which are powerful antioxidants to help control high blood pressure, reduce the risk of age-related memory loss, the risk of heart attack and Alzheimer disease. In the blue & purple colored foods are Phenolics foods such as prunes, plums, eggplant and raisins, with powerful antioxidants to help slow down the effects of aging. WHITE COLORED FOODS like garlic, scallions, leeks, onion and chives have an excellent source of Allicin, which helps to lower high cholesterol, boost immunity, helps control high blood pressure and reduces the risk of heart attacks. GREEN COLORED FOODS such as spinach, kale, mustard, kiwi, green peas, broccoli and honeydew melon are Luteins that help to reduce the risk of cataracts and macular degeneration, and maintain good vision. Also in the green colored foods are Indoles, found in broccoli, brussel sprouts, cauliflower, kale and cabbage. They are a powerful antioxidant that helps to reduce the risk of cancer and tumor growth in cancer patients.

Rhonda Walker has some excellent insight and advice on changing our eating habits to help maintain a healthy fit body that glorifies God. She wants us to personally consider some reasonable questions before eating. Do my eating habits reflect the Kingdom? Does my plate honor my body and God? Am I honoring my family by eating and/or serving these meals?

Rhonda strongly suggest that for breakfast, we would do well to replace sugar cereals with whole grain cereals like Kashi, Organic Raisin Bran and other high fiber cereals. Fiber helps to cleanse our digestive systems, saving us money spent on laxatives. We can also add organic yogurt to wheat bran or our choice of fruit. Replace white flour breads with whole wheat or sprouted whole grain bread which has no flour. Sprouted whole grain toast with butter or nut butter is another quick nutritious breakfast. Fiber also helps to sweep cholesterol out of our intestinal walls. As previously mentioned, oatmeal is a staple nutritious breakfast food. I sweeten my oatmeal with honey and I add seasonal fruits with lightly or unsalted cashews. A healthy nutritious breakfast helps to stimulate and promote consistent bowel movement.

Every family should have a juicer. Freshly squeezed juice will satisfy the desire for a sweet drink. Juices are high in sugar; therefore, it is a good idea for those who have weight issues to dilute juice with fifty percent pure water. Water is the only drink that hydrates our body, so we should drink plenty of water throughout the day. Drinking six to eight glasses of water per day will not only hydrate our bodies, but water will also help to flush toxins from our bodies. We should drastically cut back or eliminate drinking sodas altogether. And we need to stop giving them to our children. Sodas and many other beverages dehydrate our bodies. Drinking sodas contribute significantly to obesity. Sodas and many other drinks and sweet tasting foods contain High Fructose Corn Syrup, a man made sweetener, which can also be found in a majority of shelved foods. HFCS promotes obesity in children, teens and adults, because the body does not recognize it and thus the body craves more and more of it. It is important to protect yourself and your family. HFCS use to be what farmers fed their cattle and pigs to fatten them up before slaughtering them.

I was visiting a hospitalized friend and his family. My friend, who is overweight and had previously suffered from cancer, had just had emergency surgery the day before my visit for another ailment. As he finished his dinner, the nurse attendant entered his room and asked him if he wanted a diet soda? I immediately suggested to my friend that he should refrain from sodas, other foods and drinks that contain HFCS. It is important to protect yourself and your family. It would be wise to completely delete HFCS from your diet or greatly minimize it. The foods we consume play a vital role in promoting our physical and mental health.

Sugar is a cancer-feeder. When we reduce our sugar intake we cut off an important food supply to cancer cells. Sugar substitutes like NutraSweet, Equal, Spoonful, etc. are made with Aspartame which is very harmful to our bodies. A better substitute would be Manuka honey or molasses. Small portions of Cane sugar or brown sugar would even be better than regular white sugar. A high intake of sugar in children and adults can cause them to be overly hyper.

Milk causes our body to produce mucus, especially in the gastro-intestinal tract. Cancer feeds on mucus. A better substitute would be unsweetened Soya milk. Avoid drinking coffee, tea and choco-late, which have high caffeine. Green tea and white tea are better alternatives.

Cancer cells thrive in an acid environment. A meat-based diet is acidic. Fish, chicken and turkey are much better than beef and pork. Meat also contains livestock antibiotics, growth hormones and para-sites, which are harmful to our bodies.

A diet consisting of 80% fresh vegetables, whole grains with seeds, nuts, fruits and juices helps to put our bodies in an alka-line environment. Fresh vegetable juice provides live enzymes that absorbed easily within fifteen minutes to nourish and enhance growth of healthy cells. Eating raw vegetables two or three times a day also helps to provide enzymes to build healthy cells. Meat protein is difficult to digest and requires a lot of digestive enzymes. Undigested meat remaining in the intestines becomes putrefied and leads to more toxic buildup. Cancer cell walls have a tough protein covering. Eating less meat frees up the enzymes to attack the protein walls of cancer cells and allows the body's killer cells to destroy the cancer cells.

Every person has cancer cells in their body. These cancer cells do not show up in the standard tests until they have multiplied to a few billion. Cancer cells are always there but they have to multiply to a certain number to be detected by medical tests. Cancer cells occur from six to more than ten times in the lifetime of a person. An effective way to battle cancer is to starve the cancer cells by not feeding them with the foods they need to multiply. The World Cancer Research Fund, a nonprofit organization, concluded in a 1997 report on cancer and lifestyle, that there was "convincing or probable" evidence that fruits and vegetables have a preventive effect against cancers of the mouth, pharynx, esophagus, lung, stomach, colon, rectum, larynx pancreas, breast and bladder. The report suggested that 20% of cancers worldwide could be prevented if everyone just ate 14 to 28 ounces of varied fruits and vegetables every day. Fruits like blueberries, black raspberries and pomegranates may be strong cancer fighters, shrinking tumors and helping to prevent recurrence of cancer in some patients. Also, when the body's immune system is strong the cancer cells will be destroyed and prevented from multiplying and forming tumors.

Cancer is a disease of the mind, body, and spirit. A proactive and positive spirit will help the cancer warrior to be a survivor. Having the Holy Spirit within us is further strength and protection from physical and mental diseases. Anger, unforgiveness, and bitterness, causes our bodies to be in a stressful and acidic environment. In the model prayer in Matthew 6, we ask God to forgive us our trespasses as we forgive those who trespass against us. Loving and forgiving people who have wronged us is a choice that each of us needs to make. Choose to love, forgive others, and walk in the power and peace of Almighty God. Forgiveness is a powerful health remedy.

Lunch and dinner meals should include more fresh and steamed vegetables, fruits and salads. Salads made with dark salad greens like Romaine lettuce, spinach, red leaf and chicory, have more than six times the vitamin C and eight times as much beta carotene as iceberg lettuce. Eat your salads without the fattening high calorie dressings.

Eat baked or broiled meat dishes instead of fried foods saturated with artery clogging transfats, partially-Hydrogenated oils, constipating cheese, etc. A balanced meal with fruits and vegetables from the colors previously mentioned will be much more supportive of a healthier you. The American Heart Association and many knowledgeable doctors recommend eating fatty fish (salmon, halibut, mackerel, lake trout) because it is high in omega-3 fatty acids, which is comprised of two main biologically active products: EPA (eicosapentaenoic acid) and DHA (docosahexaenoic acid). For many years, EPA and DHA studies have been the subject of numerous scientific studies, including thousands of human clinical trials.

Omega-3 fatty acids are vital in the development of human cells. They are necessary in the proper development of cells involved in our brain and nervous system functions. They help produce eicosanoids, which regulate numerous body functions, including blood pressure, immune response, and the anti-inflammatory response. Fatty acids are critical for the division and maintenance of cells and the formation of healthy cell membranes. Many health experts suggest eating fatty fish at least twice each week. You can also get Omega-3 in albacore tuna and sardines. Perhaps a tuna fish sandwich on whole wheat bread with lettuce and tomatoes, or sardines, wheat crackers, fruit, and salad would be a better lunch choice than fast food burgers, fries, and nachos.

There are various dietary supplements to help lower cholesterol levels, support and promote healthy heart and blood vessel functions. Dr. Joseph C. Maroon, MD, F.A.C.S. who sits on the GNC Medical Advisory Board, strongly recommends a combination of natural supplements and regular physical fitness as powerful tools in maintaining joint function and good health. There are also dietary supplements to help you maintain a healthy digestive tract. It is important to flush and cleanse your colon periodically to prevent cancer and other harmful diseases.

Fiber rich foods are essential for keeping your colon cleansed and things moving through your intestines. A diet rich in fiber does much more than just keep you regular, it also helps with a wide range of health issues like preventing heart disease, type-2 diabetes, obesity and colon cancer. Some studies have strongly indicated that a healthy fiber intake helps to reduce breast cancer. Ideally our food intake should be 70% alkaline and 30% acidic.

There are two varieties of fiber, water soluble and insoluble. The soluble kind is found in fruits, vegetables, oats, and legumes; whereas the insoluble kind is found in wheat bran, whole-grain cereals, breads and fruits with edible skin/seeds such as strawberries and blueberries. The American Dietetic Association recommends we take 20 -35 grams of fiber per day. In the case where we don't get enough fiber in daily food intake, it is recommended that we supplement our food intake with fiber supplements. Soluble fibers help our digestion by slowing down the process so that nutrients are absorbed more gradually; thus, helping to lower cholesterol levels.

Discontinue snacks and other boxed foods that contained hydrogenated oils. Stop using margarine and shortening. Instead, use real butter and organic coconut oil in baking. Using less salt and msg in seasoning food will also promote a healthy you. Our bodies can develop bad habits from malnutritioned foods, causing our body language to send us messages demanding more of the same unhealthy, non nutritional foods. A consistent lethargic body that barely makes it through the day is in need of a more nutritious diet and perhaps vitamin supplements. An overweight body that begins to break down and malfunction in your thirties, forties and fifties is screaming for help. Don't keep putting junk food in your body and expect it to run like a thoroughbred. Break the cycle of denial, be honest and listen to your body language. The habits that we learn, good or bad, tend to stay with us for a lifetime. Why wait for a serious illness or malfunction in the body to change bad eating and drinking habits? Let's be proactive in taking care of our bodies by changing to healthier diets.

Not only what we eat is important, but equally as important is when we eat, especially our dinner meal. Always try to eat your last meal of the day at least four to six hours before your bedtime. And avoid eating late night snacks, especially chips, buttered popcorn, cookies, cake, ice cream, cheese products, etc. Discipline is the order of the day. Not only does God discipline us, but we also need to have self discipline. God's discipline and our self discipline will promote and produce healthy bodies for victorious living. Our bodies will adjust to the disciplines that we incorporate.

<u>VITAMINS AND SUPPLEMENTS</u>

There are various vitamins and supplements that can work in conjunction with a healthy diet to further promote good health, energy and wellness support. In most communities you will find a health food store with ample supply of vitamins and supplements. You can also find some products at your local drug store. My personal favorite shopping place is GNC for vitamins and supplements. GNC has its own manufacturing facility and it is committed to product **quality** and **truth in labeling.**

Choosing vitamins and supplements is a very personal choice based on individual needs. Therefore, it is important to customize your own nutritional program. Some of the factors to be considered are age, gender, health problems, health prevention, ethnicity, physical needs and deficiencies. Choose to be proactive and address your body needs before there is a breakdown or malfunction. For many years I took a dietary supplement, along with my selective eating habits to prevent prostate cancer. There are some diseases that appear to be more aggressive in a certain ethnicity group than others. Prostate Cancer is much more aggressive in Afro-American (Cushite) Men, especially when there is a history of prostate cancer in the family. My pastor and friend, Chuck Singleton, who is very proactive in health care, strongly suggested that I start a prostate health regimen, as he had, because his father had successfully survived prostate cancer. My late father had prostate cancer in his seventies; therefore, years before I started taking Mega Men 50 Plus, I chose a prostate prevention program which included taking Pygeum, Stinging Nettle, and Saw Palmetto Herbal supplement tablets twice a day.

A popular vitamin that many people take on a consistent basis is C. To get the most from vitamin C pills, divide your doses and take them twice daily. Our bodies eliminate C in about twelve hours. By splitting your daily intake into two doses you can keep your blood levels high throughout the day. If you take more than 500 milligrams of calcium daily, space the pills out during the day to enhance absorption and reduce the risk of constipation. Super B-Complex is a great dietary supplement for people working or living in stressful environments.

My sister in law, Alicia Parker, who is in the medical field, along with my wife KJoy taught me a valuable lesson about the common cold. Colds cannot be cured by antibiotics. Years ago, as many do today, people took antibacterial drugs, including penicillin to cure colds and flu, which are viral infections. There is no one drug that cures a cold but there are some good home remedies and herbal supplements that help to give relief. Hot tea with honey can soothe and temporarily relieve a sore throat. Hot chicken soup can increase the flow of nasal secretions. Saltwater gargles with 1/4 teaspoon of salt in 8 ounces of warm water can give relief, as well as homemade or store bought saline nose drops.

There are dietary supplements for men and women of all ages. And there is special emphasis for those over age fifty. Consultation with your doctor or nutritionist can assist you in getting started on the vitamins and supplements that your body needs. A good healthy diet supported by vitamins and supplements, along with proper exercise can cause your body to perform at its maximum capacity, enabling you to live better, longer and be more effective in serving your family and the kingdom of God.

EXERCISE REGIMEN

ME. Consistent exercise has been a part of my lifestyle since my early twenties. Years ago I would go to the gym, play basketball, run the track, and work out with weights. During that time I also ran on the streets in the neighborhood where I lived. Due to my competitive nature I gave up playing basketball years ago right after giving my life to Christ. I was concerned that the argumentative style and nature of the way we played basketball might compromise my Christian witness. I also stopped running on the street because running on asphalt could cause stress and damage to my ankles and knees. Now I run on dirt tracks or the treadmill. Today, at sixty-nine, I have a very active lifestyle that includes traveling, speaking all over the world, house work, working in the yard, doing sports activities with my son, and usually spending four days a week working out in the gym. My goal is to have a good quality of life for as long as I am on this earth. Physical fitness is an essential part of having a good life.

YOU. Just as I made a choice about being physically fit, you also have to make a choice. Your body is your instrument that enables you to do whatever God and you choose for your life activities. Keeping it strong and well tuned allows you to function at a high capacity as well as support your mental well being. God did not create you for a low quality of life. Nor did He design you for mediocrity. You will enjoy a high quality of life and your body will function at maximum capacity if you diligently maintain a healthy weight level, strive to avoid becoming obese, and exercise your body to build and sustain good muscle tone.

My friend, Susan Lewis, who was once a Primary Fitness Instructor, teaching Hi/Lo Aerobic classes, promotes physical exercise as a method to improve health, enhance beauty, reduce stress, promote self confidence and lessen the signs of aging. Susan and many other experts in the field believe that proper diet and physical exercise are absolutely essential to having a high quality of life.

Weight gain and obesity, often resulting in Type-2 diabetes, usually happens over a gradual period of time; therefore, exercise is not a quick fix. It takes patience, steadfastness and commitment. Most times positive results will not be seen for weeks or months; however, if one is committed to exercise, results are guaranteed. And recent studies offer strong direct evidence that physical exercise may actually help prevent non-insulin-dependent diabetes.

A daily 20-60 minute work out with cardiovascular exercises and resistance training can help you lose weight and belly fat. Belly fat is associated with insulin resistance, a condition that often precedes the onset of Type-2 diabetes. Recent studies have also shown belly fat to be associated with heart disease. Controlling weight and keeping the belly slim are necessary components for a healthier you. Pastor Gordon and Brenda Laine at Loveland, and many other churches today, have initiated programs to combat obesity and problems associated with being overweight. Some church congregations have set up work out rooms on church property, along with qualified instructors in physical training, diet and nutrition. Other church leaders have organized group and individual work out regimes for its' members at outside community facilities. Church leaders know that obesity is a serious problem in the house of the Lord. Remember, believers are the house of God, and we are to glorify and honor God in our bodies.

One way we honor God with our bodies is by keeping them trim and fit. The more proactive that we become in developing a healthier body by consistent physical exercise and healthier diets, the more we combat and destroy the destructive problems of obesity. Bad habits of improper eating and little or no physical exercise can be changed. **Change your habits and embrace a more productive lifestyle to promote a better you.** Through proper exercise and healthier eating we energize and prepare our bodies to be more available to God's service. Healthy and physical fit saints, serving the kingdom of God, truly give honor to God.

Besides exercise, the quantity, quality, and frequency of your eating can play a vital role in keeping your body weight in check and your waistline trim. Small frequent meals of food that is not refined or high in sugar or unhealthy fats are a requisite. Lean protein and plenty of fruits, vegetables and fiber will satisfy your appetite, prevent cravings, overeating, and keep your blood sugar stable. Proper diet and good physical exercise will improve your cells ability to use insulin. A consistent diet of adequate fiber and fiber supplements can help prevent Type-2 diabetes. Consult your physician or nutritionist to determine your individual needs.

Some helpful supplements for prevention of Type-2 diabetes are chromium, fiber, a multivitamin with adequate magnesium, zinc, and B vitamins. Chromium research has shown a reduced carbohydrate craving in people with depression. Low levels of magnesium are often associated with Type-2 diabetes; therefore, you would do well to boost your mineral intake. Magnesium is required for energy production and it may also improve your insulin function and help maintain healthy blood sugar levels, especially in older people. Foods that are rich in Vitamin D and magnesium can help you avoid Type-2 diabetes. Vitamin D is found in salmon, tuna, sardines, shiitake mushrooms and soybeans. The National Academy of Sciences recommends that adults should get 200-600 international units (IU) of vitamin D daily, depending on age.

In the past few years there has been a high visible concentration on obesity throughout the world. Various reports have indicated that too many people, young and not so young, are suffering and living low quality lives dictated by obesity-related ailments, such as diabetes, cardiovascular disease, mental anguish, and limb replacements. Because I know of no easy way to lovingly approach an obese person, I usually whisper a prayer asking God to open the eyes of their understanding and help them. My witness of obesity has been a great source of personal frustration for me. I find myself being deeply troubled and concerned about people who suffer from obesity because many are so easily offended and often defensive about their condition. The Holy Scriptures tell us to give the devil no place in our lives. Obesity has become a stronghold, giving the enemy place to attack the lives of faithful saints. Diet and exercise could go a long way in alleviating the obesity problem. Today, physical exercise is an absolute for all of us.

Susan and others believe that exercise does not have to be difficult. It can be as easy as walking twenty to thirty minutes a day or as challenging as running a marathon. Whatever form of exercise you choose, discipline is necessary to experience positive results. The key is to start exercising and then be consistent at doing it. Remember, discipline is a two way street between us and God. God disciplines us and we must practice self discipline.

It is estimated that as many as 12% of all deaths - (250,000) per year in America may be attributed indirectly to lack of regular physical exercise, according to the CDC. According to government guidelines, only about one in four people, exercises enough to be considered as physically active. Regular exercise inhibits, arrests, and often reverses many of the declines commonly associated with aging. A consistent regimen of three to five brisk thirty minutes walks each week can add years to your life and also life to your years.

To those living in or frequenting beach communities, walking on sand can boost your energy expenditure by as much as a third. And if you walk barefoot, it also exercises more of the muscles in the foot. Walking uphill and downhill burns more calories and expends more energy than walking on a flat terrain.

Walking also reduces the risk of strokes. A Yale University study of white male veterans, aged 50 to 60, showed that those who had inactive life styles were nearly seven times more likely to suffer a stroke than men who led moderate or very active lives. A daily walk of one mile was found to be the minimum activity for reducing stroke risk.

Walking up or down stairs, if you live in a multi-level dwelling, or work in an office buildings or department stores is a great way to get exercise and improve your overall physical fitness by 10 to 15%. If the weather is too hot or cold for walking outside, spend time in a shopping mall and combine shopping and walking. The American Heart Association sponsors walking programs in many shopping malls.

Swimming and bike riding are great alternative exercises. Both can be family activities shared together. Not being able to swim does not have to deter you from getting into the water and walking or running. Movement and activity in shallow water up to your waist or slightly higher will help exercise your limbs and develop muscle tone.

Wearing the proper shoes is essential when walking or running on any surface. When you go to purchase new exercise shoes, try to bend them. The shoe should bend where the foot bends-at the ball of the foot. If it bends at mid-foot it will offer very little support. It should not be too stiff or bend too easily. Also hold the heel of the shoe and try to move the counter (the rigid section at the back of the shoe): it should not move from side to side.

When you work out at a gym or any other facility, always warm up before stretching your muscles. Jogging in place for five to ten minutes can prepare you for your workout by gradually increasing your heart rate and blood flow. Your warm up will also raise the temperature of your muscles and improve muscle function. It will also decrease your chance of a pull muscle or sports injury. Drink cold water or a cold juice beverage during your exercise routine. Cold drinks leave the stomach more rapidly than warm drinks, thereby supplying the body more quickly with the fluid it needs. Contrary to popular belief, cold drinks do not cause cramps.

Remember, our bodies are the temple of God's Spirit, and we are to glorify God in our bodies. Eating a proper diet with vitamin supplements, engaging in continuous physical exercise will reduced stress and promote a healthy better you, which is one way to glorify God in your body. Find out what type of exercise is best for you. Consult with your physician and also your health instructor if you have a gym membership. Physical exercise is very essential as we get older, because we need to burn more calories and keep our bodies active and fit. Regular exercise burns calories and invigorates our bodies. Get started today on a consistent regimen of exercise. Your mind and body will love you for it.

CHAPTER TWELVE

THE BUSINESS YOU:

DO BUSINESS TILL I COME

Beloved, just as there is a Spiritual You and a Physical You, there must also be a Business You. We, as born again Christians, are indwelled by God's Spirit and we have power and authority to take dominion over this world. Our dominion starts in the part of the world which greatly impacts us. To be the **Awesome You** that God designed you to be demands that you take care of kingdom and natural business. Remember, God created each of us to be in **A LIMITED PARTNERSHIP FOR UNLIMITED SUCCESS!** As I said in an earlier chapter, God is the Limited Partner, who provides all the resources and we are the General Partners, who do all the work. The partnership is in no way limited in terms of power, potential, growth, success and prosperity! Nothing is too hard for our God! And as the Limited Partner, He faithfully provides all the resources, so there is no limit to our success. God has invested gifts, talents, skills in your life and mine. What are we doing with God's investment? Are we occupying, engaging in business to multiply what God has given us to bring forth great increase for His kingdom and our lives? We are stewards and brokers of God's resources and He has commanded us to do business until He comes. It is time for us to do the work of the partnership. And a significant part of doing the work is excelling in our business practices so that we can take dominion over this world.

As Christians we have a key advantage in doing business in this world system. One essential key to successful business is prayer. The first and most important step in doing our work as the General Partners is praying to our Limited Partner for directions, understanding, spiritual insight, natural insight, provisions, divine favor, and prosperity. Talking to, listening to, and following divine guidance from our Limited Partner will guarantee us success in all our business affairs. Too often in life Christians seek God for spiritual guidance, but ignore and relegate Him to a nonentity position in the daily business activities of our temporal lives. We are not of this world but we are definitely living in it; therefore, we need to become more intelligent and skillful in business negotiations. Jesus said: **"I am come that you might have life and have it more abundantly."** Abundant life is not being blessed in the spirit and broke in the natural. Abundant life is blessings in the spirit realm and the natural realm. **It is time for a drastic change in the Body of Christ. It's time for us to become the lenders and not the borrowers! It's time for us to be the "have" and no longer be the "have nots!" It's time for many of us to become entrepreneurs and land owners! We are commanded to occupy until He comes! It's time for us to engage in trade and become excellent anointed business people!** Throughout the Holy Scriptures we see examples of God in a Limited Partnership with His Created Beings for Unlimited Success. From Adams creation in the Garden of Eden, God has always provided the resources. By His divine power He spoke a world into existence. God provided all the resources to sustain abundant human life on earth. Then God made man in His image, male and female, made He them. God told man and woman to take dominion over everything that He had made. However, just before God made woman from a rib He took out of man, He put the man in the garden and told him to dress it and keep it. To dress and keep it means to be a servant husbandman and work the land. We are to observe, protect, and preserve the land. As General Partners we are the workers who work the land and have dominion over it. We also worship God, our Limited Partner, who gave us the land.

Now is the critical time for each of us to become more aware of and engage more often in good business practices. We, the church of Jesus Christ, need to do a much better job in conducting business on behalf of God's kingdom. And since the kingdom of God is within us and we are to have a kingdom mentality to establish His kingdom on earth, we need to engage in kingdom business practices in a natural world and graduate from the elementary naive practices of disengaging in business and just getting by. God did not create us nor did He save us to just get by and live from day to day just making ends meet. We were created by God and rebirthed in the Spirit of God to take dominion over this world. We are the head and not the tail. Heads occupy and engage in kingdom building business. Tails live at the mercy of others, always looking for a hand out or a helping hand. **Engaging in excellent masterful business practices is not an invitation. It is a commandment from our Lord Jesus Christ.** And He will greatly reward those of us who habitually take care of business. Doing good business and engaging in trade is a repeated activity, not a one time thing.

In Apostle Luke's inspired gospel writings, he tells us how Jesus had gone to Zacchaeus house, a chief tax collector and a very rich man. During His time in Zacchaeus house, Jesus tells him: **"Today, salvation has come to this house, because he also is a son of Abraham; for the Son of Man has come to seek and to save that which was lost."** (Luke 19:9 NKJ)

Later in his visit Jesus speaks of the Parable of the Minas: **"A certain nobleman went into a far country to receive for himself a kingdom and to return. So he called ten of his servants, delivered to them ten minas, and said to them, 'Do business till I come.' And so it was that when he returned, having received the kingdom, he then commanded these servants, to whom he had given the money, to be called to him, that he might know how much every man had gained by trading. Then came the first, saying, Master, your mina has earned ten minas.' And he said to him, 'Well done, good servant; because you were faithful in a very little, have authority over ten cities.' And the second came, saying, 'Master, your mina has earned five minas.' Likewise he said to him, 'You also be over five cities.' Then another came,** saying, 'Master, here is your mina, which I have kept put away in a handkerchief. For I feared you, because you are an austere man. You collect what you did not deposit, and reap what you did not sow.' And he said to him, 'Out of your own mouth I will judge you, you wicked servant. You knew that I was an austere man, collecting what I did not deposit and reaping what I did not sow. Why then did you not put my money in the bank, that at my coming I might have collected it with interest?' And he said to those who stood by, 'Take the mina from him, and give it to him who has ten minas.' (But they said to him,'Master, he has ten minas.') For I say to you, that to everyone who has will be given; and from him who does not have, even what he has will be taken away from him." (Luke 19:12, 13; 15-26 NKJ)

The nobleman spoken of in this parable is the Lord Jesus Christ. He has come to the earth to establish his kingdom and He has given those of us who received him as Savior and Lord, eternal life, gifts, talents, and resources to have an abundant life on earth. Just as the nobleman returned, our Lord will soon come back to this earth in the clouds. While He is gone we are commanded to do business until he comes again. Therefore, we all need to carefully examine our lives and evaluate how we are using the talents, gifts and resources that God gave us. Are we using what God gave us and occupying until He comes? Or are we allowing fear, bred out of business ignorance, to keep us on the highways of poverty, watching others navigate down prosperity expressway to viable destinations of abundance?

I truly believe that if the Lord Jesus would speak audibly to His church today, He would recognize and commend us on many things, but He would call us to task in one major area... "I know your works, love, holiness, service, faith, and worship celebrations. Nevertheless I have this against you, you have not engaged in good business practices to take dominion over the land. You have allowed the world to take advantage of you. You have allowed fear and igno-rance to keep you from managing my resources. I illustrated in a parable and clearly told you to occupy until I come. As my ambassa-dors, representing my kingdom on earth, I have anointed you, given you authority and power to engage in and do successful business until I come again to receive you unto myself. I have not given you a spirit of fear or a negative mindset about business affairs. I have empowered you to step up and become knowledgeable in the affairs of world business. Why have so many of you wasted your anointing and opted out of the business arena? Why have you disobeyed my command to occupy and do business till I come? Jesus would say: **"To those of you who have been faithful over a few things I will make you rulers of many." "My people are destroyed for lack of knowledge. Because you have rejected knowledge, I also will reject you from being priest for Me."** (Hosea 4:6 NKJ)

Beloved, we have the potential and the spiritual capacity to rise up today and walk in obedience to our Lord's command to do business until He comes. We need a kingdom mentality so that we can add to our spiritual virtues, excellent business knowledge and practices. Take note of Apostle Peter's exhortation to us: **"Grace and peace be multiplied to you in the knowledge of God and of Jesus our Lord, as His divine power has given to us all things that pertain to life and godliness, through the knowledge of Him who called us by glory and virtue, by which have been given to us exceedingly great and precious promises, that through these you may be partakers of the divine nature,** having escaped the corruption that is in the world through lust. **But also for this very reason, giving all diligence, add to your faith virtue, to virtue knowledge, to knowledge self-control, to self-control perseverance, to perseverance godliness, to godliness brotherly kindness, and to brotherly kindness love."** (2 Peter 1:2-7 NKJ)

Listen up **Awesome You** and **Awesome Me!** God's divine power has given us all things that pertain to life and godliness. That includes the natural and the spiritual realms. We do not have to fear anyone or be ignorant of anything. We can add to our faith, knowledge of business, just as we add divine principles. And we will succeed and prosper in the virtues of God and have great success in business if we walk in divine principles and persevere in godliness, brotherly kindness and love. We are partakers of God's divine nature and we have His divine power to do all things, including engaging in successful business. Therefore, we need to be mindful of how He blessed Abraham, Joseph, David, Solomon and many others throughout the Bible. God blessed these men with great favor and economic wealth.

He even raised Joseph up out of slavery in a foreign land to rule over the nation of Egypt. Joseph was in total control of the economic wealth of the great nation of Egypt. And God has continued to bless men and women of our day to go from impoverished backgrounds to great economic wealth. Our God truly desires for his saints to have and control the wealth of this land. Godly wealth should be gathered to propagate the gospel and passed down to our future generations. We should accumulate and control the wealth of the land through godly favor in wise business deals. Then we can send the gospel to every nation, feed the hungry, clothed the naked and give shelter to the homeless. Jehovah Jireh, the Lord our bountiful provider, is ready to transfer the wealth of this world into our hands.

"A good man leaves an inheritance to his children's children, but a sinner's wealth is stored up for the righteous. A poor man's field may produce abundant food, but injustice sweeps it away" (Proverbs 13:22, 23 NIV)

The inheritance we should leave to our children's children includes a good name and a godly lifestyle, prayer, biblical principles and godly examples. We should also leave our children houses, land and monetary wealth. God's word says a sinner's wealth is stored up for the righteous. We, the saints of God, are the righteous. When we engage in wise management and good business practices God will cause the wealth of the wicked to be transferred into our hands.

On the other hand the lack of knowledge, unwise management and bad business practices will cause us to lose what God has for us. Our labor, our fields can produce abundant blessings, but our inability to do business and handle the blessings of God can cause us to lose it all. **I am absolutely confident that the Lord Jesus Christ always does His part to give us the abundant life underneath the skin and in the material realm.** If we find ourselves prospering in the spirit realm but lacking in the natural realm, it is due to our mismanagement and lack of knowledge in conducting good business. Let's examine and learn some basic knowledge about conducting good business in common areas that affect all of our lives.

Tithes and Offerings. Some people may wonder why I would put tithes and offerings under The Business You. Yes, tithes and offerings, is a strong spiritual principle; however, it is also the very root of successful business for a child of God. If we are in anyway slack in living out this principle, we will never truly prosper. Our management style will suffer and our business practices and decisions will reap disaster after disaster. No one who robs God in tithes and offerings can truly succeed in life because he or she lives under a curse cloud. In this world we often see those who have not made a public profession of their faith in Jesus Christ prosper in acquiring material wealth. One common denominator that defines them is they are givers. They give away fortunes to help and bless others. They are wise stewards over what God has blessed them to acquire. And by sowing into other peoples lives they continue to reap a bountiful harvest.

When you truly learned to respect money for what it can do, then you realize that money not only blesses you, but it can be a tremendous blessing in the lives of others. Money is necessary for life, but money is not my life. **Money has been a very powerful instrument of blessings in my family's life. We have learned to see money as a blessing tool.** Nothing is more awesome or inspiring in the human experience for us with other human beings than to give a blessing. Sometimes the blessing is prayer, love, and emotional support, a helping hand, encouragement, or material gifts. Other times it is the **blessing tool of money.** It is indeed more blessed to give than to receive.

Remember, the word of God is true in the lives of believers and nonbelievers. **GOD'S WORD IS TRUE AND IT WILL NEVER RETURN VOID. IT WILL ALWAYS ACCOMPLISH WHATEVER GOD SENDS IT FORTH TO DO. GOD HONORS HIS WORD ABOVE HIS NAME AND HE CAUSES IT TO RAIN ON THE JUST AND THE UNJUST.** Unbelievers who apply the word of God in their lives will reap the benefits of God's word; whereas, believers who refuse to obey God's word will suffer loss for their disobedience. **"But this I say: He who sows sparingly will also reap sparingly, and he who sows bountifully will also reap bountifully. So let each one give** as he purposes in his heart, not grudgingly or of necessity; for God loves a cheerful giver. <u>And God is able to make all grace abound toward you, that you, always having all sufficiency in all things, may have an abundance for every good work. Now may He who supplies seed to the sower, and bread for food, supply and multiply the seed you have sown and increase the fruits of your righteousness, while you are enriched in everything for all liberality, which causes thanksgiving through us to God."</u> (2Corinthians 9:6-8; 10,11NKJ)

God's word is clear. He loves a cheerful giver who purposes in his/her heart to bless others. It is God who gives us unmerited favor to achieve and succeed that we might have abundance in every realm of life. God gives us first, seed to sow, then bread for food. However, He only continues to supply and multiply the seed we sow. Harvests in our spiritual and business lives are greatly enhanced by the seeds that we sow into the lives of others. Cheerfully sow time, talent, love, encouragement, and the **blessing tool of money** in the lives of others who have needs and watch God increase your harvest. If we grudgingly give or refuse to sow seeds of blessings, we will forfeit His grace and future bountiful crops from God. Being a cheerful giver gives us God's assurance and protection that we will be enriched in everything for all liberality. Everything includes business success and prosperity.

ME. Over the years my family and I have been faithful givers to our home churches, other ministries and individual needs. We have enjoyed feeding and clothing needy people, going into jails, prisons, and nursing homes to share God's words of hope. Giving away Bibles, ministry materials and other valuables to help those in need, is a way of life for us. For twenty years we have sponsored and continue to sponsor two children on a monthly basis because we have always believed that our prosperity was rooted in our loving desire to give generously unto others. God looks at the integrity of our hearts in our giving. And He will always cause wealth and honor to come to people who joyfully give to those in need; therefore, we continue to joyfully embrace the teaching of our Lord Jesus, who said: **"Give, and it shall be given unto you; good measure, pressed down, and shaken together, and running over, shall men**

give into your bosom. For with the same measure that ye mete withal it shall be measured to you again." (Luke 6:38 KJ)

There are three essential truths from Jesus' words in the above scripture recorded by Luke. And they help us to understand what Jesus meant when He said: **"It is more blessed to give than to receive."** (1) The act of giving is an individual choice that blesses the giver. Giving is our greatest expression of love and we have been greatly blessed with the privilege to give. If God did not continue to bless us we would not be in the position to bless others. (2) Giving opens the door to receive bountifully. Over the years we have received exceedingly, abundantly above what we have given or ever thought that we would receive. (3) Our attitude and the amount we give has greatly determined what and how we have received our blessing. We have often given sacrificially and we have never had a crisis that God did not meet in our time of great need.

One of the many valuable principles of God taught in the scriptures is found in God's question concerning tithes and offerings. This is a personal question that each of us must address: **"Will a man rob God? Yet you have robbed Me! But you say, in what way have we robbed You? In tithes and offerings. You are cursed with a curse, for you have robbed Me. Even this whole nation. Bring all the tithes into the storehouse, that there may be food in My house, And try Me now in this, Says the LORD of hosts. If I will not open for you the windows of heaven. And pour out for you such blessing that there will not be room enough to receive it. And I will rebuke the devourer for your sakes, So that he will not destroy the fruit of your ground, Nor shall the vine fail to bear fruit for you in the field, Says the LORD of hosts; And all nations will call you blessed, For you will be a delightful land, Says the LORD of hosts."** (Malachi 3:8-12 NKJ)

God said that we rob Him in tithes and offerings. The tithe belongs to God. When we pay our tithes we are simply transferring to God what already belongs to Him. In the Old Testament, God required a tenth as the tithe; however, my family and I decided that we live under the covenant of grace which is better than the Old Testament covenant of the Law. Therefore, our tithes and offerings are usually around twenty percent of our income. God's heavenly windows have remained opened to us over the years and He has never allowed the devourer to destroy the fruit of our harvest, nor has our labor ever failed to produce bountiful fruit. This is especially gratifying to me as a full time evangelist for twenty-seven years, because I have never charged a dime for ministry. When I get on an airplane or go anywhere to minister God's word, I have no idea how much I will have when I come home. Over the years God has met our every need and given us favor with business knowledge and concepts that have truly blessed my family and I to be a delightful land. Today we enjoy the blessings of God to live in an upscaled family oriented neighborhood in a comfortable and nicely furnished home, appraised at nearly a half million dollars before the economic meltdown. We drive late model cars that we own. Our son is in a private Christian School, and we are debt free, except for the mortgage on our home. We have substantial liquid cash in savings, CD's and other financial holdings. We have retirement benefits, annuities, and sufficient insurance coverage. Our God does not show partiality as it relates to salvation, nor does He show partiality in honoring His word. If you walk in the word of God, you will receive exactly what God promises. Walking in God's favor is much more rewarding than living under a curse cloud. Choose this day the path that you will walk.

You. I shared the preceding Scriptures and personal testimony so that you can get a clear picture of what God our Creator wants to do in your life. God wants **Awesome You** to prosper in every area of your life. God takes pleasure in the prosperity of His servants. Contrary to what you may have heard or been led to believe, God wants to bless you in every realm of life. In the spiritual and natural realms you need financial resources. God is not against you having money. He warns us not to allow money to occupy the throne of our heart. God alone should sit on the throne of your heart. To love anyone or anything above God, including money, is idolatry. It is the love of money that is the root of all evil. Money itself is a valuable commodity and **blessing tool** if used properly. Giving cheerfully to others is a true indication of your devotion and feelings about money. If you take delight in giving to others when there are needs in your life God is truly on the throne of your heart. God is the epitome of love and the primary activity of love is giving. For God so loved the world that He gave His only begotten Son, Jesus Christ.

Too often we allow false teaching, past history, or other emotional barriers to bind us in fear of pursuing economic prosperity. Many Christians have been led to believe that there is piety in being poor and needy. Yes, the Lord Jesus said that we would always have the poor with us. He did not say we had to be the poor. I am not saying that God wants each of us to be filthy rich. Everyone is not trained or emotionally equipped to handle great financial riches. I am saying that God wants his children to have sufficient financial wealth to build his kingdom on earth, meet our needs, and share with others less fortunate than we are. I am saying that God told us to take dominion over an oasis of material wealth that He created. If God did not want us to have abundant life which includes material sufficiency, then why did He speak into existence an oasis of plenty called the Garden of Eden, before He created Adam and Eve, and told them to replenish, subdue, and take dominion over His creation? God gave us His spirit to empower us, lead us, and equip us to rule and take dominion over the world He made for us. Being made after God's likeness means we are to operate like God. He rules over heaven. He made earth and told us to operate like He does. There is no lack, no poverty, no just barely getting by in heaven. Heaven's gates are made of one great pearl. The streets are made of gold and the Lord Jesus is preparing mansions for us to live in a gated community.

Beloved, God placed mankind in an oasis of plenty because He knows that material prosperity is a significant part of the abundant life. He wanted Adam, Eve, **Awesome You** and **Awesome Me** to rule and take dominion over the world that He created for us. Therefore, it's time to let God's anointing destroy every yoke that binds you from stepping into your economic destiny. Remember, I choose to claim God as my destiny. Therefore, I encourage you and I admonish you to: **CHANGE YOUR MIND! RECEIVE GOD'S TRUTH ABOUT YOUR FINANCIAL PROSPERITY! GOD WANTS YOU TO PROSPER! HE TAKES PLEASURE IN YOUR PROSPERITY AND HE HAS DESIGNED YOU FOR GREAT SUCCESS!**

BUDGET AND SAVE. Another factor that will greatly enhance our business life is learning how to budget and save a portion of our income. It may help you to look at saving a portion of your salary as a way of paying yourself on payday. Why work for weeks, get paid and everyone gets a piece of your paycheck but you. **WORK FOR YOURSELF AND NOT JUST FOR YOUR CREDITORS!** To do this you have to budget wisely and not spend every penny that you earn. It is always dangerous and often leads to financial disaster when you live on the cutting edge of or beyond your financial earnings. I have always tried to save a minimum of ten to fifteen percent of my income. Initially we saved money for a down payment on a house. Today, a portion of my savings goes toward retirement, my son's college education and a smaller portion is put aside for unexpected emergencies, special events and Christmas. Our Christmas spending has never carried over into the next year by way of unpaid credit cards or charge accounts. Our Christmas is budgeted and paid for before we complete our Christmas day celebration. And our celebration always involves blessing others outside of our family. I decided many years ago that I wanted to be a river, through which God's currents of blessings would flow through me into the lives of others. I have learned that it is better to be a river than a dam. Rivers are God made, dams are man made and dams stop the flow of blessings. If God's blessings flow through you, there will always be more than enough for you. Choose to be a river and allow God's blessings to flow through you to bless others. Do not be a dam where God's blessings stop and go no further than you. The quickest way to stop God's flow of blessings to you and others is to become a man made dam.

There are some very essential and important things to consider when making a budget. What is equally as important to how much money you make is how you budget and how you spend it. If you fail to have a budget plan you are planning to fail in your finances. Tithes and Offerings should be at the top of your budget plan. Always put God first. He is the source of your supply and increase. Pay yourself second by saving a portion of your salary. Many banks offer free checking accounts and you can also arrange for automatic monthly deductions from your account to your savings. It is much easier to save money when you don't see or personally handle it. Itemize your living expenses by creditor's names and dates that they need to be paid. This allows you to allocate income to expenses based on when you get paid. This also helps you to stay current on all your payments. Late payments and returned checks are always very costly and they negatively affect your credit ratings. Many people today choose to handle their budgets electronically. The same principles apply. Most families have housing, automobile, food and miscellaneous expenses.

FICO SCORES AND CREDIT RATING. We live in a world system where credit is vital for purchasing power. Therefore, our credit rating determines our FICO scores, which are relevant to our purchasing power. Depending on how we handle our finances, our credit ratings will be excellent (high), average (medium) or bad (low). Our FICO scores have a great impact on the interest we pay and the type of loans we can secure. Bad credit always equates to higher interest rates and less attractive loans. Our credit history is determined by our record of credit agreements and how we performed our part of the contract agreement. Our FICO scores and credit history is reported by three different credit bureaus. They are (1) Equifax Inc; (2) Experian; (3) Trans Union. FICO scores can go as high as 850. FICO scores in the 700-850 are excellent and they use to qualify you for 100% financing on home purchases with the most reasonable interest rates prior to the tight lending restrictions on home mortgages. Ratings in 600-700 range are average and will qualify you for most purchases at a decent interest rate. FICO's 580 and below are low. You can qualify for some important purchases but you usually pay a much higher interest rate. A low rating is the result of a bad credit history.

There are various agencies that assist in repairing credit records. Beware of those who promise to magically make all your bad history disappear. Many of the good agencies do not charge for assisting in repairing your credit because they collect from merchants that you owe. Bankruptcies and foreclosures stay in credit histories for ten years. Usually after ten years you can request that it be deleted from your files and you no longer have to declare it on your applications. By all means stay current with tax responsibilities to avoid government tax liens on your record. Government or personal tax liens can make buying anything on credit very difficult.

Paying bills on or before schedule improves your credit rating. Paying your mortgage ahead of schedule can help increase your credit score and also save you money on interest, depending on the type of loan that you have. Slow and late payments will negatively affect your rating and cause your credit limit to be lowered. Lower credit limits also cause credit scores to fall. You can help improve your credit score by cancelling zero balance credit cards. Open accounts, even with zero balances, can negatively affect your rating, because you still have access to the credit limit on the zero balance account.

CREDIT CARDS. It is good to have one or two credit cards. A credit card is essential if you need to rent a car, purchase an airline ticket or address some emergency without cash on hand. Keep your daily expenses well within your income range so that you can avoid running up heavy credit card debt. If you have good credit with a high FICO score you should not pay annual fees or high interest rates on credit cards. Because we have excellent credit with high FICO scores, I have not paid interest or an annual fee on a credit card unless I chose too. KJoy and I receive an average of three to six invitations for new credit cards every month. Most credit cards have introductory offers with special incentives that allow you to pay no annual fee and no interest for six months to a year. Many cards offer other benefits like airline mileage without travel restrictions, money back rewards, etc. Because we have an excellent credit rating I am not reluctant to demand my own credit terms. Many card companies will work with you because they want your business. Whatever I charge on a credit card I pay when the charges become due. I do not carry over balances from month to month. This also keeps me from paying interest. Please do not use a credit card for emotional spending. Credit card debt is often like quicksand. You can easily become frustrated because you are entrapped in the mire. Your despair increases when you cannot climb out of, nor can you see a light at the end of the tunnel. Stay within your spending budget and let your credit card freely serve you instead of imprisoning you.

BUYING A HOUSE. The dream and goal of many individuals and most families is to own a house. This is a reachable goal for most people. It is important to save money toward a down payment and/or closing cost. There is always a need for cash when purchasing a house. Save, save, save. My friend, Yvonne Williams, who is an excellent realtor that God placed in my family's life, has shared some of her wisdom and guidance on buying a house. The second entity needed in purchasing a house is a mortgage lender. My family and I are greatly blessed to have as a personal friend and my prayer partner, Marlow Hooper, one of the most successful brokers in the mortgage business. Marlow was the general manager of Majestic Home Loans, before stepping out to partner in his own company in the Inland Empire. Marlow also shared some valuable insights on the various kinds of loans available for residential and commercial purchases.

Once the decision has been made to purchase a house, prepare yourself by saving money and reworking your budget to accommodate a mortgage payment and minor upkeep. Then pursue an experienced realtor and lender. When you contact a lender be prepared to submit proper documentation needed to check your credit history, review your income and verify the amount of money you have in savings and any other assets. The lender can then give you a pre-approved loan that accurately shows what you can afford to buy. You can pursue your own lender; however, many experience real estate agents have good relationships with lenders and mortgage companies. A pre-approved loan and your savings helps you know how much you can spend and it will define the house you can afford to buy and the area you can live in. Pre-approved loans also encourage Realtors and sellers to take you seriously; thus, extending to you their prompt attention and a better quality of service. Now you are ready to start looking for your dream house.

Understand that as a buyer, the real estate agent does not work for you. He or she works on your behalf, but you are not paying them, the seller is. I learned this fact from buying our first house. The real estate agent did not give me information that could have enable my family and I to make a more informed decision about what price to offer for the townhouse we were buying. He did not give us Comps, telling us how long the house had been on the market and the original selling price. He did not tell us what other townhouses in the area were selling for. Although we got the townhouse for a good competitive price, I am convinced that we paid more than we had to for our first house. The real estate agent was splitting the commission with the seller's agent; therefore, it was to their advantage to sell the house for the highest price that they could get.

With that in mind, contact someone that you know and respect. Ask for a referral to a real estate agent and lender. Ask why they referred the agent and/or lender to you. If they say the real estate agent and lender will work with you and for you, then contact them immediately and tell them your goals. Many real estate agents like Yvonne Williams, take great satisfaction and pride in helping people reach their goal of buying a house. Her commission is important, it's her livelihood; but, it was not the engine that drove her efforts on our behalf.

When I looked at houses with Yvonne, she would give me Comps, sheets of information telling me the selling price, how long it had been on the market, comparing the price of the house I was considering to others in the area with similar features, rooms, square footage, age, etc. The Comps show houses that are active (currently on the market), pending (in escrow), and those recently sold over the last few months. This information comes from the Multiple Listing Service (MLS), and it is helpful to you to determine what the fair market value is. It also tells you if the house is way-over-priced. This information, along with the help of your agent, can help you to determine a good offer to make for the house. Yvonne would also do research and tell me when the current owners purchased the house and how much they had paid. In some cases she could tell me how much was owed on the house. I was totally informed and thus my family and I made a wise informed decision about the house we purchased in California. We were able to purchase a house that, at the time of this writing, is worth more than twice what we paid for it.

When dealing with your lender, always ask for a Good Faith Estimate of the cost of the loan. The Good Faith Estimate will show you the closing costs, monthly payments, interest, and loan amount. This enables you to make an informed decision concerning what you can afford. Always ask for a Good Faith Estimate whenever you put an offer on a house. The more information you have about your potential debt obligation, the wiser the decision that you can make.

There are many different types of loans available. Fixed rate loans, usually are fifteen, twenty or thirty year loans with a fixed percentage rate that does not change over the life of the loan. Adjustable Rate Mortgages (ARM) usually began with a lower interest rate, but escalates and increases over the life of the loan. Sometimes it is easier to initially get into an ARM; however, keep your credit in good shape so that you can refinance and extricate yourself from an ever increasing interest rate loan. You and your lender can best determine the most appropriate loan for you.

Once pre-qualified and you are seriously searching for a house, do not go out and start buying furniture for your house. Do not make any large purchases or a string of small purchases. This will lower your FICO score, thereby reducing the amount of money that you can qualify for.

Some definitions and additional information you need to know when purchasing a house: Closing Costs are made up of property taxes that must be paid by you for the period immediately following the close of escrow, loan insurance (if applicable), home insurance, lender fees, property taxes and any other items that must be paid before COE.

COE - Close of Escrow (i.e., the date the house becomes yours).

CMA - Comparative Market Analysis is basically the same as Comps. This term is used more to describe information that a realtor gives to a seller.

You are responsible for understanding the purchase agreement that you are signing. Some agents will go over the document with you. Others will say "sign here." It is your duty to ask questions and be informed. If you have questions, find someone reliable and trustworthy with an answer. Depending on what state you live in you will be given a disclosure statement. The disclosure will tell you what the seller knows about the house (i.e., if it floods during rain;

if it's in the path of brush fires; any recent earth movement or other potential problems.)

Once you put an offer on the house, hire a professional property inspector to go over your property. A professional inspector will alert you to any potential problems that need to be address and repaired by the seller. If the seller does not want to do the repairs then you can factor in the cost of the repairs and negotiate a lower price for the house. Please do not trust yourself or unprofessional friends to do your inspection. Hire a professional. The inspector's report and comments will give you a good idea of what you are buying into.

Finally, when you get word that your offer has been accepted, stay in touch with your agent, escrow officer and lender. Do not accept second hand information. Go directly to the source to seek your answers. Good caring real estate agents like Yvonne Williams will keep you informed, no matter how many other clients they have. If you have questions, do not hesitate to go directly to the proper source and get direct answers. Purchasing a house is a major investment; therefore, stay informed, be aware. It is your money and your debt obligation.

BUYING AN AUTOMOBILE. Another important large purchase is buying a new or used automobile-car, SUV, truck. Over the years I have learned some helpful information that has change the way I buy my autos. Before going to an auto dealership always check your credit scores, secure a pre-approved loan and know how much of a down payment you intend to pay. If you are a member of a Credit Union, AAA, AARP, or have a local bank, check to see what kind of rates you can get. In most cases you will get a better percentage rate from someone you are already doing business with than a car dealer. This enables you to know exactly what you can afford to spend and how much your monthly payments will be. This information also helps to guard against any emotional purchase. And your transaction with the car dealer is in affect a cash transaction; thus, enabling you to negotiate a much better price on the vehicle that you purchase.

You can also check out information on the cost of the vehicle that you are interested in from Consumer Report or online at Cars. com, InvoiceDealers and Yahoo!Autos. You can get helpful information that tells you how much the dealer paid for the vehicle, auto transportation cost to the dealer, cost of special features on the car, etc. Therefore, when you see the MSRP (Manufacturer Suggested Retail Price), you have a good idea of the profit built into the overall cost. The profit is always negotiable depending on the demand of the car and the time of your purchase. Many dealers get built in incentives from the manufacturers which may lower their cost for the car. Do not be afraid to negotiate. You can get a great deal on purchasing a new car.

New automobiles, for the coming year, usually arrive at the dealer's showroom sometime in early October to be available for the Christmas holiday spending. A great time to buy a new car that is the current year model is when it is nearing time for the new cars for the next year to come in. Or right after the new cars hit the showroom. All dealers want to liquidate their old inventory to make room for the new. However, always check the inventory before you negotiate your deal. If there is a large inventory of the auto in stock that you are interested in buying, you can negotiate a better deal. The car is not in demand; therefore, you should demand to pay less for the car. Remember, it's your money, don't allow the dealer to make all the demands. Most dealers will negotiate with you rather than see twenty, thirty, forty thousand or more cash dollars walk out their showroom. A pre-approved loan and your down payment is a cash deal to the dealer.

You will always be in a better negotiating position if you do not have a trade in auto to factor in the deal. If you have a car that you wish to get rid of, try selling it yourself. You can list it in the newspaper, auto trade papers, on the internet, etc. Check with AAA, your bank or other organizations that will give you a Blue Book quote on the value of your car, based on the age of your car, how much mileage and the condition of the car. Selling your car beforehand can help you with your down payment. If you do trade your car in on the new car you are purchasing, get an offer quote from the dealer before you start your negotiations on the car you are purchasing. Always take your own calculator with you if you are not fast and skilled at figuring numbers. Determine the cost that you are paying (cost of car, tax and license fees), then deduct from that total the total amount that you are receiving from your trade in. Extended warranties or any other cost you can decide on after you know your basic cost. This enables you to tract the figures and make sure that you are not being overcharged or double charged.

I personally do not advise or recommend trading in a used car that you owe money on. If you absolutely have to, make sure that you have an agreement in writing from the dealer that they will pay off the balance of your trade-in car within ten business days. Remember, until your used car is paid off, you are still responsible for the unpaid loan. GET THE AGREEMENT IN WRITING! Then the dealer is liable, not you. If the dealer refuses to give you an agreement in writing, break the deal and go to another dealer.

Buying used cars involves much of the same information that is previously mentioned. Be informed and be willing to negotiate. A pre-approved loan and down payment works just as well when buying a new auto or a used auto.

INSURANCE. There are various insurance coverages that are necessary for your protection. They are Life Insurance, Health Insurance, Homeowners Insurance, Accidental Death Insurance (if you travel extensively or work in a hazardous environment), and Auto Insurance.

Life Insurance. I am always amazed at the number of people (many clergy) who die and have no life insurance to help their remaining family. There are various types of Life Insurance Policies that you can buy. Whole Life, Universal Life, etc, are insurance policies where you pay the basic cost for the insurance coverage and a smaller portion is set aside to build up a cash accumulation savings. Your policy will break down what you pay for insurance and what goes into your cash accumulation. You can borrow against your cash accumulation value. After you have built up a significant cash accumulation, if you are unable to pay a premium, you can instruct your insurance company to deduct your premium from that account.

Another kind of policy is straight Term Life Insurance where you pay just the cost of the insurance based on the amount of coverage. Seek a Term Life Insurance Policy that has an annual renewable up to age ninety-five, with current premiums that are guaranteed for the first twenty policy years. In most cases they will increase after that. Avoid policies where the premium increases every year. After learning more about insurance, investments, CD's (Certificates of Deposits) and savings, I personally think that a Term Life Insurance policy is better than those where you pay extra above the policy coverage. I have found that you can do better and earn more with your separate investments, CD's and savings.

What determines the cost of your life and health insurance is the type of policy, amount of coverage, age and health. The younger you are the better the rate you can get in purchasing your life insurance. Your health and whether you smoke will also play a vital role in determining the cost of your life insurance policy.

Auto Insurance. When purchasing auto insurance always get full coverage, which includes liability and comprehension coverage. Liability takes care of someone else if you are at fault in an accident. Comprehension takes care of you if you are in an accident with an uninsured driver. Comprehension coverage also covers damage to your car accidentally inflicted by you or some unknown person. It is against the law in most states to drive an automobile without at least auto liability insurance.

Homeowner Insurance. Your homeowner insurance is a vital part of your home loan finance package. In most cases it is paid from your home escrow account. Each mortgage payment has monies put into your escrow account to cover insurance, taxes, etc. It is more to your advantage to include your homeowners insurance in your escrow account, rather than having to come up with a large sum of money twice a year to pay your property taxes and/or insurance premiums.

It is essential to have life insurance coverage, homeowner insurance (fire, hazard, theft liability and damage) medical health insurance, full coverage car insurance (liability and comprehension with medical). If at all possible, do not pay insurance premiums on a monthly basis. Paying monthly means you are paying extra to have someone do the bookkeeping. When buying a car, new or used, factor in the cost of your first six months premium and set it aside, along with your down payment. In most cases you pay either monthly or a six month premium. On home owners insurance you can pay monthly, quarterly, semi annually or yearly. The more times paper work has to be generated and sent to you, the more you will pay for the policy.

With all insurance policies, read them carefully and get assistance from someone you trust if you have difficulty understanding the policy. Insurance policies are a legal binding contract between the policy owner and the insurance company. Do not sign any documentation without fully understanding what you are signing.

Wills/Living Trusts. It is imperative to have a Will or a Living Trust, addressing your assets and liabilities after death. This document will state how you want whatever assets you leave behind to be distributed. Death is often unexpected and sudden; therefore, while in your right mind you should make out a Will or do a Living Trust.

Many people are drawn to making a Will, designating their desires after death. Without a Will or a Living Trust, the state where you live will make the important decisions for you, including who will raise any minor children that you may leave behind. A Will is better than nothing; however, my personal preference is doing a Living Trust. With a Will there are extensive costs for transferring your holdings to your heirs through probate. The dollar cost can be high and the time very long in the probate process.

Me. In 2003, my family and I decided to switch from a Will and we instituted a Revocable Living Trust. This is a trust that creates the entity to which you transfer ownership of your assets. It also contains our instructions for managing our assets during our lifetime and for the distribution of our assets upon our incapacitation or death. A Revocable Trust is created while you are alive and it can be changed, revoked or discontinued. The Revocable Living Trust is also a method of avoiding the probate process and minimizing estate taxes. Because our assets are owned by our Trust, no court is involved in the transfer of our assets upon my death or the death of my wife, KJoy.

Some of the benefits of a Revocable Living Trust are no requirement of newspaper notifications, our records stay private and do not become public and there is no statutory waiting period. As soon as any tax matters are settled, our assets are immediately distributed to the remaining spouse and our other beneficiaries. A dear friend, and church associate, Paul McZeal worked with KJoy and me to set up our Living Trust. Estate Planning is a very popular business today; therefore, you should not have any problems locating someone to help you plan out your estate.

Be diligent and stay informed so that you can make wise decisions in all your business affairs. We have a vital part to play in our prosperity underneath the skin (spiritual) and in the business (material) world. We are commanded to do business until Jesus comes to receive us unto Himself.

There should always be a strong growing relationship between you and God's word. Be a doer of the word, and allow sound doctrine to motivate, guide, and enhance your life. God's word will never return void but will always produce the results that God says it will. His word meets our needs, supplies our resources and satisfies our souls. **Do business until Jesus comes!**

Now that we are equipped with insight, examples, and godly principles to promote our recovery, facilitate our healing and advance our prosperity in the **SPIRITUAL YOU,** the **PHYSICAL YOU** and the **BUSINESS YOU,** it is time for **AWESOME YOU** and **AWESOME ME** to step into the **ABUNDANT LIFE** that Jesus came to earth to give us. There are no limits in abundant living. Break out on the right! Break out on the left! God would that our souls delight in His abundance! Therefore, we need to enter into **Our Season of Enlargement! For Our Best Days Are Ahead!**

CHAPTER THIRTEEN

ABUNDANT LIFE: LIVING THE MAX LIFE BY GOD'S INCREASE!

OUR SEASON OF ENLARGEMENT!

One of the amazing things about a personal relationship with the true and living God is the fact that no matter how we start the journey of life, where we may be at any given point in life, no matter our condition, our surroundings, our circumstances, God can usher us into a **Season of Enlargement.** God's desire in this life for **AWESOME YOU** and **AWESOME ME** is to take us from glory to glory. And each level of glory ushers us into a greater anointing with promotion and increase. **OUR GOD IS AWESOME and His presence, the Holy Spirit, in our lives makes us AWESOME!**

As we examine Isaac, Abraham's son of promise, we shall see some significant parallels to our own lives. Isaac was in a land of famine. I have had my times and seasons in the wilderness of life where times were tough, provisions were scarce, and the future looked bleak. But in each case God was preparing me for a new level of glory.This famine in Isaac's day was worse than the famine in his father's day. Faithful God visits him and tells him to sojourn in a land of famine. How awesome it is to have a living relationship with a loving heavenly Father. He will always show up in our time of trouble and need.

Abraham, Isaac's father, is known as the Father of Faith. In our examination of Isaac we shall see that he also was a man of great faith. He chose to listen to God, obey God, trust God, and work out his faith in a land of famine. Isaac was able to live above his situation, beyond his circumstances and capabilities by following what I call the four "I" principles. Most people, when they think of the word "I," they see it like the "me" word, as being selfish and self centered. The word I is more often a responsive word.

ME. When God called me into the ministry of evangelism, He used a familiar event from my past to reveal what He was calling me to do. He reminded me of a very popular television series called, "Have Gun, Will Travel!" God told me that I would have His gospel and I would travel. He then asked me - "will you go?" I responded by saying: "Yes Lord, I will go." On the eighteenth of November, 1989, I was standing at the altar with KJoy, my bride to be. Pastor Enoch Butler asked me: "Do you take this woman to be your lawfully wedded wife?" I responded: "I do! I do! Pastor, I sho nuff do!" The "I" word is more often a responsive word than a selfish self centered word like "me".

There are many self evident truths in the life of Isaac in Genesis, chapter twenty-six. The first four verses of Scripture tell us that there was a famine in the land, worse than the famine that was in the days of Abraham. Isaac, seeking help, went to Abimelech, king of the Philistines, in Gerar. Then the Lord appeared to him and told him not to go to Egypt, to stay and dwell in this land of famine. God promised to be with him and He would bless Isaac and his descendants. There is a valuable lesson here for you and me to learn about priority. Never seek earthly help first in our time of crisis and need. Take note of God's timing. When Isaac goes to an earthly potentate, God shows up and gives him the solution to his problem. Beloved, we should always seek divine help and guidance by first going to God in our time of need and crisis. God may direct us to an earthly being, but we should always seek him first. Ultimately, God is always the source of our blessings, whether they come through divine supernatural channels or natural earthly channels.

After God tells Isaac that He will perform the oath that He swore to Abraham, to make his descendants multiply as the stars of heaven and to give them all these lands, that all nations of the earth would be blessed through Abraham's seed, then we get insight into the first "I" principle in verses five and six. God tells Isaac that his father Abraham obeyed His voice and kept His charge, His commandments, His statues and His laws. **"So Isaac dwelt in Gerar."** (Genesis 26:6 NKJ) Isaac was **"INCLINED TO OBEY!"** He trusted God and obeyed His command to stay in Gerar. The first "I" principle that ushers us into the season of our enlargement is **"INCLINED TO OBEY!"** Regardless of circumstances, needs or hardship, we must be inclined to obey God if we desire to enter into our season of enlargement.

Isaac finds himself with a large family in a land of famine, where there is no food or provisions. He leaves his home in Hebron, goes to King Abimelech in Gerar. Gerar was the capital of the early Philistine Kingdom. Times had to be desperate for an Israeli to go to a Philistine for help. God shows up with direction and blessings. God's timing makes it clear that we should always look to the hills from whence cometh our help! **Our help cometh from the Lord!**

God tells Isaac to stay in a land of famine, and He will be with him. Isaac did not talk back. He did not try to reason with God or make a logical argument for going into Egypt. Isaac had a godly perspective and he was inclined to obey God. He had a mindset before hand to obey God. He had learned this from his father Abraham.

As a father I have learned many divine principles from studying the lives of characters in the Holy Scriptures. I find that these principles apply to our lives today. In many ways, though in a different setting, culture and time, we face many of the same challenges and have the same emotional wiring as the biblical characters. One of the evident truths between Abraham and his son, Isaac, is that the tendencies, good or bad, of the fathers often become the traits of the sons. Abraham lied and said that Sarah was his sister, not his wife. Later, Isaac lied and said to the men of Gerar that Rebekah was his sister and not his wife. Abraham, on Mt. Moriah, was inclined to obey God. He offered up Isaac, his son of promise, because God had told him to offer Isaac as a burnt offering. Abraham had faithfully waited many years for Isaac to be born. Isaac was Abraham's son of promise; however, when God told him to sacrifice Isaac as a burnt offering, Abraham did not quarrel or question God. He simply obeyed. He faithfully trusted God to provide a sacrifice. On their way up Mt. Moriah, Isaac asked his father what was the sacrifice? From a deep abiding trust in God, Abraham simply replied "The Lord will provide for himself the lamb for the burnt offering." Jehovah Jireh means, "The Lord will provide." One of God's many names comes from this story of God providing a sacrifice on Mt. Moriah. When Abraham raised his knife to slay Isaac, the Angel of the LORD (Jesus) spoke to him from heaven and said: **"Do not lay your hand on the lad, or do anything to him; for now I know that you fear God, since you have not withheld your son, your only son, from Me."** (Genesis 22:12 NKJ)

You. Over a period of time you will learn to have an abiding faith and trust in Almighty God. Godly fear is the root of obedience and the beginning of wisdom. Through diligent prayer, study and application of God's word, you can learn some divine tendencies from the Heavenly Father that will become the traits that govern your decisions and actions. God is always your first recourse. As you live out these traits before your children they will most assuredly become their tendencies. Good or bad, our children often imitate what they see us do, and much of what we say.

Isaac had seen his father walk in obedience to God; therefore; when God directed him to sojourn in a land of famine, he was inclined to obey. God told Isaac that He was going to bless him because Abraham, his father, had obeyed Him. God always displays his goodness toward those of us who obey Him. He always answers our prayers and provides for our needs and the needs of our children.

Jesus, in the garden of Gethsemane, asked God to let the cup of death and separation pass from him because He did not want to be separated from the Father. In deep sorrow and distress, He asks three times, but each time He said to the Father, "Nevertheless, not my will, but thy will be done." Nevertheless is a trust that inclines us to be obedient. It says that one is willing to allow his desires to be subjected to those of someone else. Isaac trusted God, obeyed Him and stayed in a land of famine.

Isaac introduces us to the second "I" principles. While dwelling in a land of famine he decides to sow a seed in the land. A land of famine is a cursed drought area of wilderness where nothing grows. Isaac chose to hear God, who said I will be with you and bless you, rather than be guided by the physical conditions in the land. In verse twelve, he sowed a seed in a land of famine. Isaac "**INVESTED IN HIS FAITH!**" When Isaac invested a seed in the cursed land of famine, he was not investing in the land. He was investing in his faith. God was the object of his faith and he understood the principle that God gives seed to the sower and He will multiply the seed you sow and increase your harvest. Isaac invested in God and God blessed him abundantly.

The same Jehovah Jireh who abundantly blessed Isaac when he sowed a seed of faith, will also bless you and I, exceedingly abundantly above all that we can ask or think. "**Now to Him who is able to do exceedingly abundantly above all that we ask or think, according to the power that works in us, to Him be glory in the church by Christ Jesus to all generations, forever and ever. Amen**" (Ephesians 3:20, 21 NKJ)

All generations in the church includes you and me. The power of the Holy Spirit within us and faith in the word of God before us will cause Jesus to do exceedingly abundantly above all that we could ask or think. The question is, will we invest in our faith? Will we invest and sow seeds of our time, our talent and our treasure into the kingdom of God? Will we give sacrificially and invest in God's kingdom when there is great need in our lives? How often do we, in the church, invest quality time in learning, memorizing, and being applicators of the word of God? How often do we feed the hungry, clothed the naked, give shelter to the homeless, visit those in jails and prisons? How often do we go into the world to witness our faith? And if we can't go, do we help to send others who are going? When we obey God we will follow his instructions to do unto the least of these, and go into the world spreading the gospel. Then we shall reap a great harvest here on earth and in the world to come. Investing in the kingdom of God will always guarantee us a favorable return on our investment.

Isaac had great faith in Jehovah Jireh, the Lord his provider, so he invested in his faith. And in the same year he reaped a hundredfold and the Lord blessed him. Isaac invested in his faith and God greatly rewarded him with a hundredfold blessing. God honors our faith investment and enlarges us beyond measure. We learn three significant things about Isaac after his faith investment. In verse thirteen, Isaac is referred to as the man. In Bible times and in present day vernacular, the man is someone who lives large with great abundance. First, God did multiply his seed and his harvest was so much larger than his seed faith investment. Second, Isaac, the man, began to prosper and continued to prosper until he became very prosperous. Isaac sowed one seed and he obviously continued to prosper until he became abundantly rich. He did not use schemes or trickery. He did not cheat, rob, steal or kill to get ahead. He invested in God, his faith. Third, God's enlargement of Isaac caused him to be envied by the Philistines and King Abimelech, the potentate that he had gone to for help. Abimelech obviously recognized the hand of God on Isaac and asked him to leave them. **"Go away from us, for you are much mightier than we."** (Genesis 26:16 NKJ)

God's blessings in our lives can expose what I call enemy friends. Everyone is not ready to accept God's blessings of enlargement in your life. When we walk in obedience to God's word and invest in our faith, we should expect to receive abundant blessings from God. And we should not apologize nor feel guilty about receiving the blessings of God. Having discovered some enemy friends, I have learned to lovingly tell them that they can get in on God's blessings. God is not a respecter of persons. However, if they refuse to obey God and invest in their faith, they make the choice to not be blessed by God. I choose to obey God and invest in my faith; therefore, "get use to it."

After Isaac experienced his enlargement and his abundance of blessings, he does not go shopping in Egypt. He does not go on a long cruise, nor does he take an extended vacation. What he does is introduce us to the third "I" principle. He dug again the wells that had been dug in his father Abraham's day. He got **"INVOLVED IN THE MISSION!"** The Philistines had filled all the wells with dirt that had been dug in Abraham's day. **"And Isaac dug again the wells of water which they had dug in the days of Abraham his father, for the Philistines had stopped them up after the death**

of Abraham. He called them by the names which his father had called them." (Genesis 26:18 NKJ)

Isaac did not kick back and recline on a bed of ease in a safe comfort zone. He got involved in the mission and work of his father. He dug again the wells that his father Abraham had dug. He also called them by the names that his father had called them. Isaac recognized the great legacy that his father had left him. Part of Abraham's legacy was the wells that his servants dug in his day. Isaac got involved in his father's mission and had his servants to dig the wells again. Out of great respect for his father, he also called the wells by the names his father had given them.

One of the many truths for successful living in Isaac' story, is never abandon a great legacy of good. Get involved in the mission, the ministry, the work. We would all do well to get involved in good legacies left by our forefathers. Many, including me, are walking in the blessings and the promises of God that have accrued to us by virtue of our grandfathers and grand mothers, who faithfully served God. Many of us are descendants of faithful obedient servants of God, who did not receive all that God had for them. I know that I enjoy and walk in many blessings that God has passed down to me because of my Big Mama Mattie. God's great love and faithfulness has caused Him to establish the blessings of our forefathers and mothers into the lives of their descendants. **We are greatly blessed on account of them.**

Sometimes God may call us to carry on the business, the ministry that someone else began. By all means get involved in the mission; however, we should be careful to give honor and respect to those who started the business or ministry. On a few occasions I have had the privilege to watch new pastors succeed pastors who God had anointed to do a great work. Although it is a very difficult task, the job is made easier and the people support the new pastor when he actively gets involved in the ministry, acknowledges and pays respect to the preceding pastor. Whatever the mission, we need to get involve and give tribute to those who have gone before us.

Isaac entered into his season of enlargement because he was inclined to obey God. He invested in his faith and he got involved in the mission. Isaac introduces us to the fourth "I" principle in verses nineteen through twenty-two. **"Also Isaac's servants dug in the valley, and found a well of running water there. But the herdsmen of Gerar quarreled with Isaac's herdsmen, saying, 'The water is ours.' So he called the name of the well Esek, because they quarreled with him. Then they dug another well, and they quarreled over that one also. So he called its name Sitnah. And he moved from there and dug another well, and they did not quarrel over it. So he called its name Rehoboth, because he said, 'For the Lord has made room for us, and we shall be fruitful in the land."** (Genesis 26:19-22 NKJ)

Isaac had his servants to dig new wells. He was not satisfied in just digging again, the wells that his father had dug. For Isaac to dig new wells and find springing water he had to **"INCREASE HIS COMMITMENT!"** He refused to settle for status quo. He did not want to be complacent and only enjoy the legacy of his father. Isaac was determined to establish his own legacy. My father use to tell me that I had to make my mark in life. For Isaac to establish his own legacy and make his mark, he had to increase his commitment. Continual growth and blessings from God requires and demands increased commitment on our parts. **Surely we can enjoy a triumphant moment, but don't stay in the moment. We have to increase our commitment if we want to win the battle. Too many people in life settle for a triumphant moment instead of winning the war.**

Each of us must fight against the temptation to settle in a comfort zone after God's initial blessing of enlargement. I have learned many truths from studying the life of King David. In the kingdom of God we all start life as shepherd boys or girls. If we obey God, invest in our faith, get involved in the mission, and increase our commitment, we can graduate from shepherd boys and girls to become giant killers. **Slaying giants is the work of kings and queens, advancing the kingdom of God on earth.** God enlarges us to advance His kingdom. Start from your last victory in Jesus, increase your commitment, rise up and slay the giants that stand between you and God's promises for your life. God desires to give us much more than what most people settle for.

Isaac's herdsmen increased their commitment and dug a new well. The lazy trifling herdsmen of Gerar quarreled with them, saying the water was theirs. Isaac did not quarrel with them. He named the well Esek. Esek in the Hebrew means contention. Isaac's herdsmen dug another well and found water. The same trifling herdsmen of Gerar quarreled with them, saying the water was theirs. Again, Isaac did not quarrel or fight with them over the well. He named it Sitnah. Sitnah in the Hebrew means hatred and hostility. Isaac's response and refusal to argue or fight with the herdsmen of Gerar, speaks volumes to us. We should carefully and prayerfully choose our battles. A lesson my wife is constantly teaching me. Sometimes, rather than engage in distressful actions and quarrelsome words, we should name the problem and leave it to God. Fighting and quarreling dissipates our anointing and diverts our attention from God's purpose for our lives.

Isaac knew that the hand of God was on him. He knew that envious, hateful people could not deny his blessings from God. This was evident to Isaac, because everywhere his herdsmen dug they found water. Isaac did not fight. He did not pout and he did not quit. He continued to increase his commitment. He dug a third well and no one quarreled with him or tried to claim his well. He named this well Rehoboth, which means broad place of blessings in Hebrew. Isaac kept digging wells until he came to God's broad place of blessings. Quarreling and fighting did not get Isaac and his herdsmen to God's broad place of blessings. Their increased commitment ushered them into their season of enlargement.

Sometimes in life, God will allow contention, hatred and hostility to drive us out of our comfort zone to His broad place of blessings. Too often we are quick to settle for God's good, but God is determined to get us to His best. If a job, or a relationship, that was once satisfying and rewarding, suddenly becomes a hostile environment, it very well maybe God, getting your attention so that he can get you to your Rehoboth, where He has made room for you.

Beloved, we need to examine our level of commitment. Let's do a serious assessment of our effort in the challenges of life. Many times we will find that we need to increase our commitment because we have settled into a comfort zone of past blessings. Comfort zones never inspire effort for enlargement. Increased Commitment results in enlargement. Do not recline on a bed of ease and stagnate in a comfort zone. Comfort zones are like shallow water. Increased commitment is like deep water. **We will never experience deep water blessings in shallow water living. Get out of the comfort zone!** It takes increased commitment to launch out into the deep waters where we see the wonders of God performed in our lives. Enjoy God's blessings, but don't become absorbed in a life of ease. Walk with a kingdom mentality and establish God's kingdom on earth.

Nothing pleases God more than to bless our obedience and increase our influence on the earth. God wants the world, through our living relationship with Him, to witness the difference that His love, caring and provisions make in the human experience. God would that no one be lost. He desires to showcase His awesome love for humanity through His presence in our lives. As ambassadors for Christ, we have the opportunity to experience the best of both worlds. The name of Jesus gives us acceptance in heaven and authority on earth. In Christ name we have access to all that God created for mankind. No man, no woman should be living a mediocre lifestyle. I truly hear God's words shouting out to His people today: **"Enlarge the place of your habitation!"**

This is the **Season of Our Enlargement! Be INCLINED TO OBEY GOD, INVEST IN YOUR FAITH, GET INVOLVED IN THE MISSION AND INCREASE YOUR COMMITMENT!** God has great things in store for his obedient saints. And He desires to get us all to Rehoboth, His broad place of blessings. God has made room for us. **Our Best Days Are Ahead!**

CHAPTER FOURTEEN

OUR BEST DAYS ARE AHEAD!

RISE UP SAINTS! FACE THE CHALLENGES OF THE
TIMES! LIVE EXPECTANTLY AND BE AWARE OF
THE BIBLICAL SIGNS! RISE UP SAINTS! FOR THIS IS
OUR HOUR! RISE UP SAINTS AND WALK IN ANOINTED
POWER! RISE UP SAINTS! VICTORY IS AT HAND! STEP
INTO LEADERSHIP AND TAKE DOMINION OVER THE
LAND!

We are living in challenging times and days of world conflict.
No matter how you began life's journey or where you maybe at the
reading of this book, know that our best days are ahead. Even if you
find yourself in the midst of a severe storm being tossed to and fro
by angry waves of despair, your best days are ahead. Trouble does
not last always. Cast all your cares upon Jesus. For the Lord Jesus
Christ is still telling the howling winds to hush up and the angry
waves to be still! Do not drop the anchor of your life in waters of
despair. The Lord Jesus will navigate you through the dangerous
seas to shores of safety. Raise your anchor of faith! **Our best days
are ahead!**

Today, you are a man or a woman of faith. And even in these
days that Jesus described as "the beginning of sorrows," your
abiding faith and trust in God will enable you to **Rise Up and Step
into Your Destiny!** You have been anointed and equipped to rise
above adversity and walk in a season of enlargement. From humble

beginnings and a distasteful past, you must rise to be a mighty man or mighty woman of God. God has high expectations for every one of His children. Our life on earth is an apprenticeship for a life in heaven with the triune God. So dare to have **great ambition, walk in great faith, exemplify great courage and pray great prayers,** beseeching our God to bless you and enlarge your territory.

One of the great stories in the Bible is about a man who was born of pain and sorrow. He came from humble beginnings, but he dared to seek the true and living God for a great life. He refused to allow his beginnings or his past to motivate and dictate his ambition, faith, and courage. He prayed a great prayer! God heard his prayer and granted him his request. Since our God is not a respecter of persons, this tells me that our best days are ahead. Let's examine the life of Jabez and get some miracle working insight for living a supernatural life on earth as we prepare for an eternal life in heaven.

> **"Now Jabez was more honorable than his brothers, and his mother called his name Jabez saying, 'Because I bore him in pain.' And Jabez called on the God of Israel saying, 'Oh, that You would bless me indeed, and enlarge my territory, that Your hand would be with me, and that You would keep me from evil, that I may not cause pain!' So God granted him what he requested."**
> (1 Chronicles 4:9, 10 NKJ)

In the midst of the history and genealogy of the Jewish people, God singles out Jabez, one man from some six hundred others, for special recognition and honor. God blessed Jabez to live a life way beyond average. There are only two verses of Scripture devoted to him in the Bible; however, Jabez's prayer still speaks volumes to us today. We might ask some questions: How could one from such an obscure background rise to such great prominence? And, how did he continue to be prominent throughout the days of Biblical history to present day Christianity? How do you go from being born of pain, sorrow and humble beginnings to become a superstar of the faith? Jabez is indeed a superstar of the faith. His life and his prayer touch and bless the lives of people throughout the world today, through books and sermons. How did Jabez pull it off? What made him a godly superstar? He was not a priest, not a prophet, not a judge, not a king or heir to royalty, and yet the Bible says he was more honorable than his brothers. The answers to all of the above questions are in his prayer.

As we examine his prayer we shall discover four dynamic principles that transformed his life and elevated him into the best days of his life. Take note that Jabez called on the Great God of Israel saying. Even before we discover the four principles we see two very important things that we can learn from this. Who he called on and how he called. Jabez called on the Great God of Israel, who is the true and living God. One of the most significant things about prayer is who you are praying to. Calling on the wrong gods- dead idols, will avail nothing but frustration. When the four hundred and fifty prophets of Baal called on their false god on Mount Carmel, they became very frustrated and began to cut themselves with knives until the blood gushed out of them, because their god was dead and he could not answer them. The moment that Prophet Elijah called on the God of Abraham, Isaac and Israel, the true and living God, God answered him and sent fire to consume the sacrifice and the altar, including licking up the water. Always call on the Great God of Israel. Jabez called on the God of Israel saying. He said, he did not ask. His prayer was not an interrogative question. It was an exclamatory statement of faith! In every translation that I examined I never found his statement as an interrogative question with a question mark.

Why an exclamatory statement and not an interrogative question? Jabez obviously knew about the Great God of Israel. He had heard of His great exploits on behalf of His people. Perhaps he had heard about God's response to the unbelieving spies and the camp of Israel, who refused to enter the Promised Land, saying they were like grasshoppers in their eyes and the eyes of the giants in the land. God told them they would have exactly what they said. **"As I live, says the Lord, just as you have spoken in My Hearing, so I will do to you."** (Numbers 13:28 NKJ) God frequently does exactly what we say.

Somehow, God had birthed faith in Jabez and revealed to him the teachings of Jesus in Mark's account of the gospel. Jesus said:

"Have faith in God. For assuredly, I say to you, whoever says to this mountain, Be removed and be cast into the sea, and does not doubt in his heart, but believes that those things he says will be done, he will have whatever he says." (Mark 11:22, 23 NKJ) Jabez excitedly spoke into God's hearing exactly what he wanted God to do for him. He did not doubt and God granted his request. Jabez introduces us to four dynamic principles of prayer. As we have seen in the lives of others, God gives us divine principles in groups of fours. God's word is so powerful, that even the numbers have significance. The number four always has reference to God's earthly creation. For instance, there are four regions of the earth and four seasons of the year. So we see four dynamic principles in the prayer of Jabez. He dared to have (1) great ambition. (2) He had great faith, (3) great courage and (4) he prayed a great prayer.

Despite his humble beginnings, Jabez had great ambition. His great ambition caused him to pray a prayer that defied his conditions and surroundings. His great ambition motivated him to emphatically declare his desire to be enlarged by God's presence and His blessings. He believed in and he trusted the God of Israel. There were many gods in Jabez' day, just as there are many false gods today. He was emphatic about calling on the God of Israel. He wanted more out of life, so his great ambition inspired him to ask God to enlarge his territory. Too often people are satisfied in just getting by and being in a comfort zone of having their needs met. It takes great ambition to step out of a comfort zone and demand to go to a higher level.

Jabez was aware of what God had already done for Israel. He knew that he could go to a higher level. He knew that he was connected to the God who answered the prayers of His people. God had promised Israel a land flowing with milk and honey. The land was found, by the spies, to be exactly how God had described it to be. The children of Israel, as a nation, could have been enjoying the fruit of the land. They had not obeyed God to go in and take possession of the land, because they lacked the courage and ambition. At one point they were willing to go back into slavery and settle for the hand outs of the Egyptians. Many of their leaders had disobeyed God. The people had turned against the prophets of God.

Sin was rampant and things were not well for the nation of Israel. Jabez sincerely sought after God. His great ambition overpowered his beginning, his surroundings, and the conditions in the land. No doubt this is what made him more honorable than his brothers.

You and Me. We must guard against allowing family and friends, with negative attitudes and little ambition, to influence our thinking and decision making in regards to our desires for a closer and better life with God. God wants us to be intimate with Him and have the best life on earth. He came that we might have an abundant life. Do not be afraid to dream big! Do not be afraid to rise above small beginnings! My father use to tell me to reach for the stars and make my mark in life! He was a man with very little formal education, but he became a very successful businessman and land owner. When he set his sights on something he was very tenacious in his pursuit to accomplish his goal.

It takes great ambition, a burning desire, to come from nothing and say to God, bless me indeed and enlarge my territory. Ambition is the engine that drives our efforts to achieve and get the best out of life. Getting the best out of the Christian life requires us to go deep in the word, serve the body of Christ, and seek to serve and save the lost in the world. Perhaps we should ask ourselves some questions. Are we satisfied with just being saved and having our names written down in the Lamb's Book of Life? Are we complete with just church affiliation and not an inflamed Christ relationship? Are we in the same spiritual place where we began our salvation journey? Are we still dining on the milk of the word, refusing to bite into the strong meat of the word? Are we known by our regular occupancy of pews behind stained glass windows, but conspicuous by our absence in going into the hedges and highways to compel men, women, boys and girls to come into the house of the Lord? Are we happy sailing along on a comfort ship in a safety zone of shallow waters?

Beloved, we were saved to seek to save the lost. Not only can we impact our lives, but we can also impact the lives of others. As we diligently serve God's kingdom we shall know and testify that Our Best Days Are Ahead! God has called us to launch out in the deep! It's takes great ambition to launch out into deep waters. It's out in the deep waters where we see the wonders of God performed in our lives and in the lives of others. I repeat, we will never experience deep water blessings in shallow water living!

Jabez called on the God of Israel and said: **"Oh that you would bless me indeed and enlarge my territory!"** His words indicate that his great ambition was standing on a foundation of great faith. He had faith in God and knew that He could do what he was saying. His faith in God helped him to transcend his meager beginnings. The measure of one's faith can be determined by the size of one's work and the nature and content of one's prayer. Little faith will seek little things. Great faith will not only say bless me indeed, great faith will also say enlarge my territory! In Jabez's prayer, I hear him saying my faith will not be determined by my meager beginnings, my humble background or my lack of family connections. The God of Israel is a great God; therefore, I will have great faith!

The size of our faith should be determined by the greatness of our God. Nothing is too hard for our God; therefore, as believers, we should have great faith. Great faith will enable us to overcome and move the mountain of obstacles that stand between us and the promises of God. Great faith is not determined by our titles, our position in society, our family heritage or our sphere of influence. These things may impress mankind, but God is not impressed by outward trappings. God is impressed by our hearts. The Prophet Samuel would gladly tell us that God is not impressed by our outward appearance. He learned this great lesson when he went to Jesse's house to anoint the next king of Israel. Prophet Samuel was impressed by the stature and appearance of Eliab, Jesse's oldest son. He declared that surely this was God's anointed before him. God told him: **"Do not look at his appearance or at his physical stature, because I have refused him. The Lord does not see as man sees; For man looks at the outward appearance, but God looks at the heart."** (1 Samuel 16:6, 7 NKJ)

David was not even invited to the anointing party, but when he came walking in from the sheep fields, God announced that he was the one. David had the heart of a champion and a king. Later when Israel was under siege from Goliath and the Philistine army, Eliab and the rest of Israel's army were cowards who refuse to step up and face Goliath. David spoke in the name of the God of Israel, stating that the great God of Israel would deliver them into his hands and he would cut Goliath's head off. David ran to face Goliath and the entire Philistine army. He defeated the giant and severed Goliath's head with his own sword. David did not allow his background as a shepherd boy to keep him from being a giant killer and later the greatest king of Israel. His words and actions were prompted by his great faith in the God of Israel.

Choose to see where you are, what you have and where you come from as a stepping stone and not your stumbling block. Great faith is not determined by our outward trappings. God was moved by the great faith of Jabez and David. He granted them what they said. Great faith will motivate you and me to speak our victory and not just ask for it. **We shall have what we say if we doubt not!**

It took great courage to declare what Jabez declared, when he said: **"That Your hand would be with me and that You would keep me from evil that I may not cause pain!"** We see a visible portrait of his courage in his words that your hand would be with me. Jabez wanted God to be with him. Unlike many who prayed in Biblical times and today, Jabez wanted God the Blessed One to be with him. He wanted more than the blessings of God. He wanted the Blessed One to guide him, keep him from getting caught up in evil and causing pain to others. His great courage was driven by great ambition that was standing on a foundation of great faith. The great ambition of Jabez was clothed in a suit of great courage.

Many times people seek the blessings of God, with very little regard to having God's presence with them to guide them on their journey. Wanting God with him tells us that Jabez did not want happiness without holiness. To have the blessings of God will surely make one happy for a season. However, without the Blessed One, we will not walk in holiness and bask in the joy of the Lord. God's presence in our lives guarantees us fruitful and productive travel with the strength to overcome every trial and tribulation. The joy of the Lord is our strength. Jabez knew, with God's presence, he could handle the prosperity, the new lifestyle and overcome every evil temptation. He was confident, with God's presence, that he would not get caught up in the blessings and forget his source, the Blessed One.

How often do we hear and read about people who enjoy worldly pleasures and riches? Many are caught up in evil activities that cause pain to themselves and countless others. Our news headlines are filled with stories about entertainers, sports celebrities whose lives are spinning out of control; and yet, they have access to an abundance of financial and material resources. Their lives are filled with pain and sorrow. Many are caught up in drugs and evil life-styles that cause them and others to be in great pain. If only they had a living relationship with the Blessed One and the courage to pray as Jabez prayed. I'm often reminded of the proverb: **"The blessing of the LORD makes one rich, and He adds no sorrow with it."** (Proverbs 10:22 NKJ)

When you have the blessings of God and the Blessed One guiding your life, your blessings and your life will be void of sorrow. Without the Blessed One, it's always the roll of the dice, and most times you end up losing with snake eyes. When increase and that which is design to prosper you is weighted down in sorrow, it ceases to be a blessing and becomes a curse.

The fourth dynamic principle that Jabez teaches us is to pray a great prayer. We get divine insight into the greatness of his prayer in the phrase **"That Your hand would be with me."** This word hand in the original Hebrew language means an opened hand of power, direction, means (divine supply) and fellowship. Jabez was asking for the **opened hand of God** to be with him. In doing research, I discovered two primary definitions for hand throughout the Bible. One is the opened hand of God and the other is the closed hand of God. We don't have to be rocket scientist to know which hand is the most beneficial to us. The opened hand of God that Jabez wanted was **a hand of power, direction, divine supply and fellowship.**

In his great prayer Jabez is saying, Great God of Israel, open your hand and bless me with power, direction, divine supply and fellowship. God's opened hand of blessings extends to us power; therefore, we can do all things through Christ who strengthens us. God's opened hand of blessings extends to us direction; therefore, we can trust in the Lord with all our hearts. Lean not unto our own understanding, but in all our ways trust and acknowledge Him, and He will direct our paths. His word is a lamp unto our feet and a light unto our path. God's opened hand of blessings extends to us divine supply; therefore, our God will supply all of our needs according to His riches in glory by Christ Jesus. Our God takes pleasure in the prosperity of His servants! God's opened hand of blessings extends to us fellowship; therefore, our God walks with us, He talks with us and He tells us that we are His own. We are a chosen generation, a royal priesthood, a holy nation and a special people unto our God. And the kingdom of God is righteousness, peace and joy in the Holy Spirit. God was moved by the great prayer of Jabez and He granted him his request!

We need to carefully examine our prayer life. Do we spend most of our time praying interrogative prayers? Is our ambition great and do we have great faith dressed in a suit of great courage that allows us to pray great prayers of strong declaration?! What kind of prayers are we praying? More importantly, what kind of responses are we getting from Great God of Israel?

By virtue of the fact that our names are written down in the Lamb's Book of Life, our best days are ahead! For we have graduated from spiritual poverty to godly riches. And if we dare to have great ambition, great faith, great courage and pray great prayers, we will not only have the blessings of God but we shall also have the Blessed One. Many of us are walking in a season of enlargement where the opened hand of God continues to empower us, direct us, give us His divine supply and fellowships with us. The opened hand of God is just a prayer away. Do you dare to declare His blessings and presence in your life?

Me. I personally draw great inspiration and courage from the life of Jabez. My humble beginnings and background have never been a stumbling block to me. Before Christ, I always had strong desires to have a better life. Although I was ordinary, as we all are, before accepting Jesus Christ as Savior and Lord, I was nonetheless driven to accomplish my dreams. I never lost sight of my dreams. After achieving a level of success I came to realize that my understanding of success was faulty. I was greatly disappointed and frustrated at realizing that world acclaim and monetary success did not eradicate the loneliness in my life. Having more possessions and access, without God, is definitely not the answer. I truly understand today why Jabez did not want the blessings of God without the giver of the blessing. To have the blessings of God and the Blessed One has been a great transforming factor in my life. Peace, joy and fulfillment richly abound in my life today because I have the Blessed One and His blessings. His opened hand of power, direction, divine supply and fellowship are a constant in my life. When I reflect on my past life of loneliness and misguided misery I greatly rejoice to see how God uses my family and me to represent His kingdom on earth. My wife KJoy is an anointed singer and minister of God's word. Our son Michael is an intelligent talented drummer and song writer. Today we abound with the blessings of God. We face challenges but our best days are ahead.

You. If you are not in the place of God's abundant blessings and enlargement, know that His presence in your life qualifies and equips you to live the abundant life. You have the Blessed One. And He does not impose limits on you because of your past, your lack of status in the world or your present situation. Do not settle for just being saved and a member of a church family. Dare to have great ambition, great faith, great courage and pray great prayers. God is listening! He is waiting on you to declare your blessings! Please know, with God, there are no limits and no bounds to your blessings when you walk in obedience, speak His blessings and do not doubt what you say.

Today, life is challenging. There are obstacles that we have to overcome. God allows the challenges, the obstacles to test and build our faith. God has designed and equipped you and me to overcome and live a victorious life. He has given us all things pertaining to life (material) and godliness (spiritual). As His kingdom saints we are more than conquerors anointed to live an abundant life. God's great desire is that you and I embrace His divine principles and truths. He wants us to have the peace of God and allow Him, the God of peace, to establish us as mighty victors.

Saints we honor God by living with a kingdom mentality, being a light in this world of darkness and seeking to save the lost. Start at home with your immediate family. Embrace your extended family, your home church, take your neighborhood, your city and state for the kingdom of our Lord Jesus Christ. Your past is behind you! Your "now" is in front of you! Your future is ahead of you! Living today with a kingdom mentality guarantees us victory today and **Our Best Days Are Ahead!**

We all started this life as outcasts. We all started life going down, hell bound for torment and pain. The day that we ask Jesus to save us, we received a first class ticket on a cloud, going up, heaven bound for glory and gain. **Our Best Days Are Ahead!** And one glad morning when this life is over, the trump of God will sound and Jesus will catch a cloud and descend from heaven with a shout from the voice of the archangel. He will come back down to earth to receive us unto Himself. And all the dead in Christ, they shall rise from their graves, clothed in immortality. We shall see many of our loved ones who transition from this world, waiting for the resurrection of the church and the great day of the Lord. And those of us who are yet alive, we shall be changed in the twinkling of an eye and we, along with the dead in Christ, shall be caught up to meet our Lord in the air. And we shall ever be with our Lord Jesus Christ. We shall go to heaven and live in our new mansions in a gated community, behind the Pearly Gates. We shall walk streets of gold, Hallelujah Boulevard, Glory Lane, Prosperity Avenue and Salvation Circle! God desires the best for us. He came to this world to establish His kingdom and to give us His abundant life. You don't have to wait for heaven to live a great life.

I see God as my destiny! He is my great fortune! I see His great love embracing you and me in His multitude of promises and bountiful blessings. I see His divine guidance in His word. I know His Holy Spirit dwells within me, and I sense and experience His anointed power in my daily existence. Your life and my life are hid in **AWESOME JESUS! His anointing makes us awesome! Jesus had the purpose and the passion to die for us. Now we have the privilege and the pleasure to live for him.** If you desire to go to the next level of His glory and live an abundant life now, I invite you to join me and declare these words over your life. **AWESOME YOU AND AWESOME ME! TOGETHER WE SET THE CAPTIVES FREE! TO HEDGES AND HIGHWAYS, OFF WE GO! ANOINTED, APPOINTED, LET THE GOSPEL FLOW! PURSUE THE SINNERS! RESCUE THE LOST! DISCIPLE**

OUR FAMILY, WHATEVER THE COST! AWESOME YOU AND AWESOME ME! THE HOLY FATHER'S CHILDREN ARE WE! CHOSEN, ROYAL, HOLY AND PECULIAR TO BE! AWESOME YOU AND AWESOME ME!

The best is yet to come! OUR BEST DAYS ARE AHEAD! It's time for you to RISE UP AND STEP INTO YOUR DESTINY!

Dwelling in the Presence of Almighty God!

Edified, Encouraged and Enhanced by the Word of God!

Saturated in the Compassionate Love of God!

Transformed and Triumphant in the Power of God!

Informed, Inspired and Instructed to do the Works of God!

Nurtured and Developed in the Principles and Precepts of God!

Yielded and Yoked Together with Christ for the Mission of God!

About the Author

Evangelist Christipher Joy is founder and CEO of Love Crusades Evangelistic Ministries, Inc. As a full time evangelist for the past twenty-seven years, he travels throughout the world preaching the gospel of Jesus Christ in "Celebrations of the Word." He is a graduate of The World Christian Training Center, and a participant in the Billy Graham School of Evangelism.

Evangelist Joy continues to use skills from his theatrical background in motion pictures, television and legitimate stage as a producer, writer and director of Christian plays and films. Since 2007, he has been organizing and facilitating "Life Empowerment & Financial Seminars," teaching people how to navigate through the channels of business to experience prosperity in the spiritual and natural realms of life.

Evangelist Joy is the husband of Karen D. Joy and father of his three sons, Michael, Terry and Sean. He is an anointed faithful counselor and prayer partner to many people in America and throughout the world.

You can visit his website: www.chrisjoylcem.org

Breinigsville, PA USA
08 February 2010
232125BV00001B/2/P